GW00401320

THE LANGUAGE OF FIELD SPORTS

BY

C. E. HARE

PARTRIDGE SHOOTING

From *The British Sportsman* by William Augustus Osbaldiston, 1792

CONTENTS

CONTENTS

PART III. GROUP TERMS

PART IV. BIBLIOGRAPHY

APPENDICES

INTRODUCTION

THIS BOOK owes its birth to a habit of the author—a habit of collecting. The subject was the simple one of the 'proper' term for a gathering of the various animals or birds. For twenty years there was no time except to add to the little list as information came his way. Then leisure permitted research, interest deepened, the scope of enquiry widened, until 'Group Terms' became but the *scut* to the hare of Hunting Language.

Sport is inevitably *kindled* from Nature; Smith tells us, and truly: 'a man cannot be a true sportsman who is not also a true naturalist.' Thus was the book and its title born.

Some young men—and here the author has memories of his own youth—naturally fond of sport themselves, do not happen to come of a sporting family. They lack the advantage of a relative or friend who could put them wise on such matters as the object, rules, etiquette, and peculiar language of, say, fox-hunting. Such men are shy of asking for fear of appearing foolish or ignorant, and they do not know where to look for their information. And ladies, too—though perhaps they are not so fearful of 'dropping a brick'.

It was found impossible to present the language of hunting in a suitable form without giving a short description of the several histories of the chase. But these accounts are necessarily brief; those who would go deeper into the matter and who desire a comprehensive and consecutive story are referred to vol. xxiii of the Lonsdale Library, to *Bridleways through History*, by Lady Apsley (1936), and to the Authorities mentioned in Chapter XXVI.

Strict accuracy has been aimed at and, it is hoped, attained; but the author will welcome authentic additions and criticism. The subject is inexhaustible: the more one reads the more one learns. So the *pack* is laid on, and they are away in *full cry*. *Sohowe*!

The term 'hunting' meant the chase of a wild animal in its

natural haunts. Primitive man was a hunter—for his food and his clothing—and his 'sport' was attended with far more difficulty and danger than is ours. But hunting would not be what it is if there was not an element of danger, even if that is 'only represented to-day by personal inconvenience and discomfort' (Lady Apsley).

The same spirit has prevailed through the ages. Nimrod, the first King of Babylon (about 2000 B.C.), was 'a mighty hunter before the Lord'. The Assyrians were passionately fond of hunting, and of the Persians it was said that they taught their children 'to ride, to shoot, and to tell the truth'. The Persians used to attack on foot, and ride down, wild animals in large enclosures called *paradises*. Men of every race have hunted, and for their hunting have evolved their own peculiar terms. And among the peoples of the British Isles the predominant characteristic which has persisted through the centuries is their love for Hunting.

[Since this work was started, public interest in the history and language of sport has been confirmed by the widespread popularity revealed for the recent Sports Competitions inaugurated by the British Field Sports Society.]

PREFACE

'LET US hope', wrote Folkard nearly eighty years ago, 'that the character of the English sportsman is not so far degenerated, or the respect he owes to ancient diversions so far forgotten, as to permit him any longer to persist in such cramped and improper slang as to use the inapplicable term "flock" to every, or any, description of wild-fowl. It should be borne in mind that, as we derive our laws and our purest sciences from the ancients, from the same source sprang our national sports; and the arts, systems and terms in connection with such have been handed down to us from generation to generation, because none other express so faithfully the meaning intended to be conveyed.'

There are terms inapplicable to many varieties of birds besides wild-fowl, as well as of animals and fishes. It is in the belief that the modern sportsman will be sufficiently concerned to use on all occasions the 'proper' term that this book is offered. That there is a widespread interest in the subject has been proved to the writer by the number of letters, offering help and advice, he has received from all parts of the world.

Correct speech or perfect manners do not, of themselves, make a true sportsman. 'I am sensible', said Abraham Markland, in his *Pteryplegia, or The Art of Shooting Flying*, 'there is no becoming *Sportsman* by Book. You may here find the *Rules* and proper Directions for that End; but Practice alone can make you *Masters*. *Bare Theory* may as soon stamp a *General*, as a Marksman.' The writer perceives the limitations of this work. But, just as perfect knowledge does not of itself produce practical perfection, so would no true sportsman, however expert in the field, desire to be ignorant of, or fail to use, the correct 'hunting language', by the use of which 'thereby, in a manner, all men of worth may discover a gentleman from a yeoman, and a yeoman from a villain' (Mallory).

This work has been a labour of love; its original object was to give in a correct and convenient form the proper terms for the various flocks of birds, herds of animals, shoals of fish and swarms of insects, as applied to their several species (Part III). Strictly, all terms should be 'company' terms, or nouns of assemblage—that is, words which actually mean a 'gathering together'. But it is not always so. Some terms owe their origin to the characteristics of the birds or animals, or to their cries, or refer to their progeny. Others have been copied wrongly by scribes or printers, and are now commonly employed in a form quite different from the original.

The most important ancient list of terms is the one headed 'Compaynys of beestys and fowlys' in *The Book of St. Albans.*[1] The terms were in no sense 'company' terms, as was believed by many authorities for several centuries, but just 'proper terms to be used by gentlemen and those curious in their speech'. An attempt has been made here to group the terms in a logical sequence. In all cases where the term occurs in the St. Albans list, that rendering has been given; in addition the earliest authority for each term has been noted. The special method of numbering was adopted to facilitate quick reference, and to allow room for additional terms. The 'Notes' are numbered to correspond with the terms to which they refer, and endeavour to show their original or intended meaning.

Many of these group terms might well be revived: a *trip* of geet, a *sord* or *sute* of mallard, a *host* of sparrows, a *pace* of asses, a *clowder* of cats, a *rag* of colts, and a *harras* of horses.

The writer has found his work grow upon him, and it has been expanded considerably beyond its original scope. Some particulars, which he did not intend to touch upon, were found to be so intimately blended with the main purport of this book, that their omission would have rendered it defective. It was found impossible, for instance, to omit references to such subjects as folk-lore and proverbs, though, as these form a goldmine in themselves, only a few nuggets have been offered. He feels, as did Strutt, that he must 'entreat the reader to excuse the frequent quotations that he will meet with, judging it much fairer to stand upon the authority of others than to arrogate to (himself) the least degree of penetration'. And here he would like to take the opportunity of thanking the numerous correspondents for their valuable assistance, and to tender his apologies should any source of information remain unacknowledged.

[1] This list is given in full in Chapter XXVII.

The Notes on the Authorities, besides helping to explain the nature and origin of the terms, will, it is hoped, lure readers (as the writer has been lured) to dip into the pages of some of these most fascinating works, most of which can be seen in Clubs, Public Libraries or the British Museum. Although the original intention of the writer was to deal only with sporting terms, it is felt that the work would be incomplete without a reference[1] to the terms for Persons and Objects, since such terms occur in all the old lists, and in fact are often indiscriminately mingled among those for birds and animals.

There is an old saying about 'all work and no play'. The writer has broken bounds and let his fancy (and that of others) wander freely in 'A Digression'. He trusts that readers will find relief and amusement therein, and perhaps be tempted to exercise in a like manner their own *charm* of wit. In the Parts devoted to Hunting Terms, both old and modern expressions are given. Many of the ancient terms have gone, or are beginning to die out. It is hoped that this record will serve as a reminder and a source of information.

'Critics, in general', says Daniel, 'are venomous *Serpents*, that delight in hissing; and some of them, who have got by heart a few *technical Terms*, without knowing their *Meaning*, are no other than *Magpies*.' These are strong words, but the Rev. Daniel did not mince his meat. Criticism there undoubtedly will be, but the writer believes that, by providing such a *holocaust* of terms and their meanings, he will have effectually rendered the fangs of his critics innocuous, or, if magpies, bound their beaks.

'The Compiler's first wish,' wrote the same reverend gentleman in his own Preface, 'is, that his endeavour may be approved by those, for whose use this collection is more peculiarly intended; into Every work treating upon a variety of topics, errors and imperfections will find their way; in the present, the writer fears he cannot felicitate himself in having wholly escaped them; he hopes, however, that should any be found, they will not be of importance, and that those who have the sagacity to discover, will have the candour to forgive them.' The present writer cannot do better than subscribe to these sentiments.

[1] Such reference will be found in Appendix I.

PREFACE TO SECOND EDITION

THIS BOOK has been considerably revised. In the first place, since we are here not concerned with organised games, horse-racing or the prize-ring, it has been held advisable to alter the title from *The Language of Sport* to *The Language of Field Sports* so as to indicate more accurately the contents.

The chief aim has been to simplify the lay-out. With that end in view, special attention has been paid to uniformity: all technical terms are shown in italics, most of the footnotes have been incorporated in the text, and an Index has been added. Chapters have been divided into **ANCIENT** and **MODERN,** with subheadings (in small capitals) under each. In a few chapters only, such as in Chapters III and XI, it has been necessary to make main divisions (large capitals) first; these again are divided into **ANCIENT** and **MODERN** with subheadings as necessary.

The most important additions include two new chapters (XII and XIII), on MALE AND FEMALE and THE YOUNG OF ANIMALS respectively; Sections on MODERN DEER STALKING (Ch. II), MODERN COURSING (Ch. IV), SIGHTS AND SIGHTING (Ch. VI), BIG GAME FISHING (Ch. VII); and a comprehensive GLOSSARY of TERMS FOR THE HORSE (Ch. XXII).

The following chapters have been rewritten, as they were felt to be unsatisfactory: Ch. XI (renamed) THE MUSIC OF THE CHASE, Ch. XIX CRIES OF ANIMALS, Ch. XX THE MATING OF ANIMALS, Ch. XXII (renamed) THE HORSE. Mr. Roy Beddington has again kindly revised Ch. VII on FISHING.

In Part III, those terms which, it is suggested, might be used as the correct Group Terms have been specially indicated. At the end of this Part a Summary of Genuine Company Terms has been inserted. The chapter on THE AUTHORITIES now includes an additional list of books which have been referred to or consulted. An amusing extract from J. M. Barrie's *Sentimental Tommy* introduces A DIGRESSION (Appendix I); while a new Appendix gives a Table of those terms which have two or more distinct meanings. It is hoped that this Table may be of particular interest.

Many fresh terms, both new and old, have been added, particularly under Foxhunting, Shooting, Fishing, Hawking and Appendix III. The author would here like to express his gratitude to the many who have sent him suggestions and criticisms. Of improvements there can be no end.

The author has enjoyed his research. His hope is that readers will find refreshment in these pages—and no difficulty in landing their desired fish. There is a vast shoal for drifters. Though customs die, and words change, still the ancient ways have value,

For still the heart doth need a language, still
Doth the old instinct bring back the old names.

October, 1948

NOTE. The authors of quotations throughout the book are indicated by abbreviations, e.g. '(RS.)', at the end of the quotation. The key to such abbreviations is to be found in Chapter XXVI.

Writing is þe keye of alle good remembraunce.

CHAUCER

The first pursuit that a young man just out of boyhood should take up is hunting and afterwards he should go on to the other branches of education, provided he has the means.

XENOPHON

I like to be as my fathers were
In the days ere I was born.

WILFRID SCAWEN BLUNT

Who telleth one of my meanings, is master of all I am.

EMERSON

Is there, after all, any solace like the solace and consolation of Language?

LOGAN PEARSALL SMITH

PART I

HUNTING TERMS (ANCIENT AND MODERN)

'Why you know an a man have not skill in the hawking and hunting languages now-a-days, I'll not give a rush for him. They are more studied than the Greek or the Latin. He is for no gallant's company without them.'

BEN JONSON

CHAPTER I

BEASTS OF VENERY, CHASE AND WARREN

THE BEASTS OF VENERY (OR OF FOREST) were: the Hart, the Hind, the Hare, the Boar, the Wolf.

HART AND HIND

'Some may here object,' argues Cox (1697), 'and say, Why should the Hart and Hinde, being both of one kind, be accounted two several Beasts? To this I answer, That though they are Beasts of one kind, yet they are of several seasons: for the Hart hath his season in Summer, and the season of the Hinde begins when the Hart's is over.'

(See Chapter II.)

HARE

'The Hare is a *Leveret* in the first year, a *Hare* in the second, and *a great Hare* in the third.' (RS.)

'They go *to Buck* commonly in January, February, and March, and sometimes all the warm Months. . . . If when a

Hare riseth out of her *Form* she couches her Ears and *Scut*, and runs not very fast at first, it is an infallible sign that she is old and crafty. . . . Some (and that is something strange) will take the Ground like a *Coney*, and that is called *going to the Vaut* . . . a Hare leaveth better scent when she goeth to *relief*, than when she goeth towards her *Form* . . . in the Spring-time, or Summer, a Hare will not then sit in the Bushes, because they are frequently offended with *Pismires* (i.e. ants), Snakes, and Adders, but will sit in Cornfields and open places.' (NC.)

(See Chapter V.)

BOAR

(See Chapter III, The Wild Boar; and Chapter XXIV, No. 107.)

WOLF

The last English wolf was killed in 1682.

(See Chapters III and XXIV, No. 156.)

THE BEASTS OF THE CHASE were: the Buck, the Doe, the Fox, the Marten, the Roe.

BUCK AND DOE

(See Chapter II.)

FOX

'The first year a Fox is called a *Cub*, the next a *Fox*, and after an *Old Fox*.' (RS.)

The term *litter* is applied to the young of a fox, and his underground den is known as an *earth*. The female is called the *vixen*. (Osbaldiston defines Vixen as a 'fox's cub'!)

(See Chapter XXIV, No. 123; and Chapter IV.)

MARTEN

'The Martern is so called in his second year; in the first he is termed a *Martern Cub*.' (RS.)

(See Chapter IX, Vermin, and Chapter XXIV, No. 136.)

ROE

(See Chapter II.)

THE BEASTS AND FOWLS OF WARREN were: the Hare, the Cony, the Pheasant, the Partridge, and none other saith Mr. Manwood, are accounted Beasts nor Fowls of Warren. Later on the Bustard and the Rail were added.

'My Lord *Cook*', continues Cox, 'is of another Opinion, in his *Commentary on Littleton* 233. There be both Beasts and Fowls of the Warren, saith he: Beasts as Hares, Coneys, and Roes: Fowls of two sorts, *Terrestres* (and they of two sorts), *Silvestres*, & *Campestres*. The first, Pheasant, Wood-cock, &c. The second, Partridge, Quail, Rail, &c. Then *Aquatiles*, as Mallard, Hern, &c.'[1]

'There is great difference between Beasts of Forest, and Chase; the first are *Silvestres tantum*, the latter *Campestres tantum*. The Beasts of the Forest make their abode all the day-time in the great Coverts and secret places in the Woods; and in the night-season they repair into the Laws, Meadows, Pastures, and pleasant feeding places; and therefore they are called *Silvestres*, Beasts of the Wood. The Beasts of Chase do reside all the day-time in the Fields, and upon the Hills or high Mountains, where they may see round about them afar off, to prevent danger; but upon nights approach they feed as the rest in Meadows, &c. and therefore these are called *Campestres*, Beasts of the Field.' (NC. 1697.)

According to Twici, the beasts of the forest are moved with a lymer and *enchasez*, while the beasts of the chase and all vermin are found by the hounds and *enquillez* (i.e. *roused*).

THE SEASONS OF BEASTS

'A *Hart* or *Buck* beginneth at the end of Fencer Month, which is 15 days after *Midsummer*-day, and lastest till *Holy-rood*-day. The *Fox* at *Christmas*, and lasteth till the *Annuntiation* of the *Blessed Virgin*. The *Hinde* or *Doe* beginneth at *Holy-rood*-day, and lasteth till *Candlemas*. The *Roe-Buck* begining at *Easter*, and lasteth till *Michaelmas*. The *Roe* beginneth at *Michaelmas*, and lasteth till *Candlemas*. The *Hare* beginneth at *Michaelmas*, and lasteth till the end of *February*. The season of the *Wolf* is said to be from *Christmas* till the *Annuntiation* of the Virgin *Mary*. Lastly, The *Boar* begins at *Christmas*, and continues to the *Purification* of our *Lady*.' (NC. 1697.) (The italics are those of NC.)

Sir H. Dryden, in his Notes to his edition of Twici's *Le Art de Venerie*, gives a table which agrees with the above, and adds:

Otter - - -	from Shrove Tide to Midsummer.
Badger - - - - - - -	all seasons.
Coney - - - - - - -	all seasons.

[1] Though its punctuation is very bad, the above passage, if read carefully, becomes quite clear.

He says:

Candlemas is sometimes called the Purification.
Annunciation is sometimes called Lady-Day.

The dates of the various festivals, etc., are:

Candlemas	February 2
Shrove Tide	about February 22
Easter	between March 22 and April 25
Annunciation	March 25
Midsummer	June 24
Holyrood Day	September 14
Michaelmas	September 29
Christmas Day	December 25

The *Fence Month* was for the protection of deer, the Royal game. It lasted from fifteen days before midsummer to fifteen days after; 'the time of grace', according to Strutt, began at Midsummer and lasted to Holyrood-day.

AN HEERDE. A BEVE. A SOUNDER. A ROUTE

My chylde callith *herdys* of hert and of hynde
And of Bucke and of Doo where yo hem finde
And a *Beue* of Roos what place thay be in
And a *Sounder* ye shall of the wylde swyne
And a *Route* of wolues where thay passin inne
So shall ye hem call as many as thay bene.

(St. A.)

In France the art of Venerie was first considered a science, and from France to England came the vocabulary and the ceremonies in which every man of gentle birth considered it essential to be well versed. Such knowledge was more important than correct spelling or a literary education.

This Norman hunting, together with the French language, was established with us in the 11th century; they became unfashionable at the dawn of the modern age.

The Bourbon kings of France were passionately fond of the hunt. Henry IV was probably the greatest hunter of them all. His successor, Louis XIII, may not have hunted with such zest as his father, but Salnove wrote of him that 'he made laws for hunting, regulated the times when it is useful to speak to hounds and when to blow the horn; he formed the language of hunting, making it more polite and less rough.'

FOREST, CHASE AND WARREN

A Forest, according to Manwood, was a certain territory or circuit of Woody grounds and pastures, known in its bounds and privilege, for the peaceable being and abiding of Wild Beasts and Fowls of Forest, Chase and Warren, to be under the King's protection for his princely delight; replenished by beasts of Venery or Chase, and great coverts of Vert, for succour of the said Beasts. The four principal Forests were *New*, *Sherwood*, *Dean*, and *Windsor* Forests. The chief Officer of the New Forest was the Lord Warden; under him were two distinct appointments of Officers, the one to preserve the *Venison* of the Forest, and the other to preserve its *Vert*; the former term in the language of Forest Law comprehended every species of Game; the latter signified every thing that bore a green leaf within a Forest that may cover a Deer, but especially great and thick Coverts. A Forest was fenced round with meres and bounds, such as rivers, highways, hills. It was the highest franchise.

The Officers of the Forest were: *Justice in Eyre*, *Chief Warden*, *Verderers*, *Regarders*, *Foresters*, *Woodwards*, *Agistors*, *Rangers*, *Beadles*, *Keepers*. Many of these terms are still in use, and there is an Ancient Order of Foresters (estab. 1834).

The *Purlieu* of a Forest was originally all that ground near a Forest, which being added to the ancient Forests by King Henry II, Richard I, and King John, was afterwards disafforested by the Charta de Foresta; so that it became *pur lieu*, i.e. pure and free from the laws and ordinances of the Forest.

A *Park* was a privileged place for Beasts of Venery, and other wild Beasts of the Forest and Chase; it differed from a Chase or Warren, in that it had to be enclosed. It consisted of 'Vert, Venison and Inclosure, and if it is determined in *any* of them, it is a *total* disparking.'

'A *Chase* is the same liberty as a Park, save that it is *not* enclosed, and also that a man may have a Chase in another man's grounds as well as his own, by prescription. Every Forest is a *Chase*, et quiddam amplius; but any *Chase* is not a Forest.' (RS.) A Chase was second in degree to a Forest.

A *Free Warren* was a Franchise, or a place privileged by prescription or grant from the King, for keeping Beasts and Fowls of the Warren, which appears to be only Hares, Conies, Partridges, and Pheasants. It was a minor privilege. The name *Warren* is now usually applied to grounds set apart for breeding hares and rabbits.

'There is a great difference between the *frith* and the *fell*; the *fells* being taken for the *vallies*, green *compastures*, and *mountains*; and the *friths* for *springs* and coppices.'

(*The Sportsman's Dictionary*, 1807.)

VENISON

'*Venison*, or Venaison, is so called, from the means whereby the Beasts are taken. . . . Beasts of Venary (not Venery, as some call it) are so termed, because they are gotten by Hunting.

'No Beast of the Forest that is *solivagum & novicum* is Venison, as the *Fox*, the *Wolf*, the *Martin*, because they are no meat. The *Bear* is no Venison, because not only that he is *Animal novicum & solivagum*; but because he is no Beast of the Forest, and whatsoever is Venison must be a Beast of the Forest; *sed non e converso*. On the other side, *Animalia gregalia non sunt novica*, as the Wild *Boar*; for naturally the first three years he is *Animal gregale*; and after trusting to his own strength, and for the pleasure of man, becometh *Solivagum*. He is then called *Sanglier*, because he is *Singularis*; but he is Venison, and to be eaten. The *Hare* is Venison too, which *Martial* preferreth before all others:

Inter Quadrupedes gloria prima Lepus.

'So are the *Red-Deer* and *Fallow-Deer* Venison: *vide Cook* Inst. 4. pag. 316. Give me leave to insert here out of the same Author, two Conclusions in the Law of the Forest, which follow from hence. First, Whatsoever Beast of the Forest is for the food of man, that is Venison: . . . Secondly, Whatsoever Beast is not for the food of Man, is not Venison. Therefore *Capriolus*, or the *Roe*, being no Beast of the Forest, is by the Law of the Forest no Venison unless Hunted. Nature hath endowed the Beasts of the Forest with two qualities, Swiftness, and Fear; and their Fear increaseth their Swiftness,

. . . *Pedibus timor addidit alas*.' (NC. 1697.)

(the italics are those of NC.)

VERT

'*Vert* is any thing that beareth green Leaf, but especially of great and thick Coverts, and is derived *à Viriditate*. Vert is of divers kinds: some that beareth Fruit that may serve for food both for Man and Beasts, as *Service-trees*, *Nut-trees*, *Crab-trees*, &c. and for the shelter and defence of the Game. Some called *Hautboys*, serving for food and browse of and for the Game, and for the defence of them; as *Oaks*, *Beeches*, &c. Some *Hautboys* for Browse, Shelter, and Defence only; as *Ashes*, *Poplars*, &c. Of *Sub-boys*, some for Browse and Food of the Game, and for Shelter and Defence; as *Maples*, &c. Some for Browse and Defence; as *Birch*, *Sallow*, *Willow*, &c. Some for Shelter and Defence only; as *Elder*, *Alder*, &c. Of Bushes and other Vegetables, some for Food and Shelter, as the *Hawthorn*, *Black-thorn*, &c. Some for hiding and shelter, as *Brakes*, *Gorse*, *Heath*, &c. . . .

'*Over Vert*, is all manner of high Wood.

'*Neither Vert*, is all sorts of under-wood, Brushwood is called *Cablish*.' (NC. 1697.) (The italics are those of NC.)

OLD AND OBSOLETE TERMS

(from *The Gentleman's Recreation* by Nicholas Cox,
fourth edition, 1697)

Abatures: Spots where deer have lain and pressed down the herbage (Fr. *abattre*).

Aber, making the: Disembowelling.

Blemishes: Marks placed for guidance; e.g. 'plashing down small twigs'.

Bore-Cat: Tom-cat.

Bragged: Pregnant.

Coat: When one greyhound out-runs the other and turns or wrenches, it is a *coat*, or *cote*, scoring two points; or three if the hare be bent on the outer circle.

Imbosh: Foam from the mouth of the distressed deer.

Rear: Rouse up. (See Chapter XVI.)

Wallow: Query 'wallop' = waddle.

MORE OLD TERMS

We say *How* to a *Deer*. (NC.)

Blinks: Broken boughs to mark which way a deer runs.

Cleeves: The toes of a deer.

Emprimed: Of 'a hart, when he forsakes the herd.' (Os.)
Essay: The breast or brisket of a deer.
Rechasing: Driving back the deer or other beasts into the forests whence they had strayed. 'Anciently there were offices of rechasers . . . bestowed by the king ' (Os.)
Spaid: 'A gelded beast, also a deer of three years old.' (Os.)

Stables: Huntsmen and Kennelmen with hounds in leash, stationed at allotted posts round a forest during the chase, were called *stables.* In some cases their duty was to *blench* (head back) the game. The place where these stables was 'set' was called *stable-stand.* Here also archers were sometimes posted to shoot at divers game.
Tryste: The position taken up by shooters awaiting the game within the forest (in O.Fr. termed *berceau*, *ramies* and *folies*).

(NOTE: For further old stag-hunting terms, see Chapter II.)

CHAPTER II

'ALL MANER DERE'

NOTE: A large part of the information in the following pages has been obtained from *The Master of Game*, from volumes xx and xxii of the Lonsdale Library, in which there are chapters by Mr. Eric Parker, Sir George Thursby and Colonel W. W. Wiggin, and from Lady Apsley's *Bridleways Through History*.

ANCIENT

(All *terms* are in italics)

The Greeks hunted the deer; it was the favourite sport of Xenophon—though the hunting of those days was not, indeed, what we might call 'sporting' today, for they hunted because they were hungry.

In Saxon days hunting was still looked upon as a young man's duty. N. Cox refers to the ancient practice of *leasing*, dispensing rough justice (e.g. ten strokes from a pair of hand-couples) on the spot for offences such as arriving late at the Meet, 'mistaking any term of art', or 'hollering a wrong deer and leaving the Field before the death of the deer'!

Stag-hunting proper may be said to have been introduced into England about the time of the Norman Conquest, as depicted in the mode of the Bayeux Tapestry. *Running hounds* were first employed, hunting the line by *scent* to *view*—'the fairest hunting that any man may hunt after.' (Gaston Phoebus.) In his *Livre de Chasse* Gaston clearly shows how hunting for food developed into the 'true sport of kings and princes', with all its peculiar technique and etiquette.

The first Beast of Venery held pride of place until giving way to the Hare (in winter) and the Buck (in summer) in the days of Queen Elizabeth, and finally to the Fox towards the end of the eighteenth century.

The hunting language was largely built up of terms derived from the Norman French.

TERMS USED TO DENOTE AGES OF VARIOUS DEER: (NC.)

A Male Deer (Red)	First year	a *Hinde Calf* or *Calf*
	Second year	*Knobber* (or *Knobbler*, RS.); (*bullocke*, M.G)
	When beginning to put forth the head	[1]*Pricket*
	Third year	*Brocke* (*Brocket* or *Spayard*, RS.)
	Fourth year	*Staggard*
	Fifth year	*Stag*
	Sixth year	[2]*Hart*
	If hunted by the King	*Royal Hart*
	And if he escapes	*Royal Hart Proclaimed*
A Hind	First year	*Calf*
	Second year	*Hearse* or *Brocket's Sister*
	Third year	*Hinde*
A Fallow Deer	First year	*Fawn*
	Second year	*Pricket*
	Third year	*Sorel*
	Fourth year	*Sore*
	Fifth year	*Buck of the First Head*
	Sixth year	*Great Buck*
A Doe	First year	a *Fawn*
	Second year	*Tegg* (or *Pricket's Sister*, RS.)
	Third year	*Doe*

[1] Os. says: '*Spitter*, a male deer near 2 years old, whose horns begin to grow up sharp and spit-wise; the same is also called a *brocket*, or *pricket*.' (Note.—AM. generally follows RS.)

[2] '6th year a hart of ten (i.e. a warrantable stag) and then first is he chaseable, for always before shall he be called *rascal* or *folly*.' (MG.)

A Roe-Deer -	First year - - -	[1]*Kid* or *Gyrle*
	Second year - -	*Gazelle* (or *Girl*. RS.)
	Third year - - -	[1]*Hemuse*
	Fourth year - -	*Roebuck of the First Head*
	Fifth year - - -	*Fair Roebuck*

SOME FURTHER NOTES ON THE TERMS FOR A MALE RED DEER

Twici uses *Soar* for *Staggart*, and *Great-Soar* for *Stag*, but in O.E. the hart in his fourth year was called *Stag*, and in his fifth year *Great Stag*. Twici also gives: *veel*, *broket*, *espeyard*, *sour*, and *cerf*.

In *The Master of Game* the terms are:

First year - - - -	*calf*
Second year - - -	*bulloke*
Third year - - -	*broket*
Fourth year - - -	*staggard*
Fifth year - - - -	*stag*
Sixth year - - -	*hert of x.*

SIZE OF HERDS

A Littell herde. a mydyll heerd. a grete heerd.

.xx. is a littyll herde though it be of hyndis
And .xl. is a mydyle herde to call hym be kyndis
And .lxxx. is a grete herde. call ye hem so
Be it hert be it hynde bucke or el lis doo.

(St. A.)

['And note, that twenty is the least number which maketh a herd of any deer, except the roe, which is six.' (AM.)]

Twici gives the terms as follows:

Quant des herdes sunt des bestes?
De Cerfs et de Bises, o Demys, e Deymes,
Beavie des Chevereaus, Soundre dez porcs.

(Sir H. Dryden's ed.: Daventry, 1843)

The word *bises* is from the French *biche*, the female of the hart, and must not be confused with *bisse*, *bishe*, or *bis*, which is the name for the fur of the back of the squirrel in winter.

[1] Os. varies: a roe-buck 1st year, *Gyrle*; of 2 years *Girle*; of the fourth year *Heimuse*.

What is a *beuy* of Roos grete or small.

And sex is a beue of Roos on a rawe
and .x. is a mydyll beuy full wele I it kawe
A grete beuy is .xii. when thay to gedre be
And so call hem sonnys weere that ye hem se
The moore nombur than ywis: the gretter the beuy is.
(St. A.)

THE ATTIRE OF DEER

'As to the attire of deer, or parts thereof, those of a stag, if perfect, are the *bur*, the *pearls*, the little *knobs* on it, the *beam*, the *gutters*, the *antler*, the *fur-antler*, *royal*, *fur-royal*, and all at top the *croches*.

'Of the buck, the *bur*, *beam*, *brow-antler*, *black-antler*, *advancer*, *palm*, and *spellers*. If the croches grow in the form of a man's hand, it is called a *palmed-head*.

'Heads bearing not above three or four, and the croches placed aloft, all of one height, are called *crowned-heads*.[1] Heads having double croches are called *forked-heads*, because the croches are planted on the top of the beam like forks. . . .

'All stags, as they are *furnished*, beat their heads dry against some tree or other, which is called their *fraying-post*. When a deer rubs its horns against a tree, it *frays*.' (Os.)

Compare the above with:

'Lastly, Let me speak somewhat of the attire of deer, red or fallow: the round roll next the head is called the *burr*; the main horn, the *beam*;[2] the lowest antler, the *brow antler*; next above thereunto, *bizantlers*; next above that, the *royal*; and the upper part of all, the *surroyal top*: in the buck it is thus, the *burr*, *beam*, *braunch*, *advancers*, *palm*, and *spellers*. . . .

'When they *mew*, or cast their heads, it is said they hide them in the earth so cunningly . . .' (AM.)

'If you are asked what a Stag bears, you are only to reckon *Croches* he bears, and never to express an odd number. . . .

'Their new Horns come out at first like Bunches, and afterwards by the increase of the sun's heat they grow more hard, covered with a rough skin, which is called a *Velvet-head*. . . .

'Here note, that if you geld an Hart before he hath an Head,

[1] *Crowned Tops:* 'The first head of a deer.' (Os.)

[2] The term *gutters* = the channels in the *beam*. *Mule* (Fr. *meule*) was the old name for the *burr*.

he will never bear any; and if you geld him when he hath it, he will never after *Mew* or cast it: And so, if you geld him when he hath a Velvet-head, it will ever be so, without fraying or burnishing. . . . After they have Mewed, they will begin to *Button* in March and April; and as the Sun grows strong . . . so will their Heads increase in all respects: So that in the midst of June their Heads will be *summed* as much as they will bear all the year. . . .

'Here note, that they bear not their first Head, which we call *Broches*, and in a Fallow-Deer *Pricks*, until they enter the second Year of their Age.' (NC.)

Twici calls a hart *resigned*, one whose 'head does not grow anything more'. *Tress* was the name for the extra front branch in a *staggard*.

In *The Master of Game* a head is said to be

well affeted; the modern expression is				*well proportioned.*
well opened;	,,	,,	,,	a *good spread.*
counterfeit;	,,	,,	,,	*abnormal.*

THE RED DEER

CEREMONIAL AND TERMS OF VENERY

The stag was the favourite quarry of the hunter of the Middle Ages, both in France and England; and hounds were the essence of the Chase. The best account of the ancient procedure is given in that famous book *Miroir de Phébus des desduicts de la Chase* by Gaston de Foix, surnamed Phoebus, written in the late fourteenth century. This book was translated by Edward, Duke of York, and called *The Master of Game*.

(See Chapter XXVI.)

The old Norman *veneurs* hunted *à force de chiens*. The day before the hunt the *lymerer*, who held his *lymer* (hound) in *leash* or *liam*,[1] made his *Ringwalks* searching for the *slot* of a deer. If the slot or *trace* was three fingers' breadth or more, it was a warrantable stag; if less, or the *fumes* (droppings) were small, it indicated a *rascal* (unwarrantable stag). The lymerer made *scantilon* (measure) of the slot by laying a twig over the *talon* or heel. Over night he warned the sergeant, the *yeomen berners at horse* (kennel men) and the other *lymerers*.

[1] See Chapter XXIV, No. 130.

The *Berner* was the man in charge of hounds, the huntsman or kennelman (from O. Fr. *bernier* = one who paid his dues to his feudal lord in bran from which the bread for the hounds was made). *Prickers* were the whippers-in, *chacechiens* the slippers, and *charchion* a whip.

The *lymerer* would show the *fumes* of the harboured stag to the Master on the morning of the hunt. Gascoigne describes:

> 'From out my home, my *fewmets* fyrst I drawe,
> And them present, on leaves, by hunter's lawe.'

Then the hounds were divided into *relays*—the *vauntchasse*, the *midel* and the *parfitières* (the most reliable hounds). The *lymerer* began by laying on his hound on the *fue* (track ? from the Fr. *fuite* = flight) of the hart, crying '*Ho may, ho may, hole, hole, hole!*' At the same time the lord, the Master of Game, and the other hunter blew, in turn, three *moots* (blasts) on the horn. So was the stag *unharboured* from his *ligging* or lair. (Note: the old word *ligging* is still in use in Yorkshire. In Devon it is spelt *layer.*) The *lymerer* followed, calling '*Cy va*'; when he sighted the stag he blew a moot or a *recheat*[1] and then the berner uncoupled his hounds in *relays*. If the stag was not *soule* (alone), he had to be separated from his *Esquire* (a smaller stag) or from any others. Then he was said to be *herd with rascal and folly*.

If a *relay* was unable to pick up the line, that was known as being on a *stynt*; if they hunted a heel trail, that was to run *contre*. Many were the terms used for the hart's tricks to deceive those *questing*[2] him. If he pushed up another hart and lay down in his place, that was a *blenche*[3] or a *ruse*. If he turned on his tracks, it would be a *doubling* or a *running to and fro*. If he stood in water, he went to *soil*; when he swam upstream he *beat up* the river, or downstream he *foiled down*. 'The last Refuge', says Cox, 'of a Hart sorely hunted is the Water (which, according to Art, is termed the *Soil*).'

When the hart became tired he *cast* his *chaule* (hung his head), and his *ergots* (dew-claws) made deep tracks. Then the berners let loose the *vauntlay*[4] (the last *relay* of hounds). At last the stag stood *at bay*. If he was *in velvet*, a hunter *spayed* him with a knife. Otherwise he was usually slain with an arrow. Thus was the stag

[1] See Chapter XI. [2] See Chapter XVI.

[3] *Blanche:* to head back a deer in its flight; *blanches* = tricks.

[4] *Vauntellery:* the casting off a relay of hounds before those already hunting come up.

encorned (pulled over on its side) and the *prise* (and *Mort*)[1] blown to end the hunt.

'When the hart is taken you ought to blow *four moots*,[1] and he shall be undone like as any other beast.' (Twici.)

THE CURÉE

This was the ceremony of giving the hounds their *reward* (from *cuir* = hide, on which the reward was originally given, hair side upward). The fine art of venery was peculiarly exemplified in the *breaking up* of the deer and in the *Curée*, which were performed with great care and pride. All got their share of the flesh, from lord to forester. Even the raven was not forgotten; his portion was the *oscorbin*, the gristle at the spoon of the brisket.

The word *Curée* eventually became *quarry*. These *Rights* (perquisites) were distributed with great ceremony.

He that is bid, says The Master of Game, 'should *undo* him most woodmanly and cleanly that he can and wonder ye not that I say woodmanly, for it is a point that belongeth to woodmans-craft, though it be well suiting to an hunter to be able to do it'.

Numbles: Were originally the liver, kidneys and entrails of a deer. The word became *umbles*, then *humbles*, hence came 'humble-pie'.

To *take say* was to draw the edge of the knife leisurely along the middle of the belly, to discover how fat the deer was.

THE QUARRY

'In the 16th and 17th centuries, the portion of the spoil given to the hounds was called *the reward*, but the game which a hawk caught was called the *quarry*; and the word came to mean the game at which a hawk was flown, whether it was taken or not.' (Dryden's Notes on Twici.) The hounds' reward was called the *quyrreye* (quarry), because eaten on the hide (*sur le quir*). It is therefore technically incorrect to refer to the wild animal in the course of being hunted as 'the quarry'.

BATTUES

In later days the sport degenerated, and the deer were driven by greyhounds and shot by bows. First the *harrier* (huntsman)

[1] See Chapter XI.

loosed his *teasers* to *make the rascal void* (i.e. to eliminate the smaller deer). Then the *hart hounds* were uncoupled and drove the 'wily deer' up to the *trysts*[1] (or *folies*), where they were slain by the Royal hunters (!) in full view of their ladies.

Battues (see page 52) were also held, in which the local inhabitants were employed as beaters; they formed a ring called a *tinchel*. Deer and other game were driven to a stand for the lords to shoot; this was called driving the *wanlass* (or *windass*).

These methods were only a temporary change, and the old ceremonial of the Normans was still practised in the days of James I.

'They be wonderfully perilous beasts, for with great pain shall a man recover that is hurt by a hart, and therefore men say in old saws: "after the boar the leech and after the hart the bier".' (MG.)

SOME FURTHER TERMS OF VENERY

'When a deer has been hard hunted, and then betakes himself to swimming in any river, &c., they say *he takes foil* (? soil).

'When a roe crosses and doubles, it is called *trajoining*.

'When a deer eateth in a corn or grass field, he is said to *feed*, otherwise to *browze*; and if he stayeth to look on anything, he is said to *stand at gaze*; when he forceth by upon force, he *trippeth*; and when he runs a pace he *straineth*.

'When he is hunted and leaves the herd, then he *singleth*; and when he foams at the mouth, he is *embossed*; being dead, say *he is done*.

'When a hart entereth a river or pool, which is termed the *foil*, say *she descendeth*; when you see him ready to enter water, say *he proffereth*; and for the second time, *reproffereth*; after you see where he hath trod, the water filling his footsteps, they say *here the hart defouleth*.

'When a hart or stag breaks herd, and draws to the covert, they say *he goes to harbour*, or *taketh his hold*, or *he covereth*; and when he cometh out again, that *he discovereth himself*.'

(*The Sportsman's Dictionary*, by H. J. Pye, 1807.)

'After a long run he will get *embossed* or tired, which you will know by his coat looking black. He will *tapish*, i.e. lurk, skulk, and *sink*; which latter term means lying down, with his feet close

[1] See Chapter I (end).

under his belly, and putting his nose close to the ground to prevent the scent flying, . . .' (from *The Sportsman's Directory*, by John Mayer, Gamekeeper, 1819).

THE FALLOW DEER

Some authorites hold that fallow deer were introduced into England by the Romans. They were, at any rate, hunted by the Normans, but not with the same 'ritual' as was followed in the hunting of the hart.

A buck is smaller than a hart, but larger than a roe.

'A buck's head is *palmed* with a long palming, and he beareth more tines than doth a hart. . . . They have a longer tail . . . and more grease on their haunches. . . . They are *fawned* in the month of June. . . . When the hart hath been fifteen days at rut the buck scarcely beginneth to be *in heat* and *bellow*. . . . Men go not to sue him with a lymerer nor do men go to harbour him as men do the hart. Nor are his *fumes* put in judgement as those of the hart, but men judge him by the foot or the head.' (MG.)

'There is not so much art and skill in *Lodging* a Buck, as in the *Harbouring* a Hart; . . . nor can he stay so long at *Soil* as the Hart will do: only he leapeth lightlier at *Rut* than the Hart; and *groaneth* or *troateth*, as a Hart belleth, but with a lower Voice, ratling in the Throat. And here is to be noted, they love not one another, nor will they come near each other's Layr.' (NC.)

They ran often in rings, though they were faster when first roused.

The buck was thus a less noble quarry than the hart, but—'*Buck*-Venison is incomparable Food'. A *Buck-stall* was a toil in which to take deer—could only be kept by one possessing his own Park.

Windsor Park contained a large herd of fallow deer in 1465, and they were probably driven for hunting for Henry VIII and Queen Elizabeth. 'Fallow' refers to its light colour.

THE ROE-DEER

In *The Master of Game* it is written that 'the roebuck is a common beast enough, and therefore I need not tell of his making'. But at one time, about 1800, they became nearly extinct in England.

'The roe-buck hath no season to be hunted, for they bear no

venison. . . . When they run at their ease they run with leaps, but when weary they trot and do not leap . . . (he) runneth wondrous fast.' (MG.) When hunted they often bounded back to hounds. Their hinder parts were called *target*.

'The Roe-Buck', says Cox, 'is called by the Greeks and Latins by one name, *viz. Dorcas*. These Beasts are very plentiful in Africa, Germany, and Helvetian Alps. . . . The tail of this Beast is lesser and shorter than a Fallow-Deer's; insomuch that it is doubtful whether it be a tail or not. . . . This Beast is very easie to hunt, and goeth to *Rut* (or *Tourn* most properly) in October, the extent whereof consists of fifteen days, and never parteth with the *Doe* till Fawning-time. . . .

'The Venison of a *Roe* is never out of season, being never fat, and therefore they are to be hunted at any time: only this, some favour ought to be shewn the *Doe* whilst she is big with *Fawn*.[1] . . .

'The Hounds must be rewarded with the Bowels, the Blood, and Feet slit asunder, and boiled all together. This is more properly called a *Dose* than a *Reward*.'

A Roe-deer, when taken, was not broken up in the field, but carried to the house. (See Chapter XXI.) Item of folk-lore: The roe, according to Sir Thomas Cockaine, sweats only through a vent in one of its forelegs!

Roe baiting: This was quite unlike bear or badger baiting. The practice consisted of the hunting of one particular buck, by one man (armed with a rifle) with one dog (usually an old foxhound). A good sport which has died out.

MODERN

(All *terms* are in italics)

The language of the chase has come down to us from our Norman ancestors, and the proper terms still used in the hunting of deer are of more ancient origin than those of, probably, any other sport. Deer *chew the cud*. They are the only ruminants to be found wild. Deer are said to *graze*, but Moose *browse*. The Moose is called by the Sioux Indians *mouswah* (eater of wood). It is the Elk of the Old World.

[1] *Pomeled* = spotted (e.g. the young of roe-deer). Also used to be applied to a *flea-bitten* or dappled horse.

THE RED DEER

(*Cervus elaphus.*) The terms for Deer at their various ages are but slightly altered. (Cf. the list under ANCIENT.)

Male	-	First year is known as a	*Calf*
		Second year	*Knobber*, *Knobbler* (*Pricket* for a Park deer)
		Third year	*Brocket*
		Fourth and Fifth	*Staggie*
		Sixth, Seventh	*Stag*
		Eighth	*7-Pointer*
		At Twelve	*Royal* (12 Points)
Female	-	Called *Hind Calf* up to her third year, after that a *Hind*.	
		A hind that is without calf (NOT necessarily barren) is called a *yeld hind*.	

'Only four names are applied to hinds,' writes Vesey-Fitzgerald, 'and only one of these is technical. They are old, damned, bloody and *yeld*.'

Stags are said to *roar* or *bell* at the end of September, when the rut follows. Red deer vary greatly in size and weight; a Park stag is much heavier than a Highland (a Continental heavier than both).

THE ATTIRE

The Norman names for the brow tine and the next two tines were *antler*, *royal*, and *surroyal*. Now we call them the *brow* tine, the *bay* (*bez*), and *tray* (*trez*), (termed *rights*).

The group of three tines on top is now known as *the cup*.

Summing: The complete antler—'brow, bay, tray and four-a-top'. (P. R. Chalmers.)

'The word "imperial" ' (for a stag carrying a head of more than twelve points), says Mr. Eric Parker, 'has no authority at all. Pints are imperial, not stags.' Could that have been better put? A *wilson*, for a 14-pointer, is another term to be avoided.

'A good head', says Mr. Parker, 'should be long in horn, wide in *span* and thick in *beam*. . . . In length, measured from the base of the *coronet* to the tip of the highest tine, it should be more than thirty inches. The inside *span* should approximate to thirty inches. The beam should be at least five inches. The *tine* should be long and the surface of the horn rough. . . .'

Span: The greatest distance between *beams* (inside measurement).

Length: Taken from the bottom of the *coronet*, over the *pedicle*, and up the outside of one antler to the top of the longest *tine* on top.

Beam: The circumference of the antler, between second and third tines, taken at its thinnest part.

Burr: (=*Coronet*) The swelling at base of horns, next to the skull.

Crockets: The points at the top of the horns.

Pearls: Bony swellings round the *burr*.

Tine: A branch of the antlers.

Red deer shed their horns in the spring. A new growth rises from the *pedicle*. For four months, until the complete horn hardens, the stag is said to be *in velvet*, and he rubs his horns against trees, etc., until the skin hangs in strips, and he is *in rags and tatters*. When quite stripped he is said to be *clean*.

Stags which remain without horns throughout their lives are called *hummels* (O.E. *hamelian* = to mutilate). These hornless stags are named *polled* or *humble* by Sir H. Johnston in his *British Mammals*. Stags which grow abnormal horns, a pair of single long antlers above the brow tine, are known as *switches*.

Reindeer are the only female deer to have antlers.

STAG HUNTING

In Scotland the rifle has taken the place of hound, but on Exmoor (Devon and Somerset Staghounds) red deer are still harboured and hunted by methods very similar to those of ancient days, when the Saxons properly organized the British Chase; and many of the old terms are current.

The Stag hunting season (proper) is from August Bank Holiday to October 12th; but there is also a short period of three weeks in spring, at Easter. Hind hunting is carried on from November 1 to end of February. Hinds are not harboured.

'In foxhunting you hunt *a* fox but in stag hunting you hunt *the* stag.' The harbourer, therefore, must find a warrantable stag to hunt. He *sets the covert* by *making a ring walk*. From the Meet, the first business is the *tufting*, for which about four couple of steady hounds are employed. Only if the stag is alone and in the open can tufting be dispensed with. For further notes on this procedure, see under *Fallow Deer*, below. To *tuft* is to hunt.

Entry, *Rack*. Branches broken by the deer's head.

Red deer have only one calf; whereas the Fallow produce, as a rule, two, and sometimes three, fawns.

DEER STALKING

Great was my love in youth and strong my desire towards
the bounding herds!
But now! broken, weak and helpless, their remembrance
wounds my heart.

Donald McFinley of Fersit
(the old Gaelic bard)
who sang of the wolves and deer that fell to his arrow.

The bow and arrow was supplanted by rude guns in the 17th century. The bow being noiseless, the deer-stalker could repeat his shots; but now accuracy is all-important.

Stalking, as it is known today, has only been in existence for about a hundred years. During this period many excellent books have been written, of which four may here be mentioned as representative of various aspects of the sport:

The Art of Deer Stalking (1838), by William Scrope (Ill. Landseer).
Wild Sports and Natural History of the Highlands (1851), by Charles St. John.
The Wild Red Deer of Scotland (1923), by A. G. Cameron.
Deer-Stalking (1935), by Patrick R. Chalmers.

The stalking season is from the end of August to mid October. There is 'no legal close time. But, by courtesy, a stag is not venison until he has shed his velvet.' (Chalmers.) There are two main methods of approaching the wild red deer of the Highlands—*Driving* (now in abeyance) and *Stalking*; the latter giving greater scope for skill and manoeuvre.

The deer-stalker, sometimes called the *gentleman*, is usually chaperoned by a professional *forester* (*the stalker*) and assisted by a *ghillie*. The object is to get within range (say 100 yards) of a *shootable stag* which, according to Chalmers, 'weighs from 12 to 20 stone "clean" ' (i.e. one of about 8 seasons or more; average weight 14 stone). 'The best stags, in a parcel of deer upon the move, come last.' If the stag is wounded, a dog (probably a collie; not now a deerhound) may be *slipped* to track or *bay* him. When killed, the stag is bled and *gralloched* as soon as possible, and the carcase then *saddled* on to a *pony*.

'The greater the deer the greater the fraying tree.'
(The Brothers Stuart)

TERMS

The modern terms to denote the ages of Red Deer and their attire have been given above. A *point* is not counted as such 'unless the stalker can hang the strap of his spy-glass on it'. (Chalmers.) (See p. 135.)

Black Stag: One who has been rolling in a peat hag.

Cookie: 'Their heads are very peculiar, a fork at the top, brows but no bays or trays.' (General Crealock.)

Corrie: A cup-like hollow where deer may collect.

Cromie: This type of head has an abnormal horn which bends backwards like the horns of an antelope.

Ghillie: Carries rifle (till after the *spy*), raincoat and lunch.

Gralloch: A deer's entrails; to *gralloch* is to remove them.

Heavier: (The word has nothing to do with weight. It comes from the French *Hiver* = winter, and means that the animal can be eaten in winter.) A horned stag without the ability to reproduce his species. Is said to be a better sentinel than the most suspicious hind. (Cf. a *hummel* = a hornless stag; but it can reproduce.)

March: Good Scots for a boundary.

Ponies: The light Highland farm horses or *shelts* used to carry the carcase.

Saddling: To *saddle* a stag is to sling it on to the pony's saddle.

Squire: A young stag that attaches himself as an esquire to a big old stag. (Cf. *Esquire*, p. 16.)

(Note: A stag gets up like a cow—hind quarters first.)

Deer can be *moved*; that is when a few ghillies are instructed to show themselves, 'giving their wind' to deer who are thus shifted in a required direction.

THE CARTED STAG

This travesty of the real thing was first introduced in 1728. It is a humane form of hunting and affords a good run. As the *Drag* is to foxhunting, so may the 'Carted deer' be said to compare with stag hunting proper.

When the Royal Pack hunted their quarry in Windsor Forest, hounds were permitted to hunt to the death. But it is not so now. In fact the same stag cannot often be turned out, because he soon learns that he will not be touched. About twelve minutes law is given, then hounds are laid on. When the stag thinks he has had enough, he usually *soils* in some stream, or stands at *bay*. He is then lassooed and taken quietly home in a van.

The successful conclusion of a run, whether the deer is killed or not, is termed the *Take*.

The modern hunt is the Berks and Bucks Staghounds. Red Deer only are hunted.

FALLOW DEER

Wild fallow deer are to be found to-day in the New Forest and Epping Forest, and there are many herds in private parks. Their horns are smooth and palmated at the tops, which formation first appears in their third year; at six the horns are fully developed. The buck sheds its horns in May. Park deer have, on the whole, rather a lighter coat than the wild.

In recent times, the Deputy Surveyor of the New Forest 'made out a table of the various ages of the male fallow deer with the respective names; every keeper in the Forest had this given to him and was expected to know and use the names. There is seldom any reference to these names at the present time, except the first two:

In his 1st year a male fallow deer is a				*Fawn*
2nd	,,	,,	,,	*Pricket*
3rd	,,	,,	,,	*Sorel*
4th	,,	,,	,,	*Sore*
5th	,,	,,	,,	*Bare Buck*
6th	,,	,,	,,	*Buck*
7th	,,	,,	,,	*Great Buck.*

We say three-year-old, four-year-old, five-year-old, and six-year-old, and older we call *full-headed bucks*. It is a pity the correct names are not used. All does in the New Forest are known as *old does*. The term *yeld* is not employed.

It will be noticed that this follows closely the ancient terms given by Cox and Daniel; up to the fourth year the list is the same.

Fallow deer are hunted to-day by the New Forest Buckhounds. The Forest is divided into three divisions, each under a head keeper, whose job it is to *harbour* the bucks; this is done by watching and *slotting*. The keeper reports to the Master at the meet.

The tufters are then *laid in* to a herd, or the selected buck if possible. 'The object of tufting is to single out the buck that it is intended to hunt. It has been asked why the pack cannot draw for the buck just as they draw for a fox. The answer to this is that hounds draw for a fox—any fox, but with deer it is THE ONE PARTICULAR buck that is to be hunted.'

When *roused*, the buck will almost invariably join fresh deer. When he decides to go away, that is the time to stop the *tufters* and lay on the pack. It is vital that hounds learn to stop when told; for this purpose the term used is *Hold Hard.*

'A tufter's essentials are that he must have a *good nose*, for he may be put on the line of deer that have been gone some four or five hours previously, he must *throw his tongue* all the time, have great perseverance and be obedient and stop when called.'

The pack is *held* coupled while tufting is carried on; when the pack is *unleashed* the tufters are taken back to kennels. 'Unlike a red deer, a buck will never wait for hounds to come up to him in water,' but will run on till dead beat. 'A hunted buck will *soil*, that is, roll in a pool of water, or in a stream, and in doing so will plunge straight into the pool, roll, and get up, all without a moment's delay, and go galloping on without looking or listening for hounds.'

Buck: Now used as a general term for goats and antelopes of both sexes (S. Africa). There is, also, the *Black Buck* of the plains of India.

ROE DEER

Many of these beautiful deer disappeared from our forests and woods in the war (1914-18). They were common in the South of England (where they still exist) at the beginning of this century, and have always been found in plenty in Scotland. They are no longer 'hunted', but afford good sport to the stalker. A roe drive is not sport.

They shed their horns, as a rule, in November, and *rut* in the beginning of August. The does generally have two kids.

Average weight of a good Roebuck is 40 lbs.; its horns, 6-pointed, are about 8½ inches in length.

CHAPTER III

THE WILD BOAR, THE BEAR, THE WOLF

'Hunters live in this world more joyfully than any other men.'

The Master of Game

THE WILD BOAR

ANCIENT

THE SOUNDER

What is a Sounder of swyne grete or small
¶ Twelfe make a *Sounder* of the wylde swyne
Xvi. a *medyll Sounder* what place thay be inne
A *grete sounder* of swyne .xx. ye shall call
Forr geet not this lession for thyng that may fall
Thynke what I say: my sonne night and day.

(St. A.)[1]

¶ Now to speke of the boore the fyrst yere he is
A *pygge of the Sounder* called ale haue I blis
The secunde yere an *hogge* and so shall he be
And an *hoggestere* when he is of yeris .iii.
And when he is of .iiij. yere a *beore* shell he be
From the *Sounder* of the swyne then dep*ar*trith he
A *Synguler* is he so: for a lone he will go.

(St. A.)

[1] Twelve was not always accepted as the least number to form a sounder:
'That men calleth a *trip* of tame swyn is called of wylde swyn a *soundre*: that is to say, if there be passyd v. or vj. togedres.' (*The Master of Game.*)

According to Twici, the boar was first called a '*pyg* as long as he is with his dame, and when his dame levyth hym then he is called a *gorgeaunt*, and the IIj yere he is called a *hoggaster*. . . .'

Actually it is in the third year (and not the fourth, as the rhyme in St. A. has it) that the young boar leaves the sow and becomes a solitary bachelor. In this both Turberville and Lavallée agree. 'It is curious', remarks Sir Henry Dryden, 'that the word *singular* should be used afterwards for a number of boars, when the boar is called *sengler* from *sengle*, alone, single.' But there seems no doubt that it was so used.

In Roquefort *soure* is a *company* of swine. (See Chapter XXIV, Nos. 107 and 152.)

A GREAT BOAR

MG. has a long para. on 'how to know a great wild boar'.

'And if a man see a wild boar the which seemeth to him great enough, as men say of the hart *chaceable of ten*, he shall say a wild boar of the third year that is without refusal. . . . When the tusks of a boar are great as of half a cubit or more and are both great and large of two fingers or more and there be small *gutters* along both above and beneath, these be the tokens that he is a great boar and old. . . .'

TERMS TO BE USED IN BOAR-HUNTING

'If it should be demanded what you will call a *Boar* of three years old; you may answer, He is a *young Boar which hath lately left the Sounder*. An old *Boar* you must call a *Singular*, or *Sanglier*, *that hath left the Sounder four or five years since*. In making of a report, if you are asked where the *Boar* fed the night before, you may say, he *fed* in the corn; but if in the fields or meadows, you must then say, he hath been *routing* and *worming* in such a place, or such a fern-field. Where note, that whatsoever he feeds on, excepting roots, is called *feeding*; the other is called *routing*, *worming*, *or fearning*[1]: but when he feedeth and routeth not, you must then call that *grasing*.

'The *Boar* is ever pigg'd with as many teeth at first as he shall ever have after, which will only increase in bigness, not number. Amongst the rest, they have four which are called *Tushes*, or *Tusks*, whereof the two biggest do not hurt when he strikes, but

[1] Root. A wild boar was said to *root* (or *fearn* or *worm*) when he was feeding on ferns or roots. Otherwise he was said to *feed*.

serve only to whet the other two lowest, with which they frequently kill.

'Their Season beginneth in the midst of *September*, and endeth about the beginning of *December*, at which time they go a *Brimming*.' (NC. 1697.) (The italics are those of NC.)

Grice, a young wild boar; *Shoots*, young (tame) 'swine of about three quarters of a year old'. (Os.)

HUNTING THE BOAR

Besides the deer and the hare, the Greeks also hunted the wild boar. An old boar would be located by *ring-walking*, nets were set in position, staunch hounds loosed, and the hunters advanced in line on foot, armed only with javelins or short spears.

Mr. J. E. Harting says that Britons, Romans, Saxons, and Normans all hunted the wild boar in England in turns. The failure, due to disafforestation, of their chief food (beechmast and acorns) caused the wild boar gradually to become scarce; but they were preserved in parks for hunting long after. The places where they were fed were called *Franks*. They were still hunted at Windsor in the seventeenth century by James I.

The whole of the following extract (except for the words in brackets) is from *The Master of Game*.

'They go in their love to the *brimming* (from Mid. Eng. *brime* = burning heat) as sows do about the feast of St. Andrew (Nov. 30th), and are in their brimming love three weeks, and when the sows are cool the boar does not leave them. He stays with them till the twelfth day after Christmas. . . . They *farrow* in March. . . .

'They wind a man as far as any other beast or farther. . . .

'They *root* in the ground with the rowel of their snouts which is right hard. . . . They have a hard skin and strong flesh, especially upon their shoulders which is called the *shield*. Their season begins from the Holy Cross day in September (Sept. 14th) to the feast of St. Andrew . . . they are *in grease* when they be withdrawn from the sows. The sows are in season from the *brimming time* till the time when they have *farrowed*.

'They have four tusks, two in the jaw above and two in the nether jaw; . . . men beyond the sea call the nether tusks of the boar his *arms* or his *files* . . . and also they call the tusks above *grinders* (from the French *gres*).'

Wild boar hunting in the early Middle Ages was pursued in a very similar manner to stag hunting. The huntsman sought for his boar with the *lymer*, as did the harbourer for the stag. He looked for the *traces*, and their wallowing pools and rubbing-trees. The boar was a *stinking beast* and made no *doublings*. Large savage dogs (*alaunts*)[1] were used and laid on in *relays*. When he *stood at bay* he was surrounded and killed with sword or lance. Gaston discusses at great length how to ride, and use the spear. He considered that the killing of a wild boar with a short sword from horseback was the finest sport. (Cf. MODERN PIG-STICKING.)

At the death the *prise*[2] was blown as for a stag, and hounds given their reward, called *fourail* (not curée), a mixture of bowels and bread cooked on a fire.

'When the boar is taken he shall be *undone* with the hide on' (i.e. opened up and cleaned). (Twici.)

The 'Wilde-Boar' was the fourth beast of venery, though Osbaldiston remarks that he is 'not properly termed a beast of venery, for he chiefly trusts in his strength and *tushes* for his defence, and not to his feet. . . .'

Boar hunting was common in France, where they called it *Sanglier*, 'In this sort of Hunting,' says Cox, 'the way is to use furious terrible Sounds and Noises, as well of Voice as Horn, to make the Chase turn and fly; because they are slow, and trust to their Tusks and defence: which is *Agere Aprum*, to bait the *Boar*. Yet this must be done after his Den or Hold is discovered, and the Nets be pitched.

'The Huntsmen give judgement of the Wild-Boar by the print of his Foot, by his *Rooting*. A wild Swine roots deeper than our ordinary Hogs, because their Snouts are longer; and when he comes into a Cornfield (as the *Caledonian-Boar* in *Ovid*) turns up one continued Furrow, not as our Hogs, routing here and there; and then by his soil he soils and wallows him in the myre: These are his *Volutabra Silvestria*, where his greatness is measured out; then coming forth, he rubs against some Tree, which marks his height; as also when he sticks his Tusk into it, that shews the greatness thereof. They observe the bigness of his *Lesses*, and the depth of his Den; where note, that they call his Dung by the name of *Lesses*.

'Whensoever the Boar is hunted and stands *at Bay*, the Hunts-

[1] See Chapter IV. [2] See Chapter XI.

men ride in, and with Swords and Spears striking on that side which is from their Horses, wound or kill him. This is the French Hunting: but the antient Romans standing on foot, or setting their Knees to the ground, and charging directly with their Spear, did *Opponere ferrum*, and *Excipere Aprum*: for such is the nature of a Boar, that he spits himself with fury, running upon the weapon to come at his Adversary; and so, seeking his revenge, he meets with his own destruction.'

Cox remarks that 'we have none in England'. But there were wild boar preserved in parks in his day, where the 'verie daungerous' (Holinshed) sport of hunting was still enjoyed.

THE SPEAR

'If you strike at him with your sword or Boar-spear, strike not low, for then you will hit him on the snout, which he little values; for he watcheth to take blows upon his tusks or thereabouts: but lifting up your hand, strike right down, and have a special care of your horse; for if you strike and hurt him, so will he you if he can. . . . The hunting-spear must be very sharp and broad, branching forth into certain forks, so that the Boar may not break through them upon the huntsman. . . .' (NC. 1697.)

MODERN

PIGSTICKING

From such ancient sources has evolved our modern pigsticking or hog hunting, as practised in India to-day—one of the finest sports in the world. Where is there a quarry more worthy of one's steel? A good boar might measure 30 inches at the wither; average weight, say 200 lbs.

Like foxhunting in England, which only ousted stag-hunting in popularity little more than one and a half centuries ago, pigsticking 'proper' only superseded bearsticking at the beginning of the nineteenth century.

In the South of India the animal is generally called a *hog*, and in the North a *pig*.

When 'pig' have been located, a beat is organized and the hunters are posted in *heats* of three or four at different points at the edge of the jungle (or other cover). On a boar breaking cover, when it is well clear the leader of the nearest heat gives

Ride, and the members of the heat race for *first spear* (q.v.). The signal that it is a sow (and should not be hunted) is the spear held horizontally above the head.

Then follows the sport of overcoming and killing the boar, who knows no fear, and seldom fails to charge once he has been *pricked*.

There are two kinds of spear. In Bengal a short jobbing spear is used, overhand. It is made of stout bamboo with a heavy blade and is about 6½ feet long. An *underhand* spear (about 8-9½ feet long) is used in Bombay and Deccan. It is lighter than the jobbing spear.

PIGSTICKING TERMS

First Spear: The honour of being the first to prick the boar. (Also, of the first thrust which draws blood.)

Head: The steel point at the end of the spear—about 10 inches long.

Jhow: (Urdu word for tamarisk). Favourite cover for the boar.

Jinking: A boar turns sharply to right or left (mostly to right) when closely pressed. It is then said to *jink*.

Kadir: River-bed country where pig abound. The Kadir Cup is the cup given by the Meerut Tent Club and competed for annually. The first contest was in 1874.

Pugging: Tracking boars to their lairs by their *pugs* (footmarks).

Rootings: The marks of a boar's burrowings with his snout, when searching for food. (See Footnote on p. 28.)

Squeaker: A young pig up to three years. It has dark stripes on its back and sides; and the horn of its feet is soft.

Tent Club: The name for any pigsticking club in India.

Tushes: The four projecting tusks of a boar. The upper pair are too blunt for cutting. The two lower project only about three inches, but average length is nine inches.

Tusker: Loose term for a well-grown boar.

A good man to pig: compares with the expression 'A good man to hounds'.

Three good rules, which explain themselves:

1. Better lose your boar over the horizon than chop him back into cover.
2. Keep your eye on the pig and not on the ground.
3. Ride straight, and ride like hell.

The pig is also hunted, by various means, in divers countries such as Africa, Australia and New Zealand, Germany and Albania.

In Africa there is a Bush Hog and a Wart Hog.

THE BEAR

ANCIENT

The following notes are from the fourth edition of *The Gentleman's Recreation* (Cox), in his 'Short ACCOUNT of some particular Beasts that are not Hunted in England, but in Foreign Countries':

There are two sorts of *Bears*, a greater and lesser; the last is more apt to climb trees than the other. . . .

When the she-*Bear* perceiveth herself with Whelp, she withdraws herself into some cave, or hollow rock, and there remains till she brings forth her Whelps, where without meat they grow very fat, especially the Males, only by sucking their fore-feet. When they enter into their Den, they convey themselves backward, that so they may put out their foot-steps from the sight of the Hunters.

It is commonly received as a truth (though it be a palpable vulgar errour) *That the Whelps of* Bears *at their first Littering are without all form and fashion, and nothing but a little congealed Blood like a lump of Flesh, which afterwards the old one frameth with her Tongue by licking them to her own like.* This Opinion may easily be disproved; for they are only littered blind without Hair, and the hinder-legs not perfect, the fore-feet folded up like a fist, and other members deformed, by reason of their immoderate Humor or Moistness in them.

When they are Hunted, they are so heavy that they make no speed, and so are always in sight of the Dogs: They stand not at bay as a *Boar*, but fly wallowing; but if the Hounds stick in, they will fight valiantly in their own defence; sometimes they stand up streight on their hinder-feet, and then take that as a sign of fear and cowardize: they fight stoutest and strongest on all four.

They have an excellent scent, and smell farther off than any other Beast except the *Boar*; for in a whole Forest they will smell out a *Tree* laden with Mast.

They go sometimes a gallop, and at other times an amble; but they go most at ease when they wallow . . . they use no doublings nor subtilties.

The best finding of a *Bear* is with a Leam-hound; and yet he who is without one may trail after a *Bear* as we do after a *Buck* or *Roe*, and you may lodge and hunt them as you do a *Buck*. For the more speedy execution, mingle Mastiffs[1] among your Hounds; for they will pinch the *Bear*, and so provoke her to anger, until at last they bring her to the bay.

They cast their Lesses sometimes in round Croteys, and sometimes flat like a Bullock, according to their feeding.

They tumble and wallow in water and mire as Swine, and they feed like a Dog. Some say their flesh is very good food, let who will eat it for me, who are not so nicely palated as myself.

Truly, these old sporting books make good reading. (The italics are those of NC.)

(See Chapter XXIV, No. 105.)

THE WOLF

ANCIENT

There were wolves to hunt in Twici's time. From his very nature, however, the wolf could not be tolerated in a civilized country, but it has been proved that he was not entirely exterminated in England until the reign of Henry VII. The last wolf in Scotland and Ireland is said to have been slain in the eighteenth century; and in England, the last one ever seen in Yorkshire was slain, so it is believed, in the shadow of a ruined Abbey near Leeds—by John of Gaunt. Gaston gives no less than eight chapters on the wolf; while their hunting was becoming rare in England, in France they were numerous and voracious (due to the wars), and their destruction was vital.

'There are some that eat children and men . . . they are called *wer-wolves*[2]. . . . They howl like hounds and if there are but two they will make such a noise as if there were a *route*[3] of seven or eight if it is by night, when the weather is clear. . . .

'The wolf's skin is warm to make cuffs or pilches (pelisses) of, but the fur thereof is not fair, and also it stinketh ever unless it is well tawed.'[4] (MG.)

[1] See Chapter IV.

[2] *Wer-wolf.* The name was commonly accepted to mean a man turned into a wolf, but retaining human intelligence. It is called *Bischaret* in Brittany, and *Garwalf* in Normandy.

[3] See Chapter XXIV, No. 156.

[4] *Taw* means to make hides into leather, and *tawer* the maker of white leather. There was a distinct difference between a tawer and a tanner.

'The wolf-hunters had a sporting vocabulary of their own and special cries for encouraging their hounds, the most constant of which seems to have been *harlou loulou harlou* (from *hare* (harry) the wolf). In the *Roman du Rou* the boy who is holding a greyhound sees a wolf, and cries *le leu, le leu*; hence it is possible that the *eleu eleu* of the English huntsman is a corrupted remnant of our ancient chase of the *leu* or *loup*.' (Appendix to the 1904 ed. of *The Master of Game*.)

(See Chapter XI.)

The most popular book on wolf hunting was Clamorgan's *La Chasse du Loup* (1566). Jean de Clamorgan dedicated his book to King Charles IX, and stated his opinion that the hunting of the wolf was the finest of all chases.

MODERN

RINGING THE WOLVES

This is a Russian sport, and 'as much bound by tradition as fox-hunting is in Britain.' (C. Cooper.)

The *jaeger* (professional huntsman) goes out ahead to locate the game; puts out *privada* (bait), and ascertains from the tracks where the wolves are lying up after feeding.

The wolves are then *ringed* with a rope in a circle of about one mile in circumference; the rope, to which many little red flags are attached, is hung on bushes 3 feet from the ground. A gap is left where the 'guns' take post. *Beating* begins to the accompaniment of much shouting—*Ay-kak-kak-kak-a*.

The wolves are extremely cunning hunters themselves.

CHAPTER IV

FOXHUNTING AND COURSING

FOXHUNTING

'In that word " 'unting" what a ramification of knowledge is compressed.' Surtees (*Handley Cross*).

ANCIENT

UNTIL QUITE recently fox was vermin, even though he was reckoned the third beast of the chase. In the days of *The Master of Game* fox coursing was usual; the huntsman had to hunt on foot, and a good *run* was rare; nets were placed round the *coverts*, and hounds (and greyhounds) laid on in *relays*. *Reynard*[1] stood little chance. The chief object was, not sport, but the *kill*. This spirit prevailed even to the seventeenth century. But about the middle of the eighteenth century the character of the chase began to change. This was due to a variety of causes, but particularly to the smaller size of the forests and to the fencing of fields.

Dryden, in his Introduction to Twici's *Le Art de Venerie*, has a

[1] See Appendix III.

memorable passage describing the different methods of hunting. The passage ends: 'Twici 'tis true had time to blow "trout trourourout" sundry times, to warn the gentlefolks that the hart was *unharboured*, and leisurely *recheated* on his hounds when running a burning scent; while Hugo Meynell, the "Father of Fox Hunting", had scarce time to blow one "*moot*" to tell a Leicestershire field that a Coplow fox had broken, as he *rattled* out of cover at the sterns of his gallant pack. Though, so wide the difference of the ancient and modern days, so fast the present, and so slow the past, let us not despise this noble science in its infancy. It laid the foundation of a more polished scool in a more enlightened age.'

From the pages of the sporting writers through the centuries we can trace the changing outlook on the hunting of the fox:

'I disprayse not the huntynge of the foxe with rennynge houndes, but it is not to be compared to the other hunting in the commoditie of exercise.' (Sir Thomas Elyot in *The Boke named the Governour*, 1531.) (At this time already the vast woodlands had largely disappeared.)

'To course at a Fox requireth none other Art, than to stand close and uppon a cleare wind on the outside of the covert by some bottome or place where it is likely that he will come out: and to give him head inough: . . .' but, in another place, 'For a Foxe will not willingly depart out of the covert where he hath bin accustomed to ly, but will wheele about the thicks, and thereby make you much the better pastime.' (Turberville, 1575).

'Of foxes we have some, but no great store, and also badgers . . . certes if I may freelie saye what I thinke I suppose that these two kinds are rather preserved by gentlemen to hunt. . . .' (Cockaine, 1591.)

'Foxhunting is of no small esteem, what has been wrote on this subject and what has gone by tradition was that which was practised when the Land was more woody, and when they abounded so much as to be a general nuisance.' (Blome, 1686.)

Both the above two writers give us excellent accounts of the foxhunting 'above ground'.

The first real pack of foxhounds is said to be that of Thomas Fownes, of Dorsetshire (1730); but the Charlton (now Goodwood) Hunt was the first pack to make the change from stag to fox.

'The *ffixen* of the fox is a *saute* (Fr. *sauter*, in heat; modernized version *goeth a clicqueting*) ones in þe yeere.' (MG.)

'For Foxes 'in company', see Chapter XXIV, No. 123.

Most of the modern practices have their origin from the very earliest times. As an example, stopping a fox's *earth* by inserting a faggot into the opening was the method employed, according to Roy Modus, in France six hundred years ago.

HOUNDS AND DOGS

The A.S. word *Hundas* (hound) was a general name for a dog; the dog for the chase was called *ren hund.* Gradually the word 'dog' superseded 'hound', and the latter signified 'a dogge onely as serveth to hunt.' (Gesner.)

'*Mute* was the correct term for a company of hounds, answering to our use of the word *pack.*' (Sir H. Dryden.) (See Chapter XXIV, No. 130.)

Hardel was the term used for tying couples of hounds together, ready for slipping. There used to be two *hardes* to each *relay* and not more than eight hounds in every harde. (D'Yauville.)

(The term was also for the binding of the roe-buck's legs. See Chapter XXI.)

For the Properties of a hound, see Chapter X.

NAMES FOR THE DOGS EMPLOYED IN THE SPORTS OF THE FIELD

'Theyse be the names of houndes. Fyrste there is Grehoun; a Bastard; a Mengrell; a Mastif; a Lemor; a Spanyel; Raches; Kenettys; Teroures; Butchers houndes; Dunghyll dogges; Tryndeltaylles; and pryckeryd currys; and smalle ladye's popees that bere awaye the flees and dyvers small sautes.' (St. A.)

Lymers. These were like a bloodhound, the old Southern-hound, and were led by a strap or line (*liam*) of horse hide, a fathom and a half in length. The hart was both harboured and unharboured by the sueing with a *lymer.*

Braches. Also termed *ratches* or *raches.* These were scenting hounds. They were taken in couples (of a mare's tail, and one foot between the hounds) by the *berners,* who held the *relays* of two or three couples each. A blast of two *moots* was the signal for uncoupling. (Cox says the female 'is called a *Brache.* A *Brach* is a mannerly name for all Hound-Bitches'.)

They formed *the pack,* and were sometimes called *rennyng-hounds.* 'The best hue of running hounds,' says the Duke, 'is called brown tan. I prefer them to all other kinds of hounds. . . .

There are also many kinds of running hounds, some small and some big, and the small are called *kenets* . . . and they (that) serve for all game men call them *harriers*.'

Alaunts. A ferocious breed, supposed to have been brought to Europe by a Caucasian tribe called Alani. They were used for hunting and as war dogs. There was another kind of alaunt called *Veutreres* (Veltres); they were the most savage and used for the chase of bears and wild swine. Originally they were swift greyhounds, and the men who led greyhounds (later termed *Fewterers*; *slippers* as we now call them) retained the name *veltrars* long after the name 'veltre' had ceased to mean a greyhound. In France the term for a boar-hunting pack to-day is *vautrait*.

Sir H. Dryden said that alaunts were 'bull dogs', swift, but could hunt by scent also; 'in consequence of their ferocity were used for bears and boars'. 'The true hue of a good alaunte . . . should be white with black spots about the ears, small eyes and white standing ears and sharp above. In all manner of ways alauntes are treacherous and evil understanding, and more foolish and more hairbrained than any other kind of hound. . . . And when he is well conditioned and perfect, men hold that he is the best of all hounds.' (MG.)

Greyhounds (or *Gazehounds*). 'Originally it was most likely *grehund*, and meant the noble, great, choice, or prize hound.' (Jesse.) From *gre* (Lat. *gradus*) came the English word *degree*. (Cox), 'because among all dogs they are the most principal . . . the best of the gentle kind of hounds.' (J. Caius, 1576.) In early Anglo-Norman times they were still called by their French name of *levriers*.

Greyhounds were used, in the old days, for all kinds of hunting, with or without a lymer to start the game. They were nearly always held in couples when expecting the chase.

For Points of a Greyhoumd, see Chapter X.

'The best hue is red fallow with a black muzzle.' (MG.) But at one time white was the favourite colour.

A Welsh proverb declared that a gentleman might be known 'by his hawk, his horse, and his greyhound'.

Spaniels (from Lat. *Hispaniolus*). Originally they were used for hawking and fowling. 'Another kind of hound there is that are called hounds for the hawk and spaniels, for their kind come from Spain.' (MG.)

Sometimes they were trained to be *setters* as well, when they were called *couchers* (from *coucher*, to lie down).

Turberville wrote a doggerel in praise of the spaniel in the Prologue to his Book of Falconrie:

> . . . I need not blush or deeme it my disgrace
> If hawkes and spanels I prefere and set in highest place.
>
> In roysting wise about they range, with cheerefull chappes to ground,
> To see where in the champion may some lurking fowle be found
> A sport to view them stirre their sternes. . . .

Their varieties are numerous; a popular division is: springers, cockers and water spaniels. Springers acquired their name because they were good at springing pheasants from thick cover. The cocker is so called 'from his appropriation to woodcock shooting'. (Blaine.)

Mastiffs. The name is probably derived from the M.E. *mestiv* =mixed breed, a mongrel. They were chiefly used for the protection of persons and goods.

The old type of dog under this name was quite unlike the present breed; he corresponded to the French *matin*, a big hardy dog. These were often laid on to tackle the wild boar when run by other hounds. Some mastiffs, according to MG., became *berslettis*, i.e. shooting dogs. (Fr. *bersier* =a huntsman: *bercel* =a butt or target.)

Our bulldog was known by the name *dogue* and our mastiff as *le grand dogue anglais*. The name Mastiff was not in general use in England till the eighteenth century. Osbaldiston uses the term *bandog*.

Harriers. Scenting hounds for hunting hare (from Mid. Eng. *harien* =to worry game). Originally they hunted all kinds of game. (See under *Braches*.) 'We may know thos kind of dogs by their long, large, and bagging !lips; by their hanging ears, reaching down both sides of their chaps.' (*Of English Dogs*, 1576, by Johannes Caius.)

Leviner. A hound of 'a middle kind betwixt a harrier and a greyhound', noted for 'his smelling and swift running'. (Os.)—the *limier* or *line* hound.

Lurcher. A kind of 'mongrel greyhound, with pricked ears, a shagged coat, and generally of a yellowish white colour: they are very swift runners . . . they use other subtilities, as the Tumbler does. . . .' (Os.)

Terriers. So called because they 'creep into the ground'. (Cox.) 'Hunteth the Fox and the Badger only'. (J. Caius.)

Tumblers. (From the Fr. *tumbier*, to tumble.) 'By the form and fashion of their Bodies they may be justly called *Mungrel-Greyhounds*, if they were somewhat bigger.' (Cox.) Used for taking conies by guile.

Kenet. A small hound. (See under *Braches*.)

Teasers (or Teazers). A small hound to 'tease forth' the game. Blome defines: 'A kind of mongrel greyhound whose business it is to drive away the deer before the greyhounds are slipt.' They were also used to tease forth the hart to be shot with bows.

'In Shakespeare's time hounds were divided into (1) bloodhounds or *limers*, (2) *running hounds*, (3) the *beagle* pure-bred.' (Ap.)

THE TERMS USED IN RESPECT OF THE DOGS, ETC. are as follows:

'Of greyhounds, two to make a *brace*; of hounds a *couple*.[1]

'Of greyhounds, three make a *leash*; of hounds a *couple* and a *half*.[1]

'They say, *let slip* a grey-hound; and, *cast off* a hound.

'The string, wherein a grey-hound is led, is called a *leash*; and that of a hound, a *lyome*.

'The grey-hound has his *collar*, and the hound his *couples*.

'We say a *kennel* of hounds, and a *pack* of beagles.[2]

'In the kennels or packs they generally rank them under the heads of *enterers*, *drivers*, *flyers*, *tyers*, &c.

'When the hounds, being cast off, and finding the scent of some game, begin to open and cry, they are said to *challenge*.

'When they are too busy ere the scent be good, they are said to *babble*.

'When too busy where the scent is good, to *bawl*.

'When they run it endwise orderly, holding in together merrily, and making it good, they are said to be in *full cry*.

[1] Also given by Daniel.

[2] Down to 'a *pack* of beagles' this extract from *The British Sportsman* is almost word for word the same as the distinctions laid down by Turberville, two hundred years before. See Chapter XXIV, No. 130, Notes.

'When they run along without opening at all, it is called *running mute.*

'When spaniels open in the string, or a grey-hound in the course, they are said to *lapse.*

'When beagles bark and cry at their prey, they are said to *yearn.*

'When the dogs hit the scent the contrary way, they are said to *draw amiss.*

'When they take fresh scent, and quit the former chace for a new one, it is called *hunting change.*

'When they hunt the game by the heel or track, they are said to *hunt counter.*

'When the chace goes off, and returns again, traversing the same ground, it is called *hunting the foil.*

'When the dogs run at a whole herd of deer, instead of a single one, it is called *running riot.*

'Dogs set in readiness where the game is expected to come by, and cast off after the other hounds are passed, are called a *relay.* If they be cast off ere the other dogs be come up, it is called *vauntlay.*

'When, finding where the chace has been, they make a proffer to enter, but return, it is called a *blemish.*

'A lesson on the horn to encourage the hounds, is named a *call*, or a *recheat.* That blown at the death of a deer, is called the *mort.*[1] The part belonging to the dogs of any chase they have killed, is the *reward.*

'They say, *take off* a deer's skin; *strip* or *case* a hare, fox, and all sorts of vermin; which is done by beginning at the snout, and turning the skin over the ears down to the tail.'[2] (Os.)

'When they *hunt* the game by the heel or track, they are said to hunt counter. The more common expression, however, is to say, they *run the heel*, and *ware heel*, accompanied with a crack of the whip, is the reprehension of the whipper-in. Indeed, these terms are more a matter of curiosity for their antiquity than their use, as many of them are now quite obsolete; for instance, the distinction between *pack* and *kennel*, as pack is used for every species of hounds.

'When hounds hang behind, and beat too much upon the scent, or place, they say, *they plod* (*tye* or *plod* (Halliwell)). When

[1] See Chapter XI. [2] See Chapter XXI.

they have either earthed a vermin, or brought a deer, boar, or the like, to turn head against them, they are said *to bay*.

'When the hounds touch the scent, and draw on till they rouze or put up the chase, they say *they draw on the slot*.'

(*The Sportsman's Dictionary*, by H. J. Pye, 1807.)

In Cox's time it is probable 'that his pack consisted of that cross between the Southern Hound and Northern Beagle; which cross was the foundation stock from which has been developed our modern foxhounds'. (Preface to Cox's *Gentleman's Recreation*, by E. D. Cuming.)

SOME OBSOLETE (OR LITTLE USED) HUNTING TERMS

Currant Jelly: A term used when hounds are running hare.

Left-handed: Hounds which are not always right, but apt to be wide, and fly without a scent. The sooner they are *drafted* the better. . . .

Metal: When hounds are very fresh, and fly for a short distance on a wrong scent, or without one, it is called *all metal*.

Open Bitches: Bitches to breed from, which are not *spayed* (q.v.).

Rack: For a track through a fence. (The more usual term is *Meuse*.)

Sinking the Wind: i.e. When men go down wind to hear the cry.

Spayed: Bitch hounds which were not thought good enough to breed from were sometimes spayed, i.e. they had their ovaries removed, to improve their physique.

Stroke: When hounds are drawing, and it is evident that they feel the scent of a fox, though they do not own to it.

Tight in his Tongue: Used of a hound which seldom throws his tongue, though not quite mute.

(Th. Smith.)

MORE OLD TERMS

Bawling: 'Of the dogs, when they are too busy before they find the scent good.' (Os.)

Fore-loin: 'When a hound, going before the rest of the cry, meets chase and goes away with it.' (Os.)

Pricker: 'A hunter on horseback.' (Os.)

Rout: To cheer or rate.

Untapige: A going to ground (from the Fr. *entapis* = under the carpet, i.e. easily 'bottled'—Tom Noel's Diary, c. 1769).

MODERN

FOX HUNTING TERMS

[The following authorities have been drawn on for the verification of hunting terms:

Extracts from The Diary of a Huntsman. (Th. Smith, 1838.)
The Badminton Library, *Hunting*.
The ABC of Fox-hunting. (D. W. E. Brock, 1936.)

Note. It is interesting to compare this portion with the 'Ancient'. Only the more important terms have been given.]

All on: A pack is 'all on' when every hound comprising it is present.

At fault: When hounds check they are said to be at fault.

Babbler: This is a hound which *throws its tongue* too much, when it is uncertain of the scent, or when a long way behind the leading hounds.

Bag fox: Any fox which is turned out especially for hounds to hunt. This was a common practice in the old days, but is now not recognized. (Sometimes called *Bagman.*)

Benches: The wooden platforms upon which hounds sleep in kennels.

Billett: A fox's excreta. Nearly always contains the fur of rabbits.

Blank: A covert that does not hold a fox, a day on which no fox is found, are 'blank'.

Bob-tailed: Applied to a fox which has no *brush*, or only a very short one.

Bolt: (i) To bolt a fox is to force him out of a drain or earth; (ii) of horses, to gallop away out of the rider's control.

Break: A fox 'breaks' when he leaves a covert.

Break up: Hounds 'break up their fox' when they eat its carcase.

Brush: The fox's tail. 'A Fox Tayle brush for ye Pictures, 6d.' Foxtails were used for brushes in the 17th century.

Burst: The first part of a run, if quick, is called a *sharp burst*.

Cap: (1) The black velvet peaked cap worn by the Master, Hunt Staff and Officials; (2) Money collected from Members and non-subscribers at the Meet or later in the day.

Carries a scent: Good scenting land is said to 'carry a scent'.

Carries the scent: Those hounds which are actually working out with their noses the fox's line when the pack is running are said to 'carry the scent'.

Cast: An effort made by the pack, or by the huntsman with his pack, to recover the scent at a check.

Catch hold: A huntsman 'catches hold' of hounds when he *lifts* (q.v.) the pack. The term is also used of a horse that pulls.

Challenge: A hound that *opens* is said to *challenge*, or to 'challenge on a fox'. More correctly it should be used of a hound which endorses the opinion of the first hound to *open*.

Check: Hounds check when they stop running and temporarily lose the fox's scent. The word derives from the language of Falconry. (See Chapter VIII.)

Chop: Hounds are said to chop a fox when they kill one asleep, or surprise one before he has time to escape.

Couple: Two foxhounds. A pack is, for instance, 16½ couples (but a single hound is referred to as one hound).

Couples: Two leather collars joined by steel links, used for coupling two hounds together.

Course: To course a fox is to run it 'in view'. A greyhound is said to course a hare.

Covert: All woods, unless very big, that might hold a fox. (See *Woodland.*)

Cry: The music of a pack. When the whole pack are running hard and throwing their tongues they are said to be in *full cry*. (See Chapter XI.)

Cub: A young fox. They become 'foxes' on November 1st.

Cub hunting: Carried out in September and October in the early mornings with the object of moving foxes and teaching hounds and young foxes their duty.

Cur-dog: Any dog other than a foxhound.

Dog fox: A male fox.

Doped foxes: Foxes whose natural scent has been increased by some means. Bag foxes are sometimes doped.

Double the horn: A huntsman is said to do this when he blows a succession of quick, sharp notes, e.g. when a fox is holloaed away. (See Chapter XI.)

Draft: A collection of hounds which have been drafted. To draft a hound is to get rid of it from the pack. Drafts may be 'entered' or 'unentered'. (See *Enter.*)

Drag: The line of a fox leading to his kennel ('to hunt *the* drag'). It is also the name of an artificial line ('to hunt *a* drag'), made by laying some strong-smelling substance over a certain line of country. It is not 'done' in foxhunting.

Draw: Hounds 'draw' for a fox in covert. The huntsman 'draws' a covert when he urges his hounds to look for a fox in it.

The day's draw is the area of country which the Master has planned to draw in a day's hunting, and the earths of which have been stopped.

When a huntsman separates a hound from the rest of a pack, he 'draws' it.

Dwelling: Hounds lingering too long on the line.

Earth: A fox's home underground. (See *Open* and *Putting to.*)

Earth stopper: One who goes out during the night before a day's hunting to block the entrances to the earths, while the fox is abroad. He is paid by the Hunt.

Enter: Teaching young hounds to hunt a fox is to enter them.

Feather: A hound *feathers* when it is not certain that it owns the scent, driving slowly along the line and waving its *stern.*

Field: This is the body of mounted men and women hunting with a pack.

Flags: The floor of the kennel courts. One visits hounds in kennels to see them *on the flags.*

Foil: Any smell which obliterates the fox's scent, e.g. when horses, sheep, etc., pass over the line of the fox the ground is *foiled.*

A fox is said to *run his foil* when he doubles back on his tracks.

Gone to ground: When a fox has got into an *earth* or *drain.*

Hackles up: When a hound is angry, the hair along its back and top of neck stands on end, and its stern is curved stiffly over its back.

Head: Hounds carry a *good head* when they hunt fast as a pack on a broad front.

Headed: A fox which has been caused to turn aside from his original line is said to have been headed.

Heads up: Hounds which have stopped feeling for the scent have *got their heads up.*

Heel (*Heel-way*)*:* Hounds run heel (or heel-way) when they run the line of a fox the opposite way to which he was going.

Hit the line: Used of a hound, or a huntsman in his cast, when they strike the line of the fox. 'Hounds, when they have recovered a lost scent, are said to have *hit it off.*' (Blaine.)

Hoick! Huic!: Hunting cheers, meaning 'Hark', pronounced 'Ike' or 'Ark'. (See Chapter XI.)

Hold: A huntsman, in making his cast, is sometimes said to *hold hounds round.* He may also hold them *on* or *back.* A covert that contains a fox is said to 'hold'.

Hold hard: A huntsman's *rate* to riders who press hounds too closely. (See Chapter XI.)

Hold up: One can hold up a *litter*, or a *covert* by surrounding it to prevent foxes leaving.

Hound jog: The normal pace, about six miles an hour, that hounds travel on a road.

Huic Holloa!: A cheer to draw attention to a *holloa.* (See *Tally O!* and Chapter XI.)

Kennel: A fox's bed in a *covert*, etc., above ground. (See also Chapter XXIV, No. 130, Notes.)

Lark: It is a crime to *lark* over fences, that is, to jump them when hounds are not running, or even when hacking to or from a meet.

Lift: A huntsman lifts hounds when he holds them on to a place where he thinks the fox may be, or where one has been seen.

Line: The trail of a fox. (See *Hit the Line.*)

Livery: A *livery-stable* takes in horses *at livery*—where owners can have their horses looked after, for payment. It also, generally, lets out horses on hire.

Make a pack: To count hounds.

Mark: Hounds are said to *mark the fox to ground* when they gather round and bay outside an earth or drain into which the hunted fox has gone.

Mask: A fox's head 'or *front*' (Blaine), 'but in the deer it is the *snout* or *nose*'.

Mixed pack: One containing both dogs and bitches.

Mob: To mob a fox is to surround it or to hunt it without giving it a fair chance.

Music: The cry of hounds. (See Chapter XI.)

Mute: A term to describe a hound which does not throw its tongue when on the line of a fox.

Muzzle: A hound's nose and mouth.

Nose: The ability of a hound to smell.

Open: Hounds 'open' on a fox when they first *speak* to a line in covert.

An open *earth* is one which has not been stopped.

Over-shot: The opposite of *swine-chopped* (q.v.). Of a hound whose upper jaw protrudes beyond the lower.

Own the line: Used of a hound which is on the fox's line.

Pack: A collection of hounds. (See Chapter XXIV, No. 130.)

Pad: A fox's foot. To track a fox is to 'pad' him. (See Chapter XIV.) Also the cushion-like thickenings of the soles of hounds' feet; the latter can be described as *cat's foot* (round and neat), or *hare foot* (more elongated, and generally found among fell hounds).

Peck: When a horse falls on his nose or knees, on landing over a fence, he is said to *peck*.

Pick: To pick hounds up is to *lift* them (q.v.).

Pipe: A branch or hole in an *earth*.

Point: The distance, measured as the crow flies, between two points in a run. The actual distance is described *as hounds ran*.

Pudding: The meal porridge as fed to hounds.

Put down: The expression used when a horse or hound is killed on account of old age, etc.

Putting to: Earths are 'put to' when they are closed, on a hunting morning, with the fox inside them.

Pye: A descriptive colour (lighter than tan) for a hound. It may be *lemon-*, *hare-* or *badger-pyed*. Badger pye is white and grizzled black; yellow pie, white and yellowish brown.

Rat-catcher: A kind of undress uniform consisting of tweed coat, breeches, brown field- or black butcher boots, and a bowler hat.

Rate: To reprove or scold a hound is to *rate* it.

Rattled: 'A fox well rattled, up to the first check, huntsmen tell us, is as good as half killed.' (Whyte Melville.)

Ride: A path through a *covert*.

Ringing fox: One which runs in circles, close to its home covert.

Riot: Any animal, other than a fox, hunted by hounds. When hounds so hunt they are said to riot. The *rate* is *Ware* (pronounced 'War') *Riot*. (See Chapter XI.)

Rogue: A vicious horse, that 'means it'—not a horse that merely 'plays up'.

Rounding: Cutting off the points of hound puppies' ears, a custom which is dying out.

Running: Hounds are *running* when they are actually in pursuit of a fox, though they may be only walking on a cold scent. They are not *running* when galloping to a *Holloa*.

Scarlet: The colour of a hunting coat. The terms *Red* or *Pink* are also used. One can say 'He hunts in *Scarlet* (or *Pink*)', but with 'Red' it must be 'He hunts in a red coat'.

Scent: Scent is said to be *breast high* when hounds race and do not *stoop* their heads; and *holding* when it is good enough but not very strong.

When hounds lose the scent they *throw up* their heads. Scent is *ticklish* or *catchy* when it varies from good to bad; it is *recovered* when lost and found again. (Cf. *Hit the line.*)

Hounds run almost mute when there is a *burning scent.*

Score: When the whole pack *speaks* to a strong scent.

Sinking: When a fox is very tired at the end of a run he is said to be sinking.

Skirt: A hound which cuts off corners, while other hounds are following the true line of the fox, is a *skirter.*

Speak: This is the term for a hound when it barks. (See *Tongue* and Chapter XI.)

Stain: Foil (q.v.)

Stale line: The line of a fox which has been a long time gone.

Stern: A hound's tail.

Stopping: Or *stopping out*, i.e. closing *earths* when the fox is abroad during the night. (Cf. *Putting to.*)

Stub-bred: Applied to foxes which are born above ground.

Swine-chopped: The opposite of *over-shot* (q.v.). Of a hound whose lower jaw protrudes beyond the upper.

Tail hounds: Hounds which are right behind the rest, when running. When hounds do not run abreast it is called *tailing.*

Tally O! A hunting cry made when one has viewed a fox. If the huntsman is a long way off, a shrill cry (known as a *View Holloa*) is given instead. (See Chapter XI.)

Tongue: Cry of hounds, which are said to *throw the tongue* when they speak to a line. (See Chapter XI.)

Touch the horn: To blow the horn. (See Chapter XI.)

Trencher-fed: A pack that is boarded out among the local farmers, etc. is so described. There are few such packs now.

Unentered: An unentered hound is (normally) one which has not finished one cub-hunting season. It automatically becomes *entered* on the day of the Opening Meet, and is then termed a *First season hound.*

View: The sight of a fox. To see a fox is to view it.

View Holloa, or Holloa (pronounced 'Holler')*:* The scream given when one has *viewed* a fox. (Cf. *Tally O!*)

Vixen: A female fox.

Walk: Hound puppies are out *at walk* when looked after at farms, etc.

Whelps: Unweaned puppies.

Wind: A hound is said to wind a fox, i.e. to smell it.

Woodland: A very large covert, or a large area mostly woods.

Worried: Killed by the hounds.

* * *

Listen to Daniel on foxhounds:

'There is infinite pleasure in hearing a Fox well found, the Chorus increasing from the first *Challenge*[1], and the corresponding *Hark to Chirper*, inspires a Joy more easy to be felt than described, and one Fox found with a good Drag in this lively manner, surpasses the best Hare chase that was ever ran.'

For the Music of the Chase, see Chapter XI.

THREE RECOGNISED TIPS IN THE HUNTING FIELD

£1 to the Huntsman for the brush.

10/- to the First Whipper-in for the mask.

5/- to the Second Whipper-in for a pad.

THE COUNTRY

Binder: The top (interlaced branch) of a *stake and bound* fence.

Blind: A fence, or a country, is said to be *blind* when there is much old grass and leaf hiding the natural outline of ditch and bank.

Bottom: A big ditch with (usually) a fence on one side.

Bullfinch: A thick, high and uncut fence, which cannot be jumped *over*. If straggly, it is said to be *hairy*.

Clean ground: Ground which is neither *foiled* nor stained.

Cock fences: Thorn fences trimmed very low. Horses are apt to *hurdle* them.

Cut-and-laid: A fence of which the thorns are half cut through and bent over.

Ditch: If on the near side of a fence it is *to you*, while on the far side it is *away from you*. *Open ditch* = a fence with a *ditch to you*.

[1] Technical terms:
A Foxhound *speaks* in cover, then *owns* his Fox.
The Fox *gets* a hand—the Hounds are *gaining* him.
A Hunter *cheeks* the hounds, *talks* with the head Hound.

Double: A fence or bank with a ditch on both sides.

Drop fence: A fence with the landing lower than the *take-off*.

Dry single: A bank without a ditch.

Fence: To *stand back* from a fence is to take off well away from it.

Five-barred gate: Any gate.

Flying fences: Fences which can be jumped from a gallop. In Ireland all fences which are not jumped *on and off* are known as *flies*.

Going: The nature of the ground for galloping; it may be heavy, hard, good, etc.

Headland: The edge of a field (grass or plough) near the hedge.

In and Out: Two fences close together, but too far apart to be negotiated in one jump.

Oxer: Thorn fence with a guard rail. A *double oxer* is a fence with a rail on each side.

Park railings: Any iron railings.

Plough: Arable country. A field growing crops is still 'plough'. Ploughland is said to *carry* when it is sticky.

Poached: Ground is said to be poached when the *take-off* in front of a jump is muddy and deeply cut up by horses' feet.

Rasper: Any big fence. To *swish at a rasper* is to gallop at a really thick strong fence.

Single bank: A bank with ditch on one side only.

Stake and bound: A dead hedge wattled in between strong stakes, with a *binder* (q.v.).

Timber: Posts and rails (generally). Also, anything made of wood and jumpable.

Water: A ditch (or stream) with water in it and no fence on either side is called *open water*.

Wattle: A hurdle.

* * *

Shires: Cover parts of Leicestershire,[1] Rutlandshire and Northants; the Shire Packs are: Belvoir, Cottesmore, Quorn Pytchley and Fernie.

Provinces: Any hunting country in England, Scotland and Wales, less the Midlands and Shires.

* * *

Charley: A slang term for a fox; origin, Charles Fox.

[1] A field in Leicestershire is known as a 'large grass ground'.

THE HUNTING SEASON

From November 1st to the end of March, but a few packs hunt in April. Cub-hunting is from after the harvest (end of August) to the last day of October.

The *Opening Meet* is held on the first convenient day after Nov. 1st. Packs may hunt two, three, four days a week according to the size of the pack, country, bank account etc., and to the Master's whim. Any meet over and above the usual is known as a *bye-day*, when a *cap* is not usually taken.

* * *

COURSING

ANCIENT

This is a most ancient sport, going back to the days of Solomon, who spoke of the greyhound[1] that he 'goes well and is comely in going'. After the decay of chivalry the drive or *battue* ousted the real deer hunting (in the open) of the Normans. (See Chapter II.) By the time of Queen Elizabeth (Turberville) this shooting or coursing in parks was the most popular diversion. For Coursing, the greyhounds were divided into *Teasers*,[2] *Side laies* and *Bucksets* or *Receits*. The teasers were slipt first, next the sidelayes and lastly the receits 'full in the face of the Deare'.

Speaking of Coursing, the Rev. Daniel says: 'The *Isle of Dogs*, now converting to the first *commercial* purposes, derived its name from being the *Depot* of the Spaniels and Greyhounds of Edward III, and this spot was chosen, as lying contiguous to his sports of Woodcock shooting, and *coursing* the Red Deer, in Waltham and the other Royal Forests in Essex, for the more convenient enjoyment of which, he generally resided in the sporting season, at Greenwich. . . . In ancient times three several animals were coursed with Greyhounds, the *Deer*, the *Fox*, and the *Hare*. The two former are not practised at present. . . . (The italics are those of RS.)

Sportsmen of the Middle Ages were particular about the staunchness of their hounds. A hound was termed *staunch* if he stuck to the first stag hunted, i.e. a hound who would not take the change.

'The *Laws of Coursing* were established by the Duke of *Norfolk* in Queen Elizabeth's Reign, and which were agreed to by the

[1] See *Greyhounds* under ANCIENT. [2] See *Teasers*, earlier in this chapter.

Nobility and Gentry who then followed the diversion, and have been always held authentic.

'The *Feuterer*, or person that lets loose the Greyhounds, was to receive those that were matched to run together into his *Leash*, as soon as he came into the field, and to follow next to the Hare-finder, or him that was to start the Hare, until he came to the *Form*, and no horse or foot-men were to go before, or on either side, but directly behind, for the space of about forty yards.

'A Hare was not to be coursed with more than a brace of Greyhounds.

'The Hare-finder was to give the Hare three *Soho's* before he put her from her Form, to give notice to the Dogs that they may attend her starting.

'The Hare was to have twelve score Yards Law before the Dogs were loosed, unless the small distance from cover would not admit it without danger of immediately losing her.

'The Dog that gave the first *Turn*, and during the course, if there was neither *Cote*, *Slip*, nor *Wrench*,[1] won.

'A *Cote* is when the Greyhound goes endways by his fellow, and gives the Hare a *Turn*.

'A *Cote* served for two *Turns*, and two *Trippings* or *Jerkins* for a *Cote*; if the Hare did not turn quite about, she only *wrenched*, and two *Wrenches* stand for a *Turn*.

'If there were no *Cotes* given between a brace of Greyhounds, but that one of them served the other at *Turning*, then he that gave the Hare most turns won; and if one gave as many turns as the other, then he that bore the Hare, won.

'If one Dog gave the first *Turn*, and the other *bore* the Hare, he that bore the Hare, won.

'A *Go-by* or *Bearing* the Hare was equivalent to two *Turns*.

'If neither Dog turned the Hare, he that led last to the cover, won.

'If one Dog turned the Hare, served himself and turned her again, it was as much as a *Cote*; for a *Cote* was esteemed two *Turns*.

'If all the course was equal, the Dog that *bore* the Hare, won; if the Hare was not borne, the course was adjudged dead.

'If a Dog fell in a course, and yet performed his part, he might challenge the advantage of a *Turn* more than he gave.

'If a Dog turned the Hare, served himself, and gave divers

[1] *Rick:* older term for *wrench*.

Cotes, and yet in the end stood still in the field, the other Dog, if he ran *home to the cover*, altho' he gave no *Turn*, was adjudged the Winner.

'If by accident a Dog was rode over in his course, the course was void, and he that did the mischief was to make reparation for the damage.

'If a Dog gave the first and last *Turn*, and there was no other advantage betwixt them, he that gave the odd Turn, won.

'He that came in first at the death, took up the Hare, saved her from being torn, cherished the Dogs, and cleansed their mouths from the wool, was adjudged to have the Hare for his trouble.

'Those that were Judges of the course, were to give their decision before they departed out of the Field.' (RS.)

The following list of terms which do not appear elsewhere in this book are taken from a collection of *Technical Hunting Terms* in the *Dictionary of Archaic and Provincial Words* by J. O. Halliwell (1847). Most of them seem to have some reference to Coursing.

'There is a peculiar phraseology adapted to each separate animal.' (Halliwell.)

Blink: To leave the point or back, run away at the report of the gun, etc. (See Chapter VI, *Shooting Terms.*)

Break field: To enter before you.

Chap: To catch with the mouth.

Curvet: To throw.

Doucets: The testicles or stones.

Flourish: To twist the stern, and throw right and left in too great a hurry.

Handicap: Gentleman who watches the dogs.

Hug: To run close side by side.

In and in: Too near related, as sire and daughter, dam and son, etc.

Inchipin or *pudding:* The fat gut.

Lapise: To open or give tongue.

Speans or *deals:* The teats.

To carry or *hod:* When the earth sticks to their feet.

Trip: To force by you. (Of a deer, see p. 18).

Tuel: The vent.

Vick: To make a low noise.

Watch: To attend the other dog, not endeavouring to find his own game, but lying off for advantage. In coursing it is called *running cunning*.

MODERN

Public coursing has existed since, at least, 1776 when the Swaffham Club was founded. In 1858 the National Coursing Club was formed; their Rules for Open Meetings were adopted in 1884. The most famous race is the Waterloo Cup, which originated in 1836; it is run in February at Altcar (on the Sefton Estate)—entries since 1857 limited to 64.

At each meeting there are:

Stewards: The *Flag-Steward*, who signals the Judge's decision; the *Slip-Steward*, who is responsible that the greyhounds are brought to the *slips* at the proper time.

Slipper: (Old term was *feuterer*, q.v.) Has the task of letting the dogs go when they have both fairly sighted the hare. (See *Law*.)

Judge: The principle of judging is that the greyhound that does most towards killing the hare is the winner.

THE POINTS OF THE COURSE

(1) *Speed:* One, two or three points are given according to the degree of superiority shown.

(2) The *Go-Bye:* Is where a greyhound starts a clear length behind his opponent, passes him in a straight run, and gets a clear length before him—2 points, or if gained on the outer circle, 3.

(3) The *Turn:* A change of course by the hare, when pressed, of not less than a right angle—1 point.

(4) The *Wrench:* Where the hare is bent from her line, due to the greyhound pressing her, at less than a right angle—½ point.

(5) The *Kill:* 2 points or less, according to the degree of merit displayed.

(6) The *Trip:* An unsuccessful effort to kill; e.g. where the hare is thrown off her legs, or the greyhound gets so close as to *fleck her* (q.v.)—1 point.

Various *allowances* are made for incidents such as a bad slip, a greyhound becoming *unsighted*, or the hare unduly favouring one of the dogs.

A GLOSSARY of further modern terms is given below:

Bye: A course in which, owing to the withdrawal of its opponent (an *accidental bye*), or to an odd number at the bottom of the stake (a *natural bye*), a greyhound has no opponent to meet.

Draw: (1) Of the owner—to withdraw a dog; (2) The classifying of the greyhounds prior to the running for a stake.

Enter: (Of the trainer). To show the young dog its game for the first time, and to prepare it for coursing.

Exchaning: When the dogs alternately move the hare from her course.

Fence: The act of leaping over any obstacle.

Fleck: To snatch the hare and lose hold.

Guarding: If two or more greyhounds belonging to the same owner are entered in a stake, arrangements are made for them to meet other greyhounds should they be drawn together.

Hare bearing: When she favours one of the greyhounds after a slip.

Home: A refuge for hares.

Law: The length of start given to a hare before the greyhounds are *slipped*—it should not be less than three to four score yards.

Leash: The line used to hold the dogs until *slipped.*

Lurching: Running cunning, leaving most of the work to the opponent.

Meuse: Gaps in the hedge through which a hare can escape.

Mob (by the crowd): To press a hare unfairly.

No course: When the judge has not had time to decide the comparative merits of the dogs.

Ns.: Abbreviation for 'names'—indicates that a greyhound is entered by other than its registered owner.

Produce Stakes: For puppies.

Puppy: A greyhound whelped on or after 1 Jan. of the year preceding the running season.

Sapling: A greyhound whelped on or after 1 Jan. of the same year as the running season.

Serving: When a dog turns his hare and keeps his place he *serves* himself; losing his place he *serves* his opponent.

Slips: The couples by which the brace of greyhounds are held whilst the hare is put up.

So-ho: The cry used to indicate a sitting hare. (See Chapter XI.)

Unsighted: Of the greyhound—when it loses sight of the hare, when *slipped* or during the course.

Waiting: Lying behind and waiting for a chance to kill.

Bibliography:

Fur and Feather Series ('The Hare') (1896).

Encyclopaedia of Sport (1897).

CHAPTER V

HARRIERS, BEAGLING AND OTTER HUNTING

[Certain facts and terms have been verified by reference to the Lonsdale Library, vol. xxii.]

HARRIERS

THE WORD Harrier is variously spelt *eirere*, *heyreres*, *heyrer*, *hayrers*, in early documents, and not till the sixteenth century does it take its present form. In the fourteenth century harriers were used to hunt all kinds of game (chiefly deer), and were a sort of running hound, *kenettis* (see Chapter IV), employed to 'harry' game. (A.S. *herian* and Old Fr. *herier*, to harry.) 'Let the hounds kill the fox themselves and worry and *hare* him as much as they please.' (NC.)

ANCIENT

Though as late as the sixteenth century harriers were not solely employed for the pursuit of the hare, yet for many centuries the hare had no competitor (such as the fox), and the popularity of the sport of hare hunting was unrivalled. It 'is a chase', says

Markham, 'both swift and pleasant, and of long endurance, it is also sport ever readie and equallie distributed, as well to the wealthie farmer as the greate Gentleman. It hath its beginning contrarie to the stagge or bucke, for it begins at Michaelmas when they end, and is out of date after April when they come first in season.' But sometimes 'it lasteth all the year'. (MG.)

Hare hunting proper was conducted in the old days very much as at present. The chief difference was that after the hounds (probably *raches*, [see Chapter IV]) had found the hare, greyhounds were often uncoupled and joined in the chase. In Twici's time it seems that it was customary to find and *start* the hare with a *limer*. The huntsmen carried a *rodde* instead of a crop.

Speaking of Hare Hunting, the Rev. Daniel says: 'At the most distant part of her morning's exercise, the tenderest nosed Dog can barely touch the scent, and opens a single note; as they gather on nearer towards her, many own and confirm the scent by *doubling their tongue*; when near her *form*, and the scent lies warm and strong, all double and treble their notes. The *counter trail* may be taken when Hounds are first cast off, and happen to hit about the middle of the Hare's works, or nearer the seat than her feed; there the scent lies so equal, that the dogs over eager often get upon the *Heel*; this the Huntsman will judge of by the notes his Hounds first challenge in; if they double and carry it on *counter*, they will soon signify their error by opening only *single*. . . .

'It is this ability of hearing so acutely from behind, that enables her to avoid the *Throw* of the Greyhound. . . .'

Hounds that were *entered* to hare often became hart-hounds: 'For a Hound that is a perfect good Haryer may be bold to hunt any chase, but the Hare of all games leaves the least scent behind her, but when once your Dogs have been accustomed to the Stag or Buck 'tis not easy to bring them in love with the Hare again.' (Du Fouilloux, Turberville and Blome.)

'The sport and art of hare hunting (for it is an art)', says Miss Ena Adams, 'was very popular in the 18th century, when the great landowners who had for generations kept private packs of staghounds began to turn from stag to hare, chiefly because the country was becoming enclosed and consequently more populated and the space needed for stag hunting was getting restricted.' Somerville was a hare-hunter, and he gave us the fine prose pageant *The Chace*.

The hare was thus the favourite quarry in the transition from stag to fox, which took pride of place about 1800.

THE HARE

Twici: 'Now we will begin with the Hare. And why Sir will you begin with the Hare, rather than with any other beast? I will tell you. Because she is the most marvellous beast which is on this earth. It carries *grease*, and it *croteys*, and gnaws, and these no beast on this earth does, besides it. And at one time it is male, and at another time it is female. And on that account in hunting it, a man cannot blow the *menée*[1] on the horn of it, so as one does of other beasts, as of the Hart, and of the Boar, and of the Wolf. . . . And on this account all the fine words are founded on it, when you ought to quest for it. . . .'

The ceremony of giving hounds their reward was called the *hallow*, corresponding to the *curée* in hart hunting. 'When the Hare is taken, and they are run to him, you ought to blow the *prize*, and you ought to give hounds the *halou*. What is the *Halou*? The sides, and the shoulders, and the neck, and the head . . .' (Twici.)

'Ere I speak how the hare should be hunted,' writes the Duke (MG.), 'it is to be known that the hare is King of all venery, for all blowing and the fair terms of hunting cometh of the seeking and the finding of the hare. For certain it is the most marvellous beast that is. . . . When she is female sometimes she *kindles* in three degrees, two rough, and two smooth and two knots that afterwards should be *kindles*, but this happeneth but seldom.

'It is to be known what the first word (should be) that the hunter should speak to his hounds when he lets them out of the kennel. When the door is opened he shall say loud: "*Ho ho arere*" (i.e. "Back there!" from the Fr. *arriere*), because that his hounds will come out too hastily. . . .' Then follows a long description of the Hunting Cries. (See Chapter XI.)

One of the commonest exhortations was the term *Soho!* used in hare hunting and coursing:

> All maner of beastes whatsoever chased be,
> Have one manner of woord *soho* I tell thee.
> To fulfill or unfill all maner of chase,
> The hunter in his mouth that word hase. (1586)

[1] *Menée* originally meant 'the path of a hart which is flying'. Here it appears to signify some notes on the horn to encourage hounds forward (*'hark for'ard'*). (See Chapter XI.)

'And if he (i.e. the huntsman) find (her *pricking*) he can well blow the *rights* and *holloa* and *jopey* iii or iiii times and cry loud "*le voy, le voy*" (the view, the view) . . .' (MG.)

Jopey (or *Jupper*) meant ' to whoot, showt, crie alowd'. (Cotgrave.) From the old French word *houpper*, to shout for joy. (Cf. our expression *Whoo Whoop!* when hounds roll their fox over. See Chapter XI.) (The word, possibly, may be connected with *per Jupiter*.) Here it means 'to encourage the hounds'.

Nearly all the old writers, such as Pliny, Topsell, Buffon, recall the fable that hares were all females, or of various sexes, or that their sex was interchangeable. This belief was widely held as late as the end of the eighteenth century. 'The Hebrews call the hare *arnabet*, in the feminine gender.' (Topsell.)

There were many superstitions about the hare. It was widely held, for instance, that she was an animal of evil omen, as well as the partridge, and to meet either as one started in the morning to harbour a stag would be a prophecy of a bad day's sport. (Du Fouilloux.)

(See Chapter XXIV, No. 127.)

'The hares have no season of their love (that hunters call *ryding time*) . . . for there is not a month in the year that you will not find some that be with *kindles* . . . commonly their love is most in the month of January . . . (she) beareth her kindles two months.' (MG.) (This is incorrect; it is commonly accepted that she carries her young from thirty to forty-two days.)

Cox tells us that there are four sorts of hares: some live in mountains, some in fields, some in marshes, and some have no certain place of abode. There are two to five leverets in a family, and several families in the year. The male is called *Jack*, and the female *Doe*. Hares are said never to drink, but they sometimes swim. (Modern naturalists recognize but two sorts of hare: the Brown or Lowland, and the Blue or Mountain Hare. The latter (*Lepus timidus*) is only about half the size of the brown hare (*L. europaeus*) and has a black back.)

There were two methods of finding her, says Cox, in the seventeenth century, a period when the chief sport of country gentlemen was the hunting of the hare. In *trailing* she was followed up *from relief* (i.e. from the spot where she had been feeding) to her *form*; in *beating* ('much better sport') hounds *quested* or *beat* to find her on her *form*, and when found she was given a start and hounds laid on again.

'If when a *Hare* riseth out of her Form she couches her Ears and Scut, and runs not very fast at first, it is an infallible sign that she is old and crafty.' (See Chapter I, *Beasts of Venery*.)

'When a hare runs on rotten ground, or in a frost sometimes, and it sticks to her feet, the huntsmen say, she *carries*.' (Os.)

Muse. An opening in a fence. There was an old proverb:

' 'Tis as hard to find a hare without a muse, as a woman without scuse!'

Amongst all Birds none with the *Thrush* compare,
And no Beast hath more glory than the *Hare*.
(Martial, translated by N. Cox.)

MODERN

Modern harriers may be likened to miniature foxhounds, but they have not the same temperament and require quieter handling.

Though their hunting may not provide 'thrills' equal to those of foxhunting, more opportunities occur of watching hounds work.

These packs are hunted on horseback.[1]

BEAGLING

MODERN

Many packs exist for hunting the hare on foot. These hounds stand 14 to 15 inches, and are similar to, though smaller than, foxhounds. Colours—white, black and tan most usual (no good hound is a bad colour), but dark tan, harepie, lemon and white, and blue tick are all to be found.

Green is almost universal for the hunt coat.

The language of the chase is similar to that of foxhunting, but in hunting there is comparatively little music (horn).

'*Beagles* are good', says Miss Ena Adams, 'inasmuch they are lively and game, but generally speaking they cannot hold a light scent: harriers to my mind either race a hare down without giving it a sporting chance, or on a catchy scent are flashy and are prone to lose a dying hare. The *Basset*, on the other hand,

[1] Various technical terms for the hare (which are summarized by Manwood) are given in Part II.

has a wonderful nose and is tenacious on a catchy scent or a dying hare, and he has not the speed to race down a fresh hare, so that the hares he catches are caught in fair play. . . . He has in addition the most beautiful cry of any hound, and eight couples of Basset hounds in full cry will make the welkin ring more stirringly than twenty couples of foxhounds.'

The modern Basset hound dates from about 1874, when it appears to have been introduced from France. Its head is like a bloodhound's, forehead wrinkled to the eyes, which should be kind and show the *haw* (the third eyelid in a dog or horse). Ears long, neck powerful with heavy *dewlaps*. They have a peculiar waddling gait. Colours—black, white and tan, sometimes hare-pied. Height about 14 to 15 inches.

With one exception the English packs of Basset hounds are hunted on foot.

THE OTTER

ANCIENT

At the time of *The Master of Game* the otter was 'vermin':

> And three other bestis ben of gret disport,
> That ben neyther of venery ne chace:
> In huntyng ofte thei do gret comfort,
> As aftir ye shal here in other place,
> The *grey* is one thereof with hyse slepy pace,
> The cat an other, the otre one also.
>
> (Twety.)

King Henry IV had a 'Valet of our Otter hounds', and there was a King's otter hunter as early as 1175 (Henry II).

HUNTING THE OTTER

'Men hunt them by hounds with great mastery.' (MG.)

Three or four varlets with a *limer* searched, two up and two down, the streams before daylight, looking for the *marks* and *sprainte*s, and for his *hough* or *couch* (the otter's dwelling or *holt*). The hunters would return to report, as in stag-hunting. The chief characteristic of the old hunting seems to be that every hunter carried a spear to prod at the otter when he came to *vent*: they were hunted by 'special Dogs, such as are called *Otter*-Hounds, and also with special Instruments called *Otter*-Spears . . . carry your *Otter*-Spears to watch his Vents, for that is the chief advantage . . . strive to get a stand before him where he would vent'. (NC.) The spear—they were mostly two-pronged, and called *Otter-grains*—was not dropped till about 1860.

The otter usually went up stream to feed, as the smell of the fish would be brought down to him by the water. Gesner says an otter could wind a fish at forty furlongs, but Isaac Walton is nearer the truth when he says it can smell a fish a hundred yards away. 'The otter, when he takes to water, is said to *beat the stream.*' (*The Sportsman's Dictionary*, 1807.)

MATING

'They go in their love at the time when ferrets do.' (MG.)

'An Otter and Ferret *grow salt* much about the same time, and bring forth their young much after the same manner, neither having their constant number.' (NC.)

An Otter at rutting time is said to *whine*, and when he mates he *hunteth for his kind.* (See Chapter XX.)

FOOTING AND EXCREMENTS

'She has the foot of a goose, for she has a little skin from one claw to another . . . and she has no heel save that she hath a little lump under the foot, and men speak of the *steps* or the *marches* of the otter as men speak of the *trace* of the hart, and his fumes *tredeles* or *spraints.*' (MG.)

'These Creatures are footed like your water-Fowl, having a web between their claws, and have no heel, but a round ball under the soal of their feet: and their Track is called their *Mark*, as the *Slot* of a Hart; and their Excrements are called *Spraints.*' (NC.) (See Chapters XIV and XVII.)

TERMS OF VENERY

Whelps: The young of the otter.

Marches or *Marks:* The footprints, called now the *seal.*

Spraintes or *Tredeles:* The excrements; modern—*spraints* or *wedging.*

Vent: Used by Turberville as the spot where the otter comes to the surface for air.

Couch, Hough or *Lodging:* Seventeenth century term for his dwelling; modern—*holt, couch, kennel* or *hover* (? corruption of hough).

Grease: The fat.

The otter is *cased*, i.e. the skin is drawn off him.

The otter *lodges*, goes to his lair (Dryden). (But see above and Chapter XV.)

The season for otter hunting: Shrovetide (about Feb. 22) to Midsummer.

(Appendix to MG.)

[For the remainder of the old Technical Terms, see Part II.]

The otter was a beast of 'stinking flight'.

'It is supposed by some', says Cox, 'that the Otter is of the kind of Beavers, being as it is an amphibious Creature, living both in the Water and on the Land; besides, the outward form of the Parts beareth a similitude of that Beast. Some say were his tail cut off, he were in all parts like a Beaver, differing in nothing but habitation: For the Beaver frequenteth both the Salt-water and the Fresh; but the Otter never goeth to the Salt.'

MODERN

There is a little stream called Sealy in Pembrokeshire, so named because of the *seals* or tracks of otters abounding on its banks (whence the name Sealyham for the popular breed of small terriers, which were bred with short legs to drive the otters from their holts).

To-day Foxhounds, as well as Otter hounds and terriers, are employed in England.

Otter dogs in the old days, it is believed, were a breed between the harrier and the terrier. To-day packs are very mixed, but the majority consist of true Otter hounds (originally the rough-coated *Griffon-Vendéen*, still extant in parts of France), and most of these are of the rough variety.

The otter is found by means of its overnight *drag*. 'The drag of an otter lies longer than that of any other beast of chase.' (Cameron.) When struck, it must be ascertained whether it is an up- or down-stream drag. The examination of *seals* and *spraints* helps to decide this question. The drag should lead to the *holt* where the otter is laid up, and from which it must be bolted by terriers. When the otter is *put down*, the hunt proper commences. It is not considered sportsmanlike to touch the hunted quarry with an otter-pole.

'In Otter Hunting the field can take a larger, more active and useful part than in any other form of the chase.' (Cameron.) The sport is pursued in the summer, 'when the cry of other hounds is silenced'.

A GLOSSARY OF OTTER HUNTING TERMS

(taken from *Otter Hunting*, by Capt. L. C. F. Cameron, ch. xiii, vol. xxii, The Lonsdale Library)

(NOTE: Those terms which are common to foxhunting have been omitted.)

Abroad: To *Hit an Otter abroad* is a North-country term for *Putting an Otter down* (q.v.).

Bar: The crowbar sometimes employed to move an Otter from a strong *holt.*

Beat: To *Beat the water* is an old term for when an Otter is *put down.*

Bend: The land between two reaches of a winding river, across which the Otter has travelled to gain time or avoid the current.

Bitch Otter: The female Otter.

Blooding: Marking a new member of the Field on the brow, cheeks and chin with a small piece of the Otter's flesh to *enter* him or her to the sport.

Bolt: To put an Otter out of its *holt* or *couch.*

Chain: The air-bubbles rising to the surface of the stream from the Otter's lungs or fur, when it dives or swims under water. (In some cases the chain of a tired otter is far more marked than that of a fresh one).

Coke: See *Spraints.*

Couch: The *holt* in which a bitch Otter has laid down her litter of cubs.

Cub: The young of the Otter.

Dog-Otter: The male Otter.

Double: Where an Otter has run out into a meadow and turned back towards the stream, leaving a loop of scent, it is said to be a 'double'. A *double-drag* is where an Otter has gone both up- and down-stream on opposite banks.

Down-Water: The cry used when it is found that the quarry has gone down-stream.

Drag: The trail of scent left by an Otter, by which it is traced to its *holt* or *couch.*

Foil: (1) To obliterate the scent by walking over the ground. (2) Hounds *swim the foil* when they follow the scent (or *ream*) on the water. Sometimes used for *Drag.*

Gaze: To view the Otter.

Heu Gaze: The correct cry when the Otter is viewed.

Hide: The temporary retreat of a hunted Otter, such as a tree-root, hole in the bank or heap of brushwood.

Holt: The lair of the Otter, where it lies up by day or for which it makes when pursued: often in a drain, hole in the bank, under tree-roots or in a burrow.

Hover: Same as *Hide.*

Kennel: Same as *Couch* and *Holt.*

Lay-Up: A bitch Otter is said to 'lay-up' her cubs in a couch when she produces her young.

Lodge: Same as *Couch, Kennel,* and *Holt.*

Mark: (1) When hounds bay and tear at the entrance to a holt occupied by an Otter they are said to 'Mark'. (2) Sometimes used instead of *Seal* (q.v.).

Mask: The head of an Otter.

Move: An Otter will 'move' when hounds have been taken away from a holt or drain after marking.

Notch: The cut made on an otter-pole to record a kill.

Otter-pole: A long staff of bamboo, or ash shod and capped with steel, and used by Otter hunters for wading, jumping or sounding purposes.

Out of Mark: When an Otter is lying-up in a holt whose entrance is under water it is said to be 'Out of Mark'.

Pad: The foot of an Otter.

Padding: Sometimes used for *Seal.*

Pate: Same as *Mask.*

Pelt: The skin of an Otter (anciently *Pyles*).

Put Down: To drive an Otter from its holt into the river.

Rattle: The note sounded on the horn at a kill.

Ream: Scent coming down on the surface of the water when an Otter has moved.

Riot: When Otter-hounds speak to or run deer, fox, hare, or rabbits they are said to 'riot'. (N.B. No hound can, apparently, withstand the temptation to hunt the scent of Muscovy duck.)

Rough: An Otter is said to be *lying rough* when found away from the water in a hedgerow, among undergrowth, brushwood, stick-heaps, cairns, heather, etc.

Rudder: The tail of the Otter. Sometimes wrongly called 'Pole'. (The otter has a habit of using his rudder, which is remarkably strong at the root, for poking fish out from under stones and banks.)

Seal: The foot-print of an Otter, recognizable by the marks of its five toes, to be sought in sand and mud, from which the direction in which it has travelled may be gathered. Also called *Mark* and *Spur*, and formerly *March* and *Step*. (See Chapter XIV, *Footprints*.)

Shoal To drive an Otter into shallow water.

Spraints: (from the Fr. *épreindre*, to squeeze out). The excrement of the Otter found on banks and boulders. It is agreeably scented like snuff. Also called *Wedging*, *Coke*, and formerly *Tredeles*.

(See Chapter XVII, *Ordure*.)

Stickle: Formed by the Field standing leg to leg across a shallow to keep the hunted Otter from passing to unhuntable water above or below.

Stoop: Hounds 'stoop' to the drag when they put their muzzles to the ground.

Stroke: When hounds carry the drag at racing pace or full-cry across a bend or water-meadow it is called a good 'stroke'.

Tail: To catch an Otter dexterously by the *rudder* as it forces a stickle or crosses a shallow. Not countenanced in some hunts, but sometimes necessary in order to terminate a hunt in very cold water or late in the day.

Trophies: The *rudder*, *mask* and *pads* when cut off are the 'trophies' of an Otter.

Un-kennel: To dislodge the Otter from his *couch*.

Up-water: The cry used when it is found that the Otter has gone up-stream.

Veline: The proper call on the horn when an Otter is *put down*; the Foxhunter's *Gone away!* reversed.

Vent: The Otter 'vents' when it comes to the surface to breathe.

Vent-hole: Any small hole leading into a holt above water, at which an Otter may be winded by hounds or terriers.

Visit: A dog Otter will often come up- or down-stream to 'visit' a bitch, sometimes crossing a watershed for the purpose, thus giving the chance of a long overland trail hunt.

Wash: The scent of an Otter coming from a *holt* in which it has *moved*.

Wedging: Same as *Spraints*.

CHAPTER VI

SHOOTING

ANCIENT

THE EARLY DAYS

THROUGH THE invention of gunpowder (c. 1340), and its use as a propellant, the bow and arrow disappeared and were superseded by the gun. The first use of a gun in this sport was in the 15th century—for dispatching the quarry. But it was not until the close of the 17th century that firearms came to be generally employed, so that Shooting, as a field sport, has existed for over two hundred and fifty years.

In early days it was not considered unsportsmanlike to kill birds *sitting*. 'Little more than half a century ago', wrote Lt.-Col. Peter Hawker, 'one who *shot lying* was viewed with *wonder*.'

This sportsman dedicated his famous *Instructions to Young Sportsmen* to His Most Excellent Majesty William the Fourth in

1830. The work ran through many editions and is full of sound advice 'in all that relates to guns and shooting'—advice that has stood the test of time. The author set out to explain the art of shooting and 'to give *particular directions* for (what *gentlemen least understand*) GETTING ACCESS TO WILD BIRDS OF EVERY DESCRIPTION'.

The present chapter, on the other hand, merely attempts to provide some elementary information on the game to be met with, together with the proper 'language' applicable to the art.

Mention can only be made of one other standard work—Col. Meysey Thompson's *Shooter's Catechism* (1907), one of an excellent series. How these Army men write on sport! One wonders . . . ?

Shooting, as we know it, is a comparatively modern sport, so that its language has altered little with the years.

MODERN

GAME

For the purposes of the Game Act (1831), the following are *game*: Hares, Pheasants, Partridges, Grouse, Heath or Moor Game, Blackgame and Bustards. In addition, Woodcock, Snipe, Quail, Landrail, Conies and Deer require a licence to kill, but are not game.

Wild Swan, Wild Duck, Teal, Wigeon and Capercaillie are not strictly game, but have their eggs, like those of 'game', protected by law during the breeding season.

The position of 'game' is not easy to define, and for a complete understanding reference must be made to:

The Wild Birds Protection Acts,
The Protection of Animals Act (1911),
The Game Licences Act (1860),
The Agricultural Holdings Act (latest 1923),
The Ground Game Act, and
The Hare's Act.

(Heath or Moor Game have no meaning as such; Bustards are extinct in Britain.)

THE SEASONS

For	*Open*	*Close*
Partridges	September 1	February 1
Pheasants	October 1	February 1

Blackgame (exc. Somerset, Devon and New Forest—open Aug. 31)	August 20	December 10
Grouse	August 12	December 10
Birds scheduled under the Wild Birds Protection Acts (e.g. Snipe, Woodcock)	August 1 (these dates vary from county to county)	March 1
Quail (Ireland only)	September 1	January 10
Ptarmigan	August 20	December 10
Wild Geese and Ducks	August 12 (may be extended in certain coastal areas).	February 1

BRIEF NOTES ON SOME GAME BIRDS

Partridge. There are two kinds, the Common or Grey and the red-legged or French partridge. The *Frenchman* (termed sometimes *the Guernsey*), introduced from France in 1673, is hardier—runs rather than flies when disturbed, so that he is more suitable for driving than for walking up. He flies straighter, if slower than the indigenous variety. (See Chapter XXIII, No. 35.) He differs, too, by being found in flocks, whereas among the Grey only those belonging to the same *covey* herd together; the 'red' sometimes also perch on trees. The Partridge is the slowest of our game birds on the wing, but probably has the largest vocabulary! Partridges, termed *Hungarians*, are sometimes imported and turned down to increase the stock. There is a variety of partridge in India called the Painted Francolin.

Clacking—An old term for a second hatching of Partridges. When several coveys roost together by night, they are said to *jug*. (Cf. *jucking*, Ch. XIX).

Pheasant. The O.E. 'black-neck' has been crossed by the introduction of the Chinese (or 'ring-neck'), the Mongolian, Japanese and Prince of Wales's breeds. Lately a new breed has appeared, 'the dark pheasant' (melanistic mutant). The male has a conspicuous tail, much longer than that of the female. Pheasants prefer running to flying, and are good swimmers. The cock gives a resonant crow when going to roost and when excited. A bird presented high over the guns is termed *tall*. (See Chapter XXIII, No. 37.) Pheasants, and occasionally partridges, suffer from *Gapes*, a disease caused by a worm. For latest modern varieties, see *British Game*.

Blackgame. Tradition in Scotland permits an old blackcock to be shot between August 12 and 20. Their display grounds, especially used in the spring, are known as *leks*. The Blackcock's song (as opposed to his crowing at the *leks*) is termed *rookooing*. You cannot drive blackgame. In Northumberland they are often simply called *Black*.

Grouse. The 'red' belongs only to the British Isles. The willow-grouse or *ryper* is found in Norway and Sweden. (See Chapter XXIII, No. 22.) 'Shooting grouse over dogs is delightful work.' (Eric Parker.) They can also be walked up without dogs. 'Grouse-shooting', however, refers to the shooting of driven red grouse which opens on the twelfth of August, and which is generally considered to offer faster birds and more difficult shots. Young red grouse, when emerged from their shell, are called *cheepers*; as they advance in growth they become *poults*. Grouse disease, *strongylosis*, is a disease among red grouse caused by a parasitic thread-worm. They are also subject to *Coccidiosis*, which mainly affects the poults. *Becking* for grouse is calling for them; also the name given to the explosive challenge made by Cock grouse to other Cocks or humans. The old grouse shooting quarters (or moors) were termed *Hills*. *Jag* is the correct word for the roosting of grouse.

(For Capercaillie, see Chapter XXIII, No. 4; and for Ptarmigan, No. 22.)

Woodcock. Called colloquially *cock*. It is now widely accepted that woodcock do carry their young (between their thighs). (See Chapter XXIII, No. 59.) 'The pursuit of woodcocks, with good spaniels, may be termed the *fox-hunting of shooting*!' (P. Hawker.) *Roding:* The cock's spring habit of flying low over the covert where his mate has her nest, at the same time making a curious croaking note like a frog's. Used also of wildfowl flying towards land in the evening. (From the Scandinavian *rode* = foray, excursion.)

Snipe. Provincial names for these birds are:

In Scotland - - - -	*heather-bleater.*
Ireland - - - -	*kid of the air.*
Wales - - - - -	*kid of the spring.*
Sweden, France and Finland	*sky-goat.*
Germany - - - -	*sky he-goat.*

In some places the snipe is called *air-goat*, perhaps because of the bleat-like sound of his *drumming*.

(See Chapter XXIII, No. 48, and *Drumming* under Shooting Terms (Small Game).

Only three kinds are likely to be met with in the British Isles:

Great—A rarity; never found in *wisps* (hence sometimes called *solitary*); rises silently, with a short and slow flight. Its characteristics seem similar to those of the *painted* snipe in India.

Jack—(*Judcock*, *Jetcock* or *Gid* (P. Hawker), and was frequently called *Half* Snipe). The smallest of the three. An average bag would contain about one 'jack' to four 'full'. Like the great snipe, it rises silently, and does not occur in *wisps*.

Full—(*common* or *snite*) has 14 tail feathers, compared with 16 to the 'great' and only 12 to the 'jack'. *Sabine's* is a melanistic variety of the *Common*.

'In discussing the sound uttered by snipe on being flushed, it is usual to say that it resembles 'scape-scape'. This, to my ear at least, is wholly inaccurate. I doubt whether any word can produce the sound, though I think that speaking of the '*scarping*' of snipe gives the best notion . . .' (Francis Cautley). 'Too much cover is as bad as too little,' writes the same expert, 'and the same applies to water.'

Snipe usually fly against the wind. They are occasionally driven. 'They begin to *pipe* about the first week in April.' (RS.)

Quail. 'These birds are so scarce in Britain, that to find a good *bevy* of them, and kill three or four brace, is considered as something extraordinary.' (P. Hawker.) (See Chapter XXIII, No. 42.)

Geese. Hawker gave six wild sorts which visited Great Britain: the *Bean* (variety of the Common); the *Bernacle*, *Treegoose* or *Clakis*; the *Brent*—you can 'hear them coming, like a pack of hounds in full cry'; the Common Wild or *Greylag* (sometimes called *Scotch Goose* in Ireland)—they 'may be always distinguished by their flying in a *figure*'; the Red-breasted or *Siberian*; and the *Whitefronted* or *Laughing* Goose.

According to the latest modern authority, the commonest geese now recorded in the British Isles are:

Of the Grey Geese:

The *Grey Lag* (contraction of *laggard*; denotes the grey goose that stays behind when the others depart); the *Pink-footed*; the *Bean* (the least common; see *Beanfeast*, App. III) and the *White-fronted*.

Of the Black Geese:

The *Bernicle* (i.e. the *Irish Goose*; older and better name than *Barnacle*, a name derived from the old legend); the *Brent* and the *Canada*.

(See Chapter XXIII, No. 20, Notes.)

(Note: *Mandible:* The jaw, including the horny sheaths; divided generally into *upper* and *lower*.

Nail: The inverted shield-shaped horny plate at tip of *upper mandible* in ducks, geese and swans.)

Wildfowl. (See Chapter XXIII: Coots, No. 7; Ducks, No. 14; Mallard, No. 31; Pochard, No. 40; Sheldrakes, No. 47; Teal, No. 54; Widgeon, No. 57; Wildfowl, No. 58.)

'With regard to the proper names of *land* birds, there is little difficulty in selecting them; but for those of *water* birds, and particularly *wildfowl*, there are so many provincial terms, that it would be a dull and endless task to construe the appellations given them by the decoymen, poulterers, and *gunners*, into their proper names in natural history. For example: the *dunbirds* are called *redheads* on the South and West coasts, and *Parkers* or *half-birds* in the fens. This is also a general term *here* for all birds under the size of the common wild duck. The *morillons* (or young golden-eyes, according to Leadbeater) are called *douckers* in Scotland, and *gingling curres* in the West. The *tufted ducks* are *blue-billed curres* on the Western, and *dovvers* on the Eastern coast, in many parts round which the *wigeon* are only known by the name of *winder*. The *golden-eye* is commonly called *pied curre*; and the *scaup-duck* is known by the name of *gray-back curre* in the South and West, and that of teal-drake in the North. For these, and all the various tribes of smaller wildfowl, the decoymen and poulterers have a sort of *sweepstakes* appellation, by putting them down as *dunbirds and divers*. Again, there are many absurd names for other birds, such as *Tommy Loos* for the *divers*, *Isle of Wight parsons* for the *cormorants*, and so on. . . . In short, it would be a waste of time to explain the nonsensical terms by which only birds are known in many places; and more particularly as the naturalist or sportsman should be provided with "Bewick" . . .' (P. Hawker, 8th ed., 1838—*his* italics.)

Duck. Hawker gives fifteen kinds: Bimaculated or *Clucking*; Burrough Duck or *Sheldrake*—'may be seen in what the boatmen call *troops* of from thirty to forty'; Common Wild duck—'the *male* bird of which is called *mallard*, and the young ones *flappers*. . . . When the *flappers* take wing, they assume the name of *wild ducks*. . . . You need not be at a loss to know a *wild* duck. The *claws* in the *wild* species are *black*'; *Eider*, *St. Cuthbert's* or Great Black-and-White Duck; Ferruginous Duck; *Golden-eye* (morillon); Grey Duck or *Gadwall*; *Long-tailed Duck* or Swallow-tailed Sheldrake; *Pintailed* Duck, Winter Duck, Sea Pheasant, or *Cracker* (this is the *Sprig* of California, by far the most numerous duck on the Pacific coast); *Scaup* Duck; *Shoveller*, Kertlutock, or Broad-billed Duck—they 'breed in Norfolk, where they are called "*Becks*", and, in some places, "*Scopper*-bills" '; *Tufted* Duck; *Velvet* Duck, Great Black Duck, or Double Scoter; and the Dunbird, *Pochard*, or Great-headed Wigeon.

Mr. Vesey-Fitzgerald gives the present picture clearly: 'Ducks', he writes in *British Game*, 'may readily be divided into four groups—the shelducks, the surface-feeding ducks, the diving ducks and the saw-bills.' These comprise:

Of the Shelducks (where the sexes are very alike):

The *Shelduck* and the *Ruddy Shelduck*.

Of the Surface-feeding Ducks (generally marked by a *speculum* (q.v.) and adopt an *eclipse* plumage):

The *Mallard* (its note is the well-known *quack*); the *Gadwall*; the *Teal*; the *Garganey*; the *Wigeon* (see below); the *Pintail* ('by far the fastest of our ducks'); the *Shoveler*.

Of the Diving Ducks (in flight 'feet stick out beyond the tail'):

The *Pochard*; the *Tufted Duck*; the *Scaup Duck*; the *Golden-eye*; the *Long-tailed Duck*; the *Eider Duck*; the *Scoter* and *Velvet Scoter*.

Of the Saw-bills ('quite uneatable'):

The *Goosanders* and the *Smew*.

(Note: *Eclipse dress:* Term applied to the drake's plumage when moulting in midsummer.

Speculum: A conspicuous coloured patch on the wings.)

Wigeon (*Whewer*, *Whim* or *Pandled Whew*). 'Strictly speaking,' says Hawker, 'we should say "wigeons" in the plural number, as well as "pigeons". But so generally is it the custom, among those who have anything to do with wildfowl, to leave out the *s* here, that the introduction of it feels to me like hearing a "*flock* of partridges", or a "fox's tail" (all modern sportsmen say, for the plural, "trout", and not "trouts"). . . . Our lexicographers, it appears, still spell *WiDgeon* with a *d*; Mr. Bewick spells "*wigeon*" without the *d*. I shall therefore take the liberty of following his example, under the idea that lexicographers are not gods, but men.' They are often found in the company of Brent geese; 'by far the most numerous of our game ducks . . . the punt-gunner's duck'. (Vesey-Fitzgerald.)

Swans. See Chapter XXIII, No. 52, Notes.

SHOOTING TERMS—CHIEFLY SMALL GAME

Back-break: An old term meaning to teach dogs not to worry the *cheepers.* (Blaine.)

Bag: The total of game plus *various* (q.v.) shot in one day.

Barrel: One can say 'he missed with both barrels'.

Beat: See under BIG GAME.

Blink: An old term to signify a dog passing by a bird without pointing at it. A *Blinker* is a dog which leaves its *Point* through nervousness on the approach of the 'Guns'.

Blotting out: Covering up a straight oncoming bird with the gun-muzzles.

Blow-back: Half-burnt or burning grains of powder after a 'shot'.

Bore: Calibre of a gun; measured by the number of spherical balls of lead, each exactly fitting the bore, which go to the pound.

Brace: A pair, a couple; e.g. a brace of pistols, or of partridges.

Break: Hunted game are said to 'break cover', when they come forth from a lurking place.

Brown, to: See *Firing into the brown.*

Butt: (1) A sort of *hide* for a 'Gun', usually for grouse shooting and sited in a depression. (2) The thick end of a rod, gun.

Cannons: Hawker's term for two birds killed with one barrel, deliberately chosen as they are in line.

Cast-off: The line of a gun from muzzle to butt is not straight. The butt is bent to the right, and this is called the 'cast-off'.

Choke: The narrowing of the bore of a tube at one end; commonly the left barrel of a shot-gun is 'choke'. There is *full* and *half choke.*

Clay Pigeons: Small saucers of baked clay thrown into the air from a trap; used to represent birds at a shooting school or in shooting matches.

Cock: 'The cock are in' means that the migratory woodcock have arrived.

Decoys: Stuffed birds or silhouettes (made of painted tin or wood) put out to attract wild birds.

Doll's head: A small extension of the top rib of a gun which fits into a corresponding aperture in top of breech.

Driving: Causing game to move forward towards the 'guns'; opposite to *walking up* (q.v.).

Drumming: The peculiar noise made by a snipe, generally during the breeding season, as the bird planes downwards; it is caused by the tail. ('In superstitious times (it) was called *campana coelestis*.') (RS.) The noisy spring display of the pheasant is also called *drumming*.

Field Trial: A meeting at which gun dogs are tested under field conditions by qualified judges.

Firing into the brown: Firing into the middle of a 'flock' of birds, instead of picking out a particular one.

Flankers: Men whose business it is, in driving game, to turn in such birds as show a tendency to break away from the butts.

Flight: A number of birds flying together, or the birds produced in the same season. (See Part III.)

Flighting: Term used of ducks and geese, when coming in to water in large numbers, usually at dusk.

Flush (or *spring*): To cause birds to take flight.

Following through: Bringing the gun up behind or on a bird, and continuing to swing through and ahead of it.

Game: Birds—see notes under GAME in this chapter. Animals—such as are objects of the chase, and their flesh as used for food; distinguished from meat, fish, poultry, and from the flesh of deer (=venison).

Ground game: Hares or rabbits.

Gun: A term used also for the sportsman himself with a gun.

Gunning: Shooting of game with a gun.

Hide: A small structure—to conceal a watcher or a 'gun'. (In the U.S.A. it is called a *blind*.)

Hound: To hunt with dogs.

Improved cylinder: A barrel with a slight *choke*.

Loader: One who loads both guns in turn for his 'master'.

Lock: The mechanism of a gun for exploding the charge.

Magazine: A case for cartridges.

Over and under guns: Have their barrels placed one above the other, instead of in the normal side by side position. 'A fancy weapon.' (GB.)

Pairing-time: The time when birds *tread*. (See Chapter XX.)

Pattern: A grouping of shot on a target—may be even, uneven, close, scattered.

Peg: The mark of a *stand* in grouse driving.

Planing: When birds seem to 'sail' downwards with still wings.

Poacher: One who trespasses on private grounds in pursuit of game.

Point: A gun dog is said to 'point' game when he suddenly checks and stiffens (usually with a raised front paw) and looks fixedly at some spot to his front.

Point-blank range: The greatest distance that shot will travel horizontally, when a gun is fired.

Poke: To aim at the bird (dwelling on your aim) instead of swinging the gun naturally.

Pricked: Wounded (birds).

Ranging: Gun dogs (setters and pointers) are said to 'range' when they search for game by quartering the ground in front of them.

Recoil: The backward thrust of the gun on firing.

Right and left: Two shots fired in succession, with the right and then the left barrel, at separate birds, and which 'bag' them both.

Rocketing: Applied to a pheasant which flies high and fast towards the shooter—a *rocketer.*

Rough shooting: Shooting, often single-handed and often with a dog, over an area of ground without any special preparation. On a *rough shoot*, every shot will have to be worked for.

Runner: A bird, usually a wounded one, that travels fast without flying.

Say: To allow birds (e.g. wood-pigeon) to feed without disturbing them is to let them get 'a say'.

Sewelling: The name given to one of the methods of making pheasants fly. It consists of a long cord about two feet from the ground on which is tied bits of coloured rags and feathers. The cord is kept moving by a man at one end.

Sewel: Something hung up to scare or prevent deer from entering a place; a scarecrow. (N.) (Some authorites use *Sewin.*)

Snap shot: A shot fired extremely quickly, when the shooter has only a fleeting glimpse of his mark.

Spurs: The claws of a cock pheasant.

Stand: The selected place for each gun to take up when waiting for driven birds.

Stock: (1) The amount of game on a certain area of ground. (2) The wooden portion of a gun.

Strong on the wing: Applied to birds which fly fast and boldly.

Stubble: Rough ground with the stumps of cereals left after cutting.

Tower: Used of a bird which soars almost perpendicularly after being shot. It then falls like a stone, and is usually found lying on its back. Birds tower because they are in danger of suffocation, due to haemorrhage in the throat, windpipe or lung.

Try gun: A gun which can be adjusted to fit any shooter, thus enabling the required amount of *cast-off* or *cast-on* to be measured.

Twelve-bore: The commonest type of double-barrelled shotgun. (See *Bore.*)

Various: Species of game, or other birds or animals, not specially named in the columns of a game register.

Vermin: Animals destructive to game. (See Chapter IX.)

Walking up: 'Guns' walking in line, and in silence, to *flush* partridges, etc. There may be keepers or beaters in between the guns.

Whirring: The sound of partridge's or pheasant's wings in flight.

Wild-fowling: There are two kinds: flight shooting and punt gunning.

Yackoop: Jump for the dog in the screens of a duck *decoy*.

SHOOTING TERMS—BIG GAME

Bandobast: A useful Hindustani word for any preparation or arrangement.

Bay: To chase so as to bring to bay.

Beating: When a line of men called *beaters* advances, striking at bushes, to rouse game.

Dangerous game: May be (1) thick-skinned, e.g. buffalo, elephant, rhino, or (2) thin-skinned, e.g. bear, panther, tiger.

Drag: The trail on the ground of a carcase that has been moved.

Ghooming (from *ghumna*, to turn): Prowling about silently in the jungle, usually at dawn, on foot or on a pad elephant, in the hope of seeing game. It may be called *still hunting*.

Hair trigger: A trigger which lets off the cock by the slightest touch.

Howdah: A wooden seat on an elephant.

Kill: Some animal killed by one of the carnivora. It can be either a 'natural' kill or an animal tied up for the purpose.

Machan: A platform, lashed high up in a tree, from which to watch or shoot.

Nullah: A watercourse, often dry.

Safari: A Swahili term for an expedition or caravan.

Safety slide (or *catch*)*:* When pushed forward prevents the gun or rifle from being fired. On shot guns, the act of opening the breech automatically puts the slide at *safe*. 'Non-automatic safeties should be the only kind fitted to rifles.' (GB.)

Shikar: The Hindustani term for sport (big or small game).

Shikari: Either the native expert or the European sportsman himself.

Sitting up: Usually in a machan and over a *kill*, in the hope that your quarry will approach within view or range.

Sling: A leather strap (preferably of raw hide) tied to the *eyes* on the rifle. It enables the weapon to be slung over the shoulder, and can be used round the left arm to steady the shooter when taking aim.

Stops: Men specially posted on the flanks of a *beat* to prevent the quarry breaking out.

Tree: To tree an animal is to hunt it until it climbs a tree.

SIZE OF SHOT

This varies from LG, rising through the SG's, A's and B's, to the numbers 1 to 10. They refer to the numbers of shot to the ounce. LG, for instance, has 5, B—80, and No. 6—272 to the ounce.

RIFLES

The introduction of cordite, etc., towards the end of the nineteenth century revolutionized the character of sporting rifles. The amended definitions, as given by Major G. Burrard, D.S.O., are:

Large Bore: A rifle the calibre of which is greater than .600 in.

Medium Bore: A rifle the calibre of which is not greater than .600 in. nor less than .400 in.

Small Bore: A rifle the calibre of which is less than .400 in.

Magnum Small Bore: A small bore rifle which has a m.v. of 2,500 f.s. or more.

H.V. Express, Cordite Express, Cordite Rifle, or H.V. Rifle: A medium or small bore rifle built specially to fire cordite or other nitro powder.

Express: Any medium or small bore rifle built to fire black powder only, which has a m.v. greater than 1,600 f.s. and a M.E. not less than 1,500 ft. lbs.

Miniature: Any small bore rifle which has a M.E. of less than 1,500 ft. lbs.

Note that large bore rifles are described like shotguns (e.g. 8-bore, etc.) and not by the diameter of their bore. (One could say No. 8 instead of 8-bore.)

The National Rifle Association has its headquarters at Bisley, where shooting for the King's Prize takes place annually.

SIGHTS AND SIGHTING

Sights for the rifle are of three kinds:

(1) *Open sights:* Consisting of a V-backsight (with or without *leaves*) and a foresight. Many experts recommend a standard (broad and shallow) V, and no leaves. A good pattern for the foresight is the *bead*, its object being to assist the shooter always to take the same amount of foresight, which is said to be *centered* when the aim is correct.

(2) *Peepsights* (such as the Lyman): Used instead of the V-backsight and in conjunction with the normal foresight. (Note: The shooter should not attempt to *centre* the foresight in the *aperture*, but simply to concentrate on placing the bead on the required portion of the target.) This form of sight saves eye-strain, and is quick and accurate.

(3) *Telescope sights:* Fixed either above or to the side of the rifle. They eliminate the difficulty of focussing and enable the shooter to see better in a dull light. They are, however, delicate instruments, add to the weight of the rifle and tend to spoil its balance.

Note: Standard work is Major G. Burrard's *Notes on Sporting Rifles*.

Sight Protector: A leather cover to protect the foresight, and attached by a thong to the sling eye.

For Deer Stalking, see Chapter II.

A FATHER'S ADVICE TO HIS SON

If a sportsman true you'd be,
Listen carefully to me.

Never, never let your gun
Pointed be at anyone;
That it may unloaded be
Matters not the least to me.

When a hedge or fence you cross,
Though of time it cause a loss,
From your gun the cartridge take,
For the greater safety's sake.

If 'twixt you and neighbouring gun
Birds may fly or beasts may run,
Let this maxim e'er be thine:
FOLLOW NOT ACROSS THE LINE.

Stops and beaters oft unseen
Lurk behind some leafy screen;
Calm and steady always be:
NEVER SHOOT WHERE YOU CAN'T SEE.

Keep your place and silent be:
Game can hear and game can see;
Don't be greedy, better spared
Is a pheasant than one shared.

You may kill or you may miss,
But at all times think of this:
All the pheasants ever bred
Won't repay for one man dead.

COMMANDER MARK BEAUFOY

THE CRIME

On the First of September, one Sunday morn,
I shot a hen pheasant in standing corn
Without a licence. Contrive who can
Such a cluster of crimes against God and man!

RICHARD MONKTON, 1ST LORD HOUGHTON

CHAPTER VII

FISHING

'*The study of Nature* presents itself to the angler as a part and parcel of his pursuit.' (Blaine.)

The author is grateful to Mr. Roy Beddington of 'Country Life' for his valuable advice, and for the provision of most of the terms (with their definitions) under both Ancient and Modern. The notes on the Section 'Big Game Fishing' have been kindly corrected by Mr. Harold J. Hardy of the British Tunny Club.

'I SHALL content myself in telling you that Angling is much more ancient than the incarnation of our Saviour . . . the most honest, ingenious, quiet and harmless art of Angling.' There is no sportsman who would not correctly name the author of this quotation. Izaak Walton's *Compleat Angler* (first published in 1635) is, perhaps, the best known as it certainly is one of the greatest books on sport ever written.

Space does not permit of even a few words on the history of fishing or the many famous writers on this fascinating sport.

In the following lists an attempt has been made to collect

together a selection of fishing terms, ancient and modern, which the angler is likely to use, or hear used, by the river bank or in discourse on the sport of fishing. No attempt has been made to cover sea fishing except for 'Big Game'.

[In the olden days the pleasures of the table and the art of carving were highly esteemed. Special terms for the dressing of fish are given in Chapter XXI. For Group Terms see Chapter XXV.]

ANCIENT

Ablet, Alblen: Bleak (q.v. under (2)).
Arming of hook: Shank.
Bag: Applied to line when one hair of it ran up more than the rest.
Bawk: (1) A knot in line or cast. (2) To check a fish when he bites.
Beard: That part of hook above point to prevent fish slipping off.
Bed or *Bedding:* (1) Hairs which twist 'kindly', *bed* well. (2) Eels *bed* in the mud. (3) Substance of body of artificial fly.
Bladder angling: Fishing with bladder which rises to surface (at a bite) and hooks fish.
Bley: Bleak (q.v. under (2)).
'Bobber', 'brother Bob': Term for fellow angler.
Bottom: Hair (or gut) cast.
Break: A knot in the joint of a rod.
Brogling: i.e. Sniggling. (See *Sniggle* under (4)).
Burrock: Small weir or dam where wheels were laid for taking fish.
Caralet: Form of net usually baited with worms.
Chavender, Chevin (or *Cop*)*:* Chub.
Clap bait: White maggot found under cow turd.
'Cock': A float cocks when it swims perpendicularly in the water.
Dare: Dace.
Dip: To fish with sink and draw motion.
Dippers: Droppers (q.v. under (3)).
Drab: Contraption of iron and four hooks useful for saving tackle fast in bottom.
Drabling: Method of catching barbel.
Drag: An instrument to disentangle the line (cf. *drag* under (4)).
Drift: When four or more Anglers are in company together, they are called a *drift*.

Dub: To make an artificial fly. (See under (3).)

Dull: Snare for catching trout.

Eldrin: Brown trout.

Fence month: Close season.

Flew: Old form of trammel net.

'*Follow the rake*': Term for gudgeon feeding after river bed was raked.

Gad: Small pike.

Gape: Mouth (of pike). (Cf. *Gape* under (3).)

Gartaman: One who owns an open weir where fish are taken.

Garth: Fish dam.

Gildard: The link of a line.

Gilse: Old spelling of *Grisle* (q.v. under (2)).

Gogger: Gaff. (Cf. *Cleek* under (3).)

Grabble: Fishing on the grabble is when the line is sunk with a running *plummet* fast to the bottom, so that the hook-link plays in the water.

Ground angling: Fishing with a leaded cast without a float.

Ground plumbing: Gauging depth of water with a *plummet* (q.v. under (3)).

Haltering: Snaring. Means of catching pike or poaching other fish by slipping noose attached to rod over head or tail.

'*Hang a fish*': The Angler is said to hang a fish when he has fastened the hook in him.

'*Hovers*': Trout waiting on edge of fast water in great numbers ready to dash at food brought down by stream.

'*Huxing for pike*': Fishing with bladders to each of which line and hooks are attached. A form of *live-baiting* similar to *trimmering* (q.v. under (4)).

Jury of flies: 'Flyes wyth whyche ye shall angle to ye trought and grayling.'

Kink: A line kinks in trowling, when it is twisted between the top of the rod and the ring.

Kipper time: 3rd–12th May, when salmon fishing was prohibited in River Thames.

Landing hook: Gaff (q.v. under (3)).

Lave: To throw water out of a pond, etc.

'*Laying on the water*': Always fishing.

Leash of fish: Three (also modern).

Leather mouthed: Fish with teeth in throat.

Leger line: See *Ledgering* (under (4)). (Lat. *lego* = I layout.)

Link: Two or more hairs twisted together. (See under (3).)
Load (a line): Put shot, etc., on it.
Luce: Pike.
Mid-water fishing: Fish at depth under surface but not on bottom.
Muddle: To stir up bottom, when Gudgeon fishing.
'Off': Applied to fish after spawning.
Palmer: Hackle fly.
Peg line: Trimmer (see under (4)).
Phinnock, Pinnock: Sea trout (mis-spelling for *Finnock* (q.v.)).
'Physician of the fish': Tench.
Pink: Young grayling.
Pouch: (1) As applied to pike after swallowing prey. (See *Gorge* under (3).) (2) Creel.
Prickle-back: Stickleback.
Prime: Fish are said to prime when they leap out of the water.
Quoil: Gather up line with thumb and 'two next fingers' in small rings of equal size.
Rank hooks: Hooks with too large a *gape* (q.v. under (3)).
River fox: Carp.
River sheep: Roach.
Runners: Bits of quill for fixing float to line.
Rush-grown: Tapered, as applied to rods.
Salmon-hunting: Spearing salmon on horseback at low tide.
Salmon pipe: Engine for catching salmon.
Scouer (mod. *Scour*) *worms:* Clean worms (e.g. by leaving for a time in moss). Also applied to yellow eels which are kept in keep-box to purge themselves before despatch to market.
Scouers and *sharps:* Shallow places in rivers.
'Scratching for barbel': Stirring up the bottom before barbel fishing.
Sharpling: Stickleback.
Sheer: To have your hook 'bit off' by a fish.
Shett: Young grayling.
Shoal: Any great number of fish together (also modern).
Shoemaker: Tench.
Shoot: A fish 'shoots' when it swims away in fright.
Skirlings: Samlets, lasprings, fingerins—young salmon.
Spud: Spike at butt end of rod for insertion in ground.
Sput net: Caralet (q.v. above).
Stand, A: Convenient place to fish at.
Stew: Fish pond (also modern).

Strike: A pike 'strikes' when it seizes a bait (also modern).
Sun-lestering: Spearing (especially eels) in the sun.
Thrash: Anything which swims down the water and incommodes the angler.
'*Tied up*': Applied to a hooked fish which had weeded itself or become entangled in a snag.
Toss angling: Fishing with a worm and drawing bait along surface without a float.
Tripping bait: Allowing bait to move just touching the bottom.
'*Troll at home*': To cast near the bank from which the fisherman is fishing.
Trout binning: Stunning fish by striking rocks and stone under which fish are lying with heavy instrument.
Umber: Grayling.
Veer your line: Let it off the reel after striking.
Walking bait: Live bait.
'*Weigh a fish out*': To lift it out without using a landing net.
Whip: To cast artificial fly, drawing it gently over the surface (cf. under (4)).
Whitefish: Roach, dace, bleak and gudgeon were so classified.
Wince, Winch, Wheel: Reel.

MODERN

(1) REPRODUCTION

Alevin: Trout or salmon after emerging from *ova* (yolk sac attached).
Baggot (*bagget, baggit* or *bagot*): Unspawned salmon after usual spawning time.
Beak: Neb (q.v. under (2)); applied to a salmon at and after spawning time (cf. *Kip*).
Clean fish: Fresh run (q.v.), as applied to salmon.
Cock: Male fish.
Fry: Fish between *alevin* and yearling stage.
Gled: Baggot (q.v.).
Gravid: Full of *ova*.
Hatchery: Fish farm.
Hen: Female fish.
Judy: Kelt.
Kelt or *Kipper:* Unclean fish, which has not recovered from spawning.

Kip: Male salmon's *beak* (or nose) at spawning time. (See ***Neb*** under (2).)

Ligger: Kelt.

Maiden: A fish which has never spawned.

Mended (Kelt): *Kelt* getting into better condition in the river.

Milt: Fish's semen (or sperm). *Milter:* a male fish.

'Old Soldier': Male salmon after spawning.

Ova: Eggs of fish.

Pea fish: Gravid (q.v.) hen fish.

Rawner: Vide *Baggot.*

Redds: Spawning beds.

Red fish: A fish which has adopted its spawning livery.

Ripe fish: Ready to spawn.

Roe: Ova of fish.

Shedder: Vide *Baggot.*

Slanger: Kelt.

Slat: Kelt (see *Kelt*).

Spawn: The eggs of fish or frogs when ejected. To ***spawn***='to produce or deposit eggs.'

Spawning: Process of shedding and fertilizing ova accomplished by hen and cock.

'Spent fish': After spawning.

Strip (a fish): To squeeze out *ova* or *milt.*

Yolk sac: Umbilical food sac carried by ***alevin*** when it emerges from *ova.* It is retained for some time.

(2) NAMES AND PARTS

Adipose fin: Fin without rays on backs of salmon family proximate to the tail.

Air bladder: Enables fish to raise or lower themselves in the water by letting air in or out.

Alderman: Chub, also large trout.

Anal fin: Fin near anus on under side of fish.

'Banker': Trout lying close in to bank.

'Black neb': Sea trout.

'Black tail': Sea trout.

Bleak: Small freshwater fish, often used as bait for Thames trout.

Brown trout: Trout common to our fresh waters—non-migratory (cf. *Sea trout*).

Bull salmon: Well-mended salmon kelt.

Bull trout: Name applied to old and large sea trout.
Cannibal: Fish that preys on its own species.
Caudal fin: Tail.
Coarse fish: Any fish other than game fish. Called *coarse* from the coarseness of its flesh. In U.K. any fish outside the Salmon family.
'*Dolly Vardon*': Char.
'*Educated*' *trout:* One which has got to know the ways and wiles of fishermen.
Elver: Young eel ascending river.
Finnock: Sea trout.
'*Fish*', *A:* Salmon.
'*Fork tail*': Grilse.
Game fish: Term usually applied to members of the family *salmonidae.*
Gib: Beak of lower jaw of salmon or trout.
Gillaroo: A species of trout with teeth in its throat.
Gills: Breathing apparatus of fish.
Gilse, grilse: A salmon which has spent one winter in the sea. (Vide *Peal.*)
Good fish: Applied to fish worth catching.
Graining: Dace.
Grey fish: Sea trout.
Grig: Small eel.
Herling: Sea trout (in most parts of U.K. = young sea trout).
Jack: Pike. (See under (3).)
Migratory fish: Fish who leave the river for the sea at some period of their lives.
Mort: Sea trout.
'*Nanny nine holes*': Lamprey.
Neb: Nose (especially *beak* of cock fish).
Orange fin: Young sea trout.
Parr Marks: Thumb-like marks on the sides of young salmon and trout.
Parr: Young salmon after it has got rid of its umbilical sac.
Peal: Sea trout (west country), grilse (Ireland, etc.).
Penk: Minnow.
Pugg (or *Pug*): Third year salmon.
Rainbow trout: So named because colours resemble those of rainbow. Introduced from America.
Salmon spring: Smolt (q.v.).

Salmon trout: Name used by fishmongers for sea trout or pink-fleshed brown trout.

Schooler: Sea trout.

Sea lice: Insects found on the bodies of fresh-water migratory fish.

Sea trout: Trout which migrate to the sea as smolts, but return to fresh water where they spawn.

Sewin or *Sewen:* Sea trout, also applied to *grilse* in certain parts of Eire.

Skegger: Term for the more modern *grisle.*

Slob trout: Sea trout; also applied to brown trout in estuary.

Smolt: Young salmon or sea trout going to sea for first time, silvery (also termed *smout*, etc.).

'*Sounds*'*:* Entrails.

'*Springer*'*:* Spring salmon. Enters river from sea in spring.

Sprod: Sea trout smolt.

'*Square tail*'*:* Sea trout.

Stale fish: Migratory fish which has been some time up the river.

Umber: Grayling.

Whitefish: Sea trout.

Whitling: Sea trout.

Yellow fin: Sea trout smolt.

NOTE: The stages in the life of the salmon generally recognised are, in ascending order, *ova*, *alevin*, *fry*, *parr*, *smolt*, *grisle*, salmon.

(3) TACKLE, LURES, AND CASTING, ETC.

Agate rings: Rings of rod (through which line passes), lined with agate.

Amadou: Fungus—used for drying flies.

'*Backing*'*:* Light silk line spliced to dressed line to act as reserve (wound *first* on reel). '*Down to the backing.*'

Bait: Lure for catching fish.

Bend: (Of a hook).

'*Bird's nest*'*:* Resulting tangle after an over-run, while spinning.

Blow line: Undressed silk line or length of floss silk used especially in *dapping*. Allowed to be carried out by wind over water, thus keeping fly riding realistically on surface.

Bob fly: The top fly of a wet fly cast of two or more flies.

Brandling: Type of worm used for fishing.

'*Bundle of sticks*'*:* Fishing rod (Gloucester).

'Bungle' a cast: To make a bad cast.

Butt: End of the rod grasped by the hand or hands.

Button: Rubber button affixed to butt end of rod to prevent it galling the hand or body.

Cast: Casting line or *leader*, transparent two or three yards of line made of gut or gut substitute, attached to running line or collar.

Check: The brake on a reel.

Cleek, Clip, Clep: Gaff (q.v.).

Collar: Twisted gut, joining cast to running line.

Creel: Basket for carrying fish caught.

Devon minnow: An artificial minnow used for *spinning* through which gut or wire to hold hooks is threaded.

Disgorger: A wooden or metal instrument, V-shaped at end, for removing hooks from fish.

Dressed line: Prepared line, waterproofed, etc.

Dropper: Any fly tied to short piece of gut affixed at right angles to cast above tail fly.

Drop minnow: A minnow used with a 'sink and draw' motion.

Dub, dubbing: Hair or other material attached to waxed thread for purposes of making body of fly.

Dun: Natural fly before it has undergone its final change.

Eel tail: Bait used for *spinning*.

Eye of a fly: Metal or gut loop through which gut is passed to make fly fast to cast.

Ferrule: The *male* ferrule is the solid end of the joint of a rod. The *female* is the hollow socket into which the male ferrule fits.

'Fine': Applied to light tackle (e.g. *'fine cast'*, cf. *'heavy cast'*).

Flies on gut: Flies having no metal eyes but strands of gut spliced to the shank of the hook.

Flight (of hooks): Two or more triangles form a flight.

Float: Made of wood, quill or cork, etc., used (1) to keep bait from bottom, (2) to show, by its submersion, a bite.

Gaff: Sharp hook attached to stick for extracting played-out fish from water.

Gape: Bend of hook. (Cf. *Gape* of pike, under (2).)

'Garden fly': Worm.

Gentles: Maggots.

Gimp: Twisted wire and silk.

Gorge: Swallow completely (*gorge hook*, used in dead bait fishing).

Green Drake: Green-coloured Mayfly (sub-imago stage).

Guffin: Ground bait (Cornish).

Hackle: Neck feather of bird used in fly making. The hackle is wound round the body of the fly to represent legs and antennae.

Haf Net: Similar to *lave* net.

Imago: The final or *spinner* state of a fly.

'Iron', An: Hook.

'Jack': Male stonefly. (See also under (2).)

Kettle: Receptacle for holding live fish to be used as bait.

'Killing' bait or fly: A successful bait or fly.

Landing-net: Net used for extracting fish from the water after *playing.*

Lave net: Like a large shrimping net worked by one man wading. Used for netting salmon in Severn estuary.

Leader: Vide *Cast.*

Light: Applied to tackle (as *fine*).

Link: Single strand of gut.

Lip hook: Hook used to put through the lip of bait when *live baiting.*

Live baiting: Fishing for another fish with a live fish.

Marrow spoon: Spoon used for putting down fish's gullet to see what it has been feeding on.

'Mount' a cast: Put fly on to it (and tie *droppers* to it, when fishing with more than one fly).

Nymph: Larva of a fly.

Paste: Mixture of bread, or other ingredients, and water used as bait in *bottom fishing.*

Plug: American *wobble bait.*

Plummet: Weight attached to end of line or cast to gauge the depth of the water.

Point: (1) Top joint of rod. (2) Fine piece of gut (about 18") tied to end of cast.

'Priest': Instrument for killing fish.

'Put up' (a fly): Put on a fly.

Quill: Float.

Quill body: Body of artificial fly made of feather quill (usually peacock) wound round.

Rent-cane: Split-cane, as used in rod manufacture.

Runt: A form of *Plug* bait.

Shank (of a hook): Straight part of wire.

'Shepherd's crook': A desirable result of casting a dry fly, when the fly, line and cast rest on the water in the shape of a crook.

Shot: Lead pellets affixed to cast to sink bait.

Sinker: A weight for sinking the bait.

Sliced hook: A barb cut half way down shank of hook, to support a worm and prevent it bunching.

Snap tackle: Used for live baiting for pike.

'Snatcher': (1) Tailer, see *Tailer.* (2) Man who 'snatches'.

Sneck bend (of hook): The point of the hook not in same line as the *shank.*

Spear: Spike affixed to end of rod for inserting in ground.

Spent gnat: Imago mayfly after laying eggs.

Spey cast: Casting without bringing fly behind fisherman so as to avoid obstacles.

Spinner: (1) *Imago* fly. (2) Spinning bait. (3) He who spins.

Spinning: Fishing with revolving bait.

Spoon: Spinning bait shaped like spoon (without handle).

Swim: E.g. to swim a worm, or a bait = allow it to descend with the current.

Swim, A: (1) A place to *swim* a bait for coarse fish. (2) A place where fish may be expected to lie.

Switch Cast: Cast without bringing the fly behind the fisherman.

Swivel: Attched to line, trace or bait to prevent 'twisting' of line and aid *spinning.*

Tackle: Fishing gear.

Tag: Short tail of artificial fly.

Tail fly: Fly tied on bottom of cast (when using more than one fly).

Tailer: Weapon forming wire noose used for landing salmon, used for purpose of saving *kelts* from injury.

Top: Top joint of rod.

Topping: Feather of Golden Pheasant tied on top wing of fly.

Trace: Wire or gut length between line and bait with a *swivel* at either end, used in *spinning.*

'Treble': (Vide *Triangle*).

Triangle: Three hooks soldered or welded together.

Troll: To trail a fly or bait behind a boat.

'Tying' flies: Making artificial flies.

'Wagtail': Form of spinning bait.

Wiggler: Form of *wobble bait.*

Wire: (1) Hook. (2) Snare (q.v. under (4)).
Wobble bait: Bait which wobbles.

(4) GENERAL FISHING TERMS

Algae: Microscopic plant life, seen by fishermen as green scum.
Backing up: Fishing a pool from the bottom towards the top by casting across and walking slowly backwards and upstream, a few steps at a time.
Bait fishing: Fishing with any lure other than a fly.
Basket: '*Basketful*' = a catch of fish. '*To basket*' = to catch.
'*Be faston bottom*': Catch in the bottom of the river when fishing.
Bite: A fish '*bites*' in *bottom fishing*, '*rises*' in fly fishing (when it breaks the surface), '*gives a pull*' when the taking of fly or bait is only *felt* by angler.
Bottom fishing: Fishing with a bait on or near the bed of river.
Brace: Two fish.
'*Bulging fish*': Fish not quite breaking the surface when rising.
Burning the waters: A means of poaching salmon by night. By means of a light fish are speared.
Bustard fishing: Night fishing with artificial moth (called *bustard*) practised in River Eden.
'*Chuck and chance it*': To fish without knowing that a fish is lying where the cast is made, or fishing when no rise has been seen. Usually fishing *wet fly* downstream.
Clay ball fishing: Disguised hook in ball of clay only allowing bait to show.
Clodding, or *clotting:* Means of catching eels by a ball of worms, threaded on worsted.
'*Cocking*' *a fly:* Making a fly sit up well on the water when *dry fly fishing*.
'*Come again*': Term for a fish, *biting*, *rising* or *giving pull* again. (See under *Bite* above.)
'*Comingshort*': Not taking fly properly. Not taking a proper hold of it.
Common fishery: A public right to fish in tidal waters.
Coracle fishing: Fishing from a wicker boat, reminiscent of those used by early Britons. (Mostly in Wales.)
'*Covering*' *a fish:* Getting bait or fly over where fish is lying.
Creeper fishing: Fishing with the natural creeper or stone fly.
Cross-lining (means of poaching): One rod each side of river connected with line carrying many flies or baits.

Croy: An artificial pier, placed to make lies for fish.

'Cruising': Applied to trout taking a fly here, a fly there, never in the same place.

Cruives: Dam with fish trap.

'Curse': Fisherman's curse—minute diptera, on which trout like to feed, much to fisherman's annoyance as 'curse' is difficult to imitate.

Dapping (daping): Fishing with a *blow line* with live or artificial fly, allowing wind to carry out line, and allowing fly to float or dance realistically on the water.

'Dead rod': Rod left unattended.

Dibbing: Vide *Dapping.*

'Drag': State when fly is moving at a pace or direction different from that of the stream. 'There is an awful drag.'

Drogue: Canvas bag attached by two ropes to steady boat while drifting.

'Drowning the fly': Trout sometimes sink dry fly without taking it.

Drowning or *'Drenching' the line:* Fish turns upstream from below fisherman and force of stream holds the line.

Dry fly fishing: Fishing with a floating fly.

Eel weir: Weir where traps are placed for catching running eels on way to sea.

'Entry': Good 'entry' of a *wet fly* into the water.

Fishing: (1) 'Blind' (vide *Chuck and chance it*). (2) *'the water'* (i.e. covering the water or 'chuck and chance it'). (3) *'the rise'*, fishing when the fish are rising. (4) *'the fall'*, fishing during the fall of spent gnat or *spinners.*

Flashy river: River which rises and falls quickly.

'Flog the water': See *'Whip the water'.*

Fly board: Used in trout streams for encouraging fly to breed.

Foul hooked: Hooked otherwise than in the mouth.

'Fouled my line': 'Got mixed up with my line.'

Fresh, freshet: Rise in the level of the river.

Fresh run: Just up the river from the salt water.

Furunculosis: Fish disease attributable to bacillus, usually producing boils and blains on fish.

Ghillie, gaffer: The fisherman's helpmate.

'Grass' a fish: Land a fish.

Greased line fishing: Fishing with the floating line.

Groyne: Croy.

Grue or *Brue:* Snow or ice water.

Guddling: (Vide *Tickling.*) Means of poaching trout.

Gumping: As *Guddling.*

Handline, To: Pull in fish by hand without winding reel—'Handlining a trout from the weeds.'

Hang a fly: By raising the point of the rod, the fly is made to dangle over a fish.

Harling: Trolling (River Tay). A fly or bait trailed behind boat rowed by *ghillies*; usually stone fixed to butt of rod.

Hatch: (1) A frame with movable boards for varying quantity of water in stream. (2) 'Hatch' of fly.

'*Head and tail rise*': Describes motion of fish coming to surface, first its head and then its tail breaking the surface.

Heavy fish: Large fish.

Hook, To: Succeed in embedding hook in fish's flesh.

'*Jigging (fish)*': A fish, when being *played*, that pulls 'jag' 'jag' on line.

Keir: Wooden *croy.*

Ladder (salmon): Artificial work to assist Salmon over difficult or unjumpable weir or falls.

Leap (salmon): Falls where the Salmon jump.

Leash: Three fish.

Ledgering: Bottom fishing with the weight above the hook. Lead rests on bottom.

Leister = spear.

Level (applied to cast or line): Untapered.

'*Lies*': Places where salmon will stop on their way upstream.

Liming: The act of throwing lime into streams (poaching) which kills or renders fish unconscious.

Limit: Minimum length of fish which may be retained or number allowed to be caught.

Long line: Used in fishing for eels, especially in Ireland.

'*Lose*' *a fish:* Term used when a hooked fish gets off or breaks the tackle.

Mending the line: By a circular arm movement straightening out bellied line. Especially used in *greased line fishing.*

Minnowing: Trout when feeding on minnows.

'*Move*' *a fish:* Make him take notice of the fly or bait.

'*Not a fin*': 'Nothing doing.'

'*Off*': 'He's off!' = lost. Also '*Off the feed*'; '*Off the rise*'; '*Off the take*'; '*The rise is off*' (finished).

'*Otter*': A line to which are attached many flies and a leaded board, which can be made to go out by pulling the line. Used in poaching.

Pass: Vide *Ladder.*

Paternostering: Form of '*bottom*' *fishing.* Weight below hook or hooks.

'*Play*'*:* Process after hooking a fish when trying to bring him to *gaff* or net, etc.

Pollution: Fouling of rivers by effluent, etc.

'*Portmanteau*'*:* Very large fish.

'*Pricked*'*:* Fish hooked and lost.

Pull: Feel when a fish takes bait or fly under water. 'I had a good pull.'

'*Pumping a fish*'*:* Lifting and lowering rod in *playing* a fish, which is deep in the water, with the object of raising him to the surface.

Puts and Putchers: Basket-like traps—tier upon tier—used for catching salmon (Severn estuary).

'*Putting down*'*:* Frightening fish sufficiently to make him swim away or cease to rise.

'*Raise your point!*'*:* Raise the point of the rod.

Recovery: Getting back the line from the water.

Reel in: Wind in the line.

Ring: (Of a rise.)

Rise: Fish coming to surface.

Run: (1) A pool, usually fast moving water. (2) The taking out of line by hooked fish, especially applied to the first movement of a pike after it takes a live bait. (3) Line *runs out* through the rings of a rod.

'*Running salmon*'*:* Salmon swimming up a river.

Scringer = poacher.

Several fishery: Ownership of fishery without adjoining land.

Shade fishing: Vide *Dibbing.*

Shooting the line (in casting): Allowing quantity of line, held in the hand, to run out through rings at the forward motion of the rod.

Shrimping (trout): Feeding on fresh-water shrimps.

Smoking: Water 'smoking' = mist rising.

Smutting: Fish taking minute black flies, or *fisherman's curse.*

'*Snagging*' (for pike): Foul hooking intentionally with a *triangle.*

Snap fishing: Live baiting for pike with tackle arranged for striking as soon as fish takes bait.

Snare: Method of catching a pike: a running noose of copper wire is attached to a tapered pole guided over fish's head or tail and jerked tight. (Vide *Wire.*)

Snatch: Foul hook intentionally.

Sniggle: To fish for eels with worm on needle instead of hook.

Snitchering: Jerking out eels with the roughened blade of a sickle lashed to a pole.

St. Anthony's school: Late run of salmon.

Steeple Cast: Making backward cast straight up above angler, to avoid obstacles behind.

Stickle: Small eddies or runs in river.

Stoning a fish: To move him when sulking by throwing stones.

Stone a pool: Throw stones in to drive salmon up to a required spot, much used in poaching.

Strike: Sharp jerk to drive hook into fish's flesh. Also the strike of a pike at a bait.

'Stripped my reel': Took out all the line.

'Stuck' in a fish: Playing a fish. Also *'He came unstuck'* (i.e. he got off).

'Suffer a break': Lose a fish after hooking it, because the tackle breaks. *'He broke me.'*

'Swelled line': Special taper of line.

Tailing (fish): Applied usually to trout, grubbing on the bottom. Cf. *tailing a fish* = landing by grasping tail end of fish.

'Take' a fish: Kill a fish.

'Taking up their quarters' (trout): For the evening rise.

Thrash the water: Keep on casting violently, and indifferently, when fishing.

Tickling: Means of poaching trout. Tickling their bellies and then throwing them out of water with hands. (Vide *Guddling.*)

Tight lines: Term used by one fisherman to another wishing the other 'Good luck'.

'Touch' a fish: To feel it for an instant on the hook.

Travelling: Used of *migratory fish* moving upstream.

Trimmering: Means of catching fish (pike) by means of live bait on line attached to V-shaped stick, stuck and left in bank.

'Turn' a fish: To cause it to change direction. The expression to *turn a fish over* is used in salmon fly-fishing when fish is hooked, comes to the surface but then is lost.

Undercut cast: Underhand cast.

'Weeded': Fish hooked having taken refuge in weeds.

Wet fly fishing: Fishing with a sunk fly.
'*Whip the water*': Keep on fishing indifferently.
'*Working the fly*': Keeping the fly moving.

FISHING RULES: (1) All fish under 7 inches (other than very small fry for bait) must be returned to the water. (2) Fishing for trout (other than with an artificial fly or minnow) is not permitted before June 1.

BIG GAME FISHING

TUNNY

This fish is a giant member of the mackerel family. It is called *Tuna* in the Pacific; the fish are smaller there (average under 200 lbs.). Found off Scarborough and the Dogger Bank (August and Sept.), and in Cornish waters (Oct. to Dec.); also off the coasts of Norway, Denmark, Nova Scotia, California, Turkey and New Zealand. Average weight, say 600 lbs. (The *Albacore* and *Bonito* (which may be the *King fish* of Trinidad) are names for fish of the same family as the Tunny.)

Tackle: Rod—6′6″ (max.); weight limit 44 oz. (British Tunny Club rules).
Line—500 yds. of 54's suggested.
Trace—should be of wire (15 to 20 feet long).

Some sort of brake for the reel is required—preferably one operated by a slipping clutch; also a leather thumb brake operating directly on the line; the latter for holding the fish only.

Harness. This is essential. It consists of leather or stout webbing; is slipped over the shoulders and attached to the rod by hooks. The butt end of rod fits into a *Rodrest,* which is screwed into the front of the seat between the angler's legs.

Tunny fishing in British waters is of recent origin (1930), but the world's record was broken here in 1932. (It is now held in the U.S.A.—a fish of 927 lbs.; caught Aug. 1940.) Fishing is done in England from a motor-boat, or *coble* (open or decked)—plus a rowing-boat. The tunny follow the herring shoals, so the quarry must be sought near the drifters, liners or trawlers. Fishing is, usually, only begun when a tunny is spotted. Mackerel is the best bait.

When *hooked*, during the first *run* it is important merely to *brake* sufficiently to stop the reel *overrunning*. The tunny is a great fighter—he will tow the boat; as much line as possible must be got back during the pause between rushes. He does not jump out of the water like a Sword-fish or Tarpon. If he swims to the sea-bed (=*sounds*), he must be raised by *Pumping*. This consists of lifting the rod (to nearly 70°), then quickly lowering the *tip* while reeling in—and repeating the operation. (See under (4) above.)

In America some additional aids are used:

Teaser: A fish-shaped wooden lure (with no hook), towed 50 to 100 yards behind the boat.

Chumming: Strewing the water with ground bait. (This is also now used in England.)

TARPON

'When he raiseth himself up the mighty are afraid.
He maketh the deep to boil like a pot.'

JOB

This is not a British marine fish.

It is found in the Atlantic and Indian Oceans, but not the Pacific; also off the coasts of Africa and Northern Australia (where it is known as *Ox Eye*). It is often called the *Silver King.* Average weight, about 100 lbs.; length about 6 feet.

Formula (for fish not being with roe):

$$\text{Weight (lbs.) (approx.)} = \frac{\text{Girth (inches)} \times \text{Length (inches)}}{800}$$

The males are usually smaller than the females, but more active.

The tarpon is fond of fresh water. It is a great jumper—sometimes it leaps ten or twelve times after being hooked. Its chief enemy is the shark.

Tackle: Rod—with 12-oz. tip and 18-thread line is satisfactory.
Reel—should be large enough to hold 600 feet of 24-thread.

Tarpon belt: Is required to house the end button of the rod. (Also used for halibut, shark, and skate fishing.)

Sea motor-boats are usually employed for this sport. To gain line after hooking the operation of *pumping* is, as a rule, necessary. (See above.)

Render: Used of a line running off a reel.

Priest: Best type is a piece of iron piping.

Still fishing: The boat is anchored. The bait is cast into the selected water, and 20 to 30 feet of line is unreeled and coiled.

Cork fishing: The bait is suspended about 10 feet below a net cork, which is permitted to drift in the tideway up to 60 feet from the boat.

NOTE: It has been said that a fish can only be considered *struck* when it jumps or is seen on surfacing, and *hooked* when it is *fast* for two or more jumps.

OTHER SPECIES OF LARGE SPORTING FISH

Halibut: Found chiefly off the Faroe and Orkney Isles, and in Irish and Scottish waters. They grow up to 600 lbs., but about 200 lbs. would be the limit for rod and line. This fish often *strikes* himself.

Shark: They are the 'vermin' of the sea. They give the best sport round our home waters after Tunny and Halibut. The three species chiefly met with are:

Porbeagle: Found in Irish waters, and off Scarborough. Weight—up to 300 lbs. Generally fished from an unanchored boat.

Blue: Found in Western British waters—up to 7 feet and 100 lbs. Faster than the porbeagle, and the best fighter.

Tope: = small shark or large dog-fish. Gives good sport all round our coasts, especially the Thames estuary and the South coast. Local name *Sweet William* in the West of England. Average—weight 50 lbs., length 5 feet. Season—June to August; bait—squid, mackerel or herring.

Barracuda (-couta): A large fish of the Perch family—6 to 10 feet. Found in seas off the West Indies.

Swordfish: The upper jaw of this fish is sharp like a sword. It occurs occasionally in the North Sea, but is found chiefly in New Zealand waters. Gives great sport.

NOTE: Whaling has not been covered owing to lack of space. But—Read *Moby Dick* by H. Melville.

[Chief authorities consulted:
Lonsdale Library, Vol. XVII—*Sea Fishing*.
Tunny Fishing for Beginners, by F. Taylor (1934).]

CHAPTER VIII

HAWKING

'It is easier to train a gun than a hawk.' (Old saying.)

[A large part of the information on this sport, together with the Glossary of Terms at the end, has been obtained from *Falconry and Falcons* (1934) by Arnold Fleming, to whom the author is deeply grateful for permission to consult his work. Actual quotations from this source are acknowledged by the letter (F.).]

ANCIENT

THE HISTORY AND LANGUAGE

HAWKING IS one of the oldest, as it was once the most select, of the sports of all nations. It appears to have been known in China about 2000 B.C. The Persian kings hawked after butterflies with sparrow and 'starrs' (starlings). The Muscovian emperours *reclaimed* eagles to let fly at hindes, foxes, etc. Blaine shows proof that falconry was practised by the Roman Britons in the sixth century (*An Encyclopaedia of Rural Sports*, 1840); Lady Apsley gives the date as about A.D. 860. The sport was re-introduced into England by the Normans. It recalls the romance and chivalry of the Middle Ages. 'At one time it was the sole prerogative of kings and princes, but later it became a national recreation.' (F.)

In the fifteenth century the main occupations of our ancestors, both mentally and bodily, were hunting and hawking. As civilization progressed and the population increased, so did 'game' gradually die out and 'the sport of kings' (as hawking was once termed) decayed with it. The introduction of fire-arms dealt the final blow, so that the tradition of this fascinating sport was kept alive by but a few enthusiasts. The old term for a Falconer was *Austringer* (Ostringer).

There was a proper etiquette and a peculiar vocabulary for Falconry; from its 'language' many idioms have been borrowed, and some have passed the test of time. 'We still use two terms—a hawker and a cadger. Originally the hawker was one who perambulated the countryside peddling trained hawks and spaniels. The cadger, who carried the frame for the hooded birds, was the humblest servant of the chase: his name has ever since been a term of reproach.' (F.) (See *Cadge.*)

One of the earliest treatises on hawking is contained in the first portion of the *Book of St. Albans.* The Dame gives precise instructions: a young hawk is not hatched, but *disclosed*; hawks do not breed, but *eyer*; they do not build their nests, they *timber* them. . . . When the young first left the nest, they were *Bowesses*, also *Branches*, *Bougher*, or *Bower*; and when they could fly, they were *Branchers.* When the young were caught (with nets), you first had to *ensile* them (sew up their eyelids with needle and thread). When tame, they were said to be *reclaimed.* A hawk *rejoiced* when it sharpened its beak and shook its feathers after a meal. A great variety of terms are given for the movements and habits of the birds, and for every part of their bodies. A hawk, for instance, does not *catch* a partridge, it *nommes* it; it is never *ill*, it is said to have *ungladness.* 'You shall say, *Cast* your Hawk to the Pearch, and not *Set* your Hawk upon the Pearch.' (J. Guillim, 1632.)

In the ancient days there were four branches of the chase, the Heron, Brook, Field and Crow. The cry *au vol* is now being revived.

THE RANKING

The different species of Hawks were appropriated to the various ranks and stations of life:

An *Eagle* for an Emperor.
A *Gerfalcon* for a King.
A *Peregrine* for an Earl.
A *Merlyon* for a Lady.
A *Goshawk* for a Yeoman.
A *Sparehawk* for a Priest.
A *Muskyte* for 'an holiwater clerke'.

(St. A.)

The Porkington MS. puts it in rather more detail:

Ther havkes byñe *of the tovr*
A *garfavkoñ* and A *tarsselet* A *garfavkoñ* for a kynge
A *favkoñ jentyl* & a *tarselet jētylle* for a pryns
A *favkoñe of the roche* for a duke
A *favkon* perygryne for a norle
A *basterd* for euyry lord
A *sakor* & a *sakorret* for a kny3te
A *lannyr* and a *lanneret* for A squyer
A *marlyoñ* for a lady
An *hobby* for a yovnge squyer
This byne havkys *of the tour* that fleythe frove the *lur*

(P.)

To complete:

The *Kestrel* was for knave or servant, and
The *Sparehawk* was for the clergy or a retainer.

The *Hawk of the tower* belonged to the upper classes, the *Merlin* was reserved for ladies, while the *Goshawk* was for yeomen.

Hawks were *cast*, but goshawks were *let fly*.

(See Chapter XXIII, No. 24, Hawks.)

The 'victims', too, were pursued by their appropriate hawks, e.g. the snipe by the *tercel*, the partridge by the *goshawk*, even the lark by the little *merlin*.

THE TERMS OF FALCONRY

How oft, with loving hand,
Have I the *Pelt* for *Falcon-gentle* held!—
Then fed, she *rouzed* and *mantled*; and anon
Feaked on my glove, while I did smooth her *mailes*,

Her *petty-single* with a soft plume touched;
Meanwhile, with right good will, she *pruned* herself.—
Full oft I told her of a Hern at *seidge*:
Then were we friends; and when the drousy night
Talked to the world of stars in its bright dreams,
I loved to deem she *jouketh* well in it.

(NC., 2nd ed., 1677.)

A LIST OF OLD TERMS

(Taken mainly from *The British Sportsman* by W. Aug. Osbaldiston, 1792, and NOT included in the SELECTED GLOSSARY on page 108. Those marked * are from *Encyclopaedia of Sport*, 1897.)

Bate: Of a hawk, 'when she striveth to fly from the fist'. (Guillim.)

Bewits: 'Pieces of leather to which the bells of a hawk are fastened and buttoned to his (*sic*) legs.'

Block: The perch, covered with cloth, on which a bird of prey is kept.

Branch-stand: 'The making a hawk leap from tree to tree, till the dog springs the partridge.'

Brayl (or *Brail*): 'A piece of leather slit, to put upon the hawk's wing to tie it up'—to prevent her from *bating*.

Cancellier: 'When a light-flown hawk in her stooping turns two or three times upon the wing, to recover herself before she seizes.'

**Canker:* Tumour on the hawk's throat.

**Croaks:* A sort of cough.

Entermewer: 'A hawk that changes the colour of her wings by degrees.' (Cf. *Intermewed.*)

Enterpen: Of a hawk 'when her feathers are wrapped up, snarled, or entangled'.

Enterview: The second year of a hawk's age.

Foots well: Kills her quarry strongly on the ground.

Frill: To tremble or shiver.

Frounce: A disease—when the tongue swells, 'they lose their appetite, and cannot close their *clap* (q.v.). Some call this eagles bane, for they seldom die of age, but of the overgrowing of their beaks.'

Garden: 'To put a hawk on a turf of grass to chear her.'

**Gauntlet:* Leather glove worn by falconer.

Get in (or *make in*): To approach a hawk and lift it from its quarry.

**Hunger-trace:* A line which appears across the feathers of a hawk that has been starved.

Ink: 'The neck of any bird that the hawk preys upon.'

Intermewing: The *mewing* from the first change of coat till it turns white. (See *Entermewer.*)

Juke: The same as *Ink.*

**Keeks:* See *Croaks.*

Lunes (or *Lowings*): 'Leashes, or long lines, to call in hawks.'

Mayl: To pinion hawk's wings.

**Mount:* To *wait on* high.

Pendant feathers: Those 'that grow behind the thighs of an hawk'.

Pip: A distemper.

**Pitch:* The highest point to which a hawk rises when *waiting on.*

Plumage: The feathers under a hawk's wing.

Prune: Of a hawk, to pick herself.

**Put over:* To digest by passing food from crop to pannel. (See Fleming's GLOSSARY.)

Rabate: 'When, by the motion of the bearer's hand, she recovereth the fist.' (Guillim.)

Reclaim (old meaning): To call a hawk back to the fist. 'The *sparhawk*, *gos-hawk*, &c. are reclaimed with the voice; the *falcon* only by shaking the lure.' (But see Fleming's GLOSSARY.)

**Ring:* To *mount* in wide circles.

Rouse: Of a hawk, to shake herself.

**Ruff:* To strike game without seizing it.

Rye: A disease, which may turn into the *frounce* (q.v.).

Sere: 'The yellow between the beak and the eyes of a hawk.' (Mod. *cere* (q.v.).)

**Serve:* To put out the quarry from cover for the falcon waiting overhead.

Sliming: 'Of a hawk, *muting* long-ways in an entire substance without dropping anything.'

**Snurt:* See *Rye.*

Strike: To knock the bird, break its neck in the air and fly on.

Sweep: When she wipes her beak after feeding, she is said to *sweep.* (Cf. *Feaking.*)

**Tiring:* Piece of tough food given to hawk to keep it busy. (Cf. *Tyring.*)

Tyrrits: Slip-rings for fastening the *lunes* to the fingers.

Varvels: Small silver rings fastened to the end of *jesses*, and usually engraved with the owner's name.

Warble: When a hawk crosses her wings over her back after *mantling*, she is said to *warble her wings.* (Guillim.)

MODERN

To-day, with the wonder of modern 'flight', interest in falconry has revived, though the sport, at one time as aristocratic as heraldry, is now shorn of its former pageantry. It is chiefly practised upon the moors of Scotland, and the peregrine is the most usual variety of falcon flown.

'Peregrines,' writes the Hon. G. Lascelles in *English Sport* (1903), 'may be divided into two classes, each containing falcons and *tiercels*; that is to say, hand-reared hawks taken from the nest, termed *eyesses*, and wild caught hawks, taken after they have been preying for themselves at large for at least several months—often for two or three years: these are termed *passage hawks*, and the older ones *haggards*.'

The language of falconry is *full summed* with such technical terms. Those mainly in use to-day are given below. Perhaps a little knowledge is better than none at all. For instance, one could 'reclaim' with 'pride' that a goshawk does *not* soar or hover like a long-winged hawk; that a falcon is never *he*.

SOME VERY COMMON TERMS

Eyesses: (From Fr. *niais*, a chick.) Fledglings captured by setting a snare baited with some dainty.

Eyrie: The nest of a raptorial bird. (May be derived from the German *ey*, an egg; or from the Welsh *eryr*, an eagle.)

Fly: The hawk's pursuit after game is called *flying*; a hawk *flies at fur* or *at plume* or *feather*.

Hooding: Confining the head of a hawk in a soft leather cap. 'The enuring the hawk to this head gear is technically called *making to the hood*.' (Blaine.)

Jess (*Gesse*): A short strap round the legs of a hawk, by which she is held and let fly. (N.)

Lure: A bait to recall a hawk. Sometimes called a *drawer*. It consisted of a bundle of feathers and meat on the end of a string.

Mew (From Lat. *mutare*, to change), to moult. (Also, of deer, to shed their antlers.) 'The Royal Stables at Trafalgar Square, where the National Gallery now stands, were called the Mews, because they were erected on the site where the royal hawks formerly *mewed*. Hence the term Mews became later to be accepted as the Stables.' (F.) The Master of the Mewhouse was the royal title corresponding to the Master of Game.

Put in: Game when it takes to a hedge to evade pursuit is said to be *put in.*

Seamed: Was a want of condition; *inseamed,* perfect condition.

Stoop: The sudden descent of a hawk on its prey. (See *Quarry.*)

Tackler: Another term for a *hack-hawk.*

Whistle: 'By this sound the falconer dispatches his hawk from his fist, and he *lures* her back again to the fist by the same. The *hallo* is used by others for similar purposes.' (Blaine.)

A SELECTED GLOSSARY

(from *Falconry and Falcons,* by Fleming)

Arms: Legs of a hawk from the thigh to the foot.

Bare-faced: Unhooded.

Bathing: Action of a hawk when it refreshes itself.

Beak: Upper crooked part of the bill.

Beams: Long feathers of the wings.

Beating or *bating* (Fr. *se battre*): Fluttering the wings when bird strives to fly off the perch.

Bind: To seize the prey in the air and come down with it.

Bob: To shirk the *hood.*

Bolt: To fly from fist.

Booze or *Bousing:* Drinking freely, yet desiring more.

Cadge: A padded wooden frame, formed of four narrow boards, on which hawks are transported.

Camber: Concavity of the underside of the wing in a fore and aft direction.

Carries: When bird flies off with *quarry.*

Castings: Pellet of feathers given to a hawk to purge her *gorge.*

Casting a hawk: Holding the hawk's wings in your hand by the shoulder, so close that it may not beat them if you force anything on it.

Cawking-time: Coupling-time of hawks.

Ceasing: Fast hold a hawk takes with its talons.

Cere: Wax-like skin above the beak.

Cessel: First long feather of the wing.

Checks: When hawk changes bird in pursuit.

Clap: Nether part of beak.

Clitch: Adhere, become thick.

Coll: Embrace or clasp.

Concavity: Camber of wing.

Concha: Shell-shaped depression around the eye.

Coping: Paring the claws or beak when over-grown.

Cowering: The quivering of a young hawk's wings in obedience to an older hawk.

Crabbing: Quarrelling among hawks as they sit by one another.

Cray: A disease.

Creance: Long cord which secures the hawk while being trained to the first *lure*.

Crines or *Crivets:* Small black feathers like hairs about the cere-eyelids.

Crock: Cramp.

Cutell: Third long feather of the wing.

Deck-feathers: Two centre feathers of the tail.

Disclosed: As chicks peep through the shell, newly hatched.

Dropping: *Mewting* of a hawk directly downwards, and not jerking it forwards.

Endew or *Endue:* To digest, not only discharging the *gorge*, but also cleansing the *pannel*.

Engout: Feathers having black spots.

Enseamed: In good condition, no superfluous fat; purging of *glut* or grease.

Enter a hawk: When it begins to kill.

Feaking: Wiping the beak after feeding (old term = *sniting*).

Fellenden: Intestinal worms.

Flags: Shortest feathers next the shoulder; also the 'principals' in the wing.

Fly on head: The hawk is said to do this when, missing her prey, she sets out again.

Full-summed: Completely moulted. (Cf. *Summed*; see note at end of GLOSSARY.)

Gate: Elevation whence to stoop at the quarry.

Gleeming: Throwing up filth after *casting*.

Glut: Filmy substance that lies in the *pannel*.

Gorge: Crop, craw, or first stomach.

Gurgiting or *Gurgiping:* Suffocating, by whatever cause or kind of meat.

Hack: State of liberty in which young long-winged hawks are kept before pairing; early stage of training. A hawk *flies at hack*.

Hackle: Feathers at back of neck.

Haggard: A wild adult (over a year) captured bird that has preyed for itself.

Imping: Repairing broken feathers with slender wire.

Intermewed: When a hawk's first moult colour is altered from red to white, the second year. (Cf. *Entermewer* (old term).)

Jouk or *Jenk:* To sleep.

Lessens herself: Half-closing the wings to *stoop.*

Long open: Second of the long feathers of the wing.

Mailes: Breast feathers.

Make-hawk or *Quarry-hawk:* An old staunch hawk, used for instructing the young.

Makes-out: When the hawk goes forth at check.

Manning: Making a hawk endure company.

Mantling: Lowering one wing and then the other down over the legs, stretching the wings.

Mark, keep her: Wait at the place where she lays game till retrieved. Soar above the quarry.

Mutes: Droppings.

Nares: Small holes in the *beak,* nostrils.

Pannel: Lower stomach.

Passagers: Under-a-year wild hawks.

Pelt: Prey hawk has killed.

Petty-singles: Small toes of a hawk.

Pill or *Pelf:* That which is left of the prey after the hawk is fed.

Plume: General mixture of colour and feathers whereby hawk's age or health is known.

Pluming: Dismantling prey of feathers.

Pounces: The claws of the front toes. [Hence 'to *pounce*'. The mod. *Talon* includes the *pounce.*]

Pride: To be in good flesh and heart.

Principals: Quill feathers.

Put-up, Put-over: Cast-off from the wrist.

Quarry (Fr. *curée*)*:* Live game at which hawks *fly.* (See note on *Curée,* Chapter II.)

Rake-out: To fly out too far without soaring.

Ramage: When bird preys for itself, difficult to *reclaim.*

Rangle: Gravel given to bring down the stomach.

Raping: Clawing or scratching.

Rases: Scrapings or shreddings.

Reclaim: Make hawk gentle and familiar.

Sails: Wings.

Sarcels: Outer pinion feathers.

Searce: Strain.

Seeling: Closing the eyes of a new hawk with a thread through the eyelids.

Sharp-set: Hungry.

Snyting: Sneezing.

Sore-hawk or *Red-hawk:* So called from the time the bird is taken from the eyrie till it has received maturer feathers.

Summed: When hawk has all its plumes and is ready to be taken from the *mews*.

Tassel: Male peregrine or goshawk.

Towers: When bird lifts up her wings.

Train, A: Something living or dead tied to the *lure* to entice the hawk to it.

Trains: Tail.

Trussing: When hawk raises a bird aloft, and soaring with it, at length descends to the ground. Also, tying the wings to the body.

Tyring: Giving the tough leg or pinion of a pigeon for hawk to pluck at.

Unstrike the hood: To draw the strings so that hood may be readily pulled off.

Urives: Nets for trapping *passage* birds.

Wait-on: When hawks soar in circles above their master's head.

Wake: To sit up all night with newly-caught hawk in order to tame it.

Weathering: Airing hawk in an open courtyard while attached by leather thongs to an upright round wooden block.

Wreath: Fore part of neck.

Yarak: An eastern term signifying that short-winged hawks were fit and lean.

NOTE: Mr. Arnold Fleming writes (Sept. 1946): 'A hawk does not "moult" as arboreal birds, for it must be always fit to hunt for food. Perhaps the term "moult" does not express as it might the casting off of old feathers to give place to the new. But I have so far failed to find a better word. . . . It will be of great interest to many English bird watchers to learn that the white-tailed sea-eagle, or hawks, are again in the Firth of Clyde wheeling among shoals of herring. Also the Icelandic Gerfalcon—the large curlew-coloured falcon—killing a herring or other gull daily. These are rare visitors, and have been noticed for these last two years around our Western shores (of Scotland).'

HAWKING AND FALCONRY

It seems advisable to clear up the difference between the conventional and the technical methods of considering this subject. Blaine puts the matter very well: 'In many of the old sporting treatises, hawk and hawking are terms of much more frequent occurrence than falcons and falconry . . . nevertheless . . . the hawk is only a subordinate member of the falcon family. . . . We shall only remark, that the old writers use the word hawk for falcons of every degree on almost every occasion, but they make use of the term falconer, in many instances, to designate him who makes use of the hawks, although in many others the term hawker is employed.'

There were:

(1) The 'long-winged hawks of the lure' or falcons, i.e. peregrine *falcon*, *gyr-falcon*, *merlin*, *hobby*, etc. They were reserved, at first, for those of high estate, and their use was 'true, or noble, falconry'. These were the hawks of high flight (*rowers*).

(2) The 'short-winged hawks' or 'hawks of the fist', i.e. *kestrel*, *sparrow-hawk*, *goshawk*. These 'take their prey by *raking*, that is, by seizing on it near the ground'. (Blaine.) They 'do not *fly* for *flyng* sake'. These were the hawks of low flight (*sailors*).

When dogs were used to flush or point the game, the falcon *waited* above; the birds were not flushed until the falcon had *reached her pitch*, ready to *stoop*.

Hawks were furnished with *hood*, *jesses*, *swivel*, *leash* and *bell*.

THE BIRDS THEMSELVES

Thus speaks Auceps, in the 'conference betwixt an ANGLER, a HUNTER, and a FALCONER, each commending his Recreation'. (*The Compleat Angler*, by Izaak Walton, 1653):

'To return to my Hawks . . . you are to note, that they are usually distinguished into two kinds: namely, the Long-winged and the Short-winged Hawk; of the first kind, there be chiefly in use amongst us in this nation:

The *Gerfalcon* and *Jerkin*,
The *Falcon* and *Tassel-gentle*,
The *Laner* and *Laneret*,
The *Bockerel* and *Bockeret*,
The *Saker* and *Sacaret*.
The *Merlin* and *Jack Merlin*,

The *Hobby* and *Jack;*
There is the *Stelletto* of Spain,
The Blood-red Rook from Turkey,
The *Waskite* from Virginia.

And there is of Short-winged Hawks:

The *Eagle* and *Iron*,
The *Goshawk* and *Tarcel.*
The *Sparhawk* and *Musket*,
The French *Pye* of two sorts.

'These are reckoned Hawks of note and worth, but we have also of an inferior rank:

The *Stanyel*, the *Ringtail*,
The Raven, the Buzzard,
The Forked *Kite*, the Bald Buzzard,
The *Hen-driver*, and others that I forbear to name.

'Gentlemen, if I should enlarge my discourse to the observation of the *Eires*, the *Brancher*, the *Ramish Hawk*, the *Haggard*, and the two sorts of *Lentners*, and then treat of their several *ayries*, their *mewings*, rare order of *casting*, and the renovation of their feathers; their *reclaiming*, dieting, and then come to their rare stories of practice; . . . it would be much, very much pleasure to me.'

There follow a few notes on the different species of hawks; for full particulars the reader is referred to Mr. Fleming's book.

Falcon. (From Lat. *falx*, a sickle; suggests the scythe-like curve of its beak.) 'Every falcon is included under the term of hawk, but every hawk is not a falcon.' (F.) It has a toothed bill, and dark-coloured eyes. There is also a curious structure, called the *Pecten* (or comb), found in the interior of a falcon's eye; it is shaped like a fan, and has a special value in connection with the bird's remarkable vision.

The female must not be called a hen, but a *falcon* (or *slight* falcon). It is a third larger than the male, which is termed the *tiercel-gentle* (or *tassel*).

The male of the *Gerfalcon* (or Iceland falcon (Blaine)) is called *jerkin.*

'The female of all byrdes of praye is ever more huge than the male, more ventrous, hardie and watchful, and the female peregrine has given her name to the gentle art of falconry, because the falcon doth pass all other hawkes in boldness and curtesie and is most familiar to man of all other byrdes of praye.' (Turberville.)

Osprey is a fish-hawk. Its cry is 'killy-killy'. (See App. III and Chapter XXIII, No. 17, Eagles.)

Peregrine. (From Lat. word meaning 'pilgrim'.) It is the lord of the hawk family, and is sometimes called *Cliff-hawk.* Its young are ruddy-coloured. When the male brings food for the young, his mate flies to meet him and the prey is changed over in the air; this process is termed the *pass.* The male is called *Tiersel* or *Tassel.*

Goshawk. Erroneously called *Goosehawk* in Scotland. It prefers fur to feather. In the old days it was termed the *cook's bird,* as it was the main hope of a well-stocked larder. The male is the *tiercel.* They are flown straight from the hand, and do not require a *lure* to persuade them to return.

Buzzard. In Scotland this bird is called 'the little eagle of the hills'. Turberville describes them as 'base bastardly refuse hawks, which are somewhat in name, but nothing in deed'. 'It is like a cat on wings.' (F.)

Hobby. From the Fr. *haut-bois,* due to its liking for high woods. The male was called *jack* or *robin.* (Blaine.)

Kite. Also called *Puttock,* and in some parts *Gled* or *Glead* (O.S. *glida,* from its gliding flight). A boy's paper kite derives its name from this bird.

Kestrel or *Windhover.* Also termed *Stannel* or *Standgale.* It is 'nature's helicopter'. (F.)

Sparrow-hawk. The male is termed *Musket.*

Merlin. The smallest of the hawks. It is often called the *Stone Falcon,* and the male a *Blue Hawk.* Male = *jack-merlin* (Blaine.)

Harrier. So called because it 'harries' its victim. 'They would seem to form a connecting link between the Owl and the Buzzard.' (F.)

Hen Harrier. The sexes show a marked difference in plumage and colour.

Montagu's Harrier. Sometimes called the *Ash-coloured Falcon.*

Marsh Harrier. Also known as the *Dutch Hawk,* and termed sometimes, in error, the *Moor Buzzard.*

Lanner (male *Lanneret*) *Saker* (male *Sackeret*)	Probably not separate species, but geographic races of the Peregrine falcons.

'The ages also were known by arbitrary terms, as the female yearling was called a *red* falcon; the male a *red* tiercel, and when *reclaimed* (i.e. trained) was a gentil or gentle hawk of any kind, though afterwards by corruption *gentil* was used as the proper name of an individual falcon.' (Blaine.)

CHAPTER IX

VERMIN

Polecat—Marten—Stoat—Weasel
Badger—Beaver—Wild Cat

THE TERM *Vermin* may be taken to cover the *Mustelinae*, i.e. the Polecat, Marten, Stoat and Weasel. In addition, the Badger, Beaver and Wild Cat may well be included in this chapter.

The Otter is covered by Chapter V.

'Vermin' is very often just a 'point of view'. For example, so destructive are the Upland Geese to the precious grass in the Falkland Islands (three geese eat as much as one sheep, and it takes five acres to graze a sheep) that these birds are treated as 'vermin'. In Scotland, hooded crows and black-backed gulls are 'vermin' on the grouse moors; and the Kite (or Gled) in Wales. And what of Rabbits?—and of Rats, of Jackdaws, and of Wood-pigeons?

Because certain mammals are mentioned in this Chapter it is NOT intended to suggest that they should be shot, or even kept down. Mr. Vesey-Fitzgerald has some excellent chapters on this subject in Part Six of his *British Game*. All sportsmen and game-keepers should ponder and digest the whole of his 'gamy' first paragraph which ends: 'If you must use the word vermin confine it to the rat and the rabbit, creatures that are not only enemies of game but of game-preservers.' Agreed—the word has been retained here solely for its ancient origin and its brevity.

Of the predatory birds, Mr. Vesey-Fitzgerald sums up: 'There are certain birds which should *never* be shot. They are the kestrel, the brown owl, the barn owl, the long-eared owl and the short-eared owl, the buzzard, the rough-legged buzzard and the honey-buzzard, the hobby and the osprey.' As the chief enemies of game he votes for:

Mammals: (1) Brown Rat. (2) Fox. (3) Grey Squirrel.

Birds: (1) Carrion Crow. (2) Hooded Crow. (3) Raven.

(But note: the Fox, besides being valuable for hunting, is a deadly enemy of the rat.)

'Ground game,' he says, 'are vermin not game . . . their numbers should be kept under control.' Rabbit-infested ground will hold neither partridges nor woodcock. And 'the woodpigeon can only be regarded as vermin'. As regards game preservation he concludes: 'It is always as well to try to preserve a sense of proportion as well as game.'

POLECAT

This is the *Fitchew* or *Fitchet* (from the O.Fr. *fissau*). It was also called *Foumart* or *Foulmart* from its unpleasant smell. Topsell (Gesner) calls it *Fitch* or *Poul-cat*.

The names *Filchet*, *Fitchet* and *Fulimart* were applied in the early days indiscriminately to the Ferret and the Polecat. The 'ferret agrees with the fitchet in many respects', says Thomas Pennant (*British Zoology*, 1776), and some even believed would mate with it. Juliana Barnes, in the *Book of St. Albans*, speaks of the *Fulmarde* as one of the rascal beastes of the chase, and Strutt classes it as one of the animals of rank, or fetid, flight. The Foumart was hunted—and mated with a ferret—by Capt. N. W. Apperley (grandson of 'Nimrod').

'A fetid mouse of Pontus' (Dr. A. Lyttleton's *Dictionary*).

The last stronghold of the Polecat is in Central Wales.

MARTEN

This is allied to the Canadian sable.

Other names for this beautiful animal are: *sweetmart*, *mart*, *martern*, *martron*, *marteron*, *matron*, *martlett*; also *Pine Marten* and *Marten Cat* and *Mertrick* (Pennant).

In the old days it was ranked, like the Wild Cat, as vermin, but 'not to be sought purposely'.

It is 'the sweetest vermine that is hunted . . . so soone as they light upon the sent . . . (the hounds) will double their mouths, and teare them together'. (CK.)

Topsell gives: *Marder*, *Martel* or Marten, and divides them into two, the 'Beech-Martins' (*Foins*) and the 'Fir-Martins'.

The marten is now practically extinct in England.

(See Chapter XXIV, No. 136.)

STOAT

J. G. Millais gives a list of local names for this animal: *Foumart*, *Fomart*, Weasel (Suffolk), *Royal Hunter* (Oxford), *Hob*, White Weasel, Big Weasel and *Whittret* (Scotland); also *Clubstart* (Yorks), *Lobster*, *Lobstart* (Norfolk), *Clubtail* (Lancs and Lincolnshire) which refer to its stumpy tail. The provincial name *Lobster*, according to Harting, was given because of its peculiar 'lobbing' motion when running.

Sir H. Johnstone says: 'It was called the Stoat, or Stot-Weasel, meaning the bigger, more pushing, energetic of the two beasts.' The name, however, is thought by some to be derived from *stot*, which once implied any male animal. *Stot* nowadays implies sexlessness, say, a *steer*.

In Ireland the stoat is known as *Weasel*, 'a wonderful little animal, which runs like a fox, dives like an otter, climbs like a cat, doubles like a hare, and which will stand before hounds for hours and beat them'. (Irish Sportsman.)

There are packs of 'Weasel' Hounds in Ireland. They are staunch to stoat, but only suitable for hunting in country that is fairly clear of rabbits.

It is the *Ermine*, from its snowy winter fur; and its tail, compared with the weasel's, is long, and always black at the end.

WEASEL

Some of the names given by J. G. Millais in his *British Mammals* for this animal are: *Kine*, *Cane*, *Beale* (Sussex and other counties), *Ressel*, *Rezzels* (Yorks), *Mousehunt*, *Mousehunter* (Norfolk), *Whitethroat* (male), *Fair*, *Fairy-hound*, *Lonnenan*, *Game Rat*, *Whitrick*, *Whittret*, *Mouse-weasel*, and *Futteret* (Scotland).

There seems to be no doubt that the word *chyme* and a 'weasel' are identical. Variants of chyme are *Kine* (Hants and Surrey),

Crane (Hants), *Kyme* (Sussex), *Skene* or *Keen* (Kent), *Cane* (Gilbert White's *Selborne*). Gilbert White wrote in a 'Letter to Thomas Pennant' (dated March 30, 1768): 'Some intelligent country people have a notion that we have in these parts a species of the genus muctelinum, besides the weasel, stoat, ferret, and polecat; a little reddish beast, not much bigger than a field mouse, but much longer, which they call a 'cane'. This piece of intelligence can be little depended on . . .'

Note by the editor in an edition of White's *Selborne*: '*Cane* is a provincial name for the female of the common weasel, which is usually one-fourth smaller than the male.' There does not appear to be, actually, any very marked difference in the size of the two sexes.

Pennant gives: *Fitchet*, *Fitchel* or *Fitchew*, but in these early days the various species of animals, especially the smaller kinds such as the weasel tribe, had not been properly sorted out.

This animal is smaller than the Stoat, and has a short tail which is the same colour as its body (tawny brown). It is not believed to exist in Ireland. (See under STOAT above.)

THE BADGER

ANCIENT

In *The Master of Game* there is a chapter on 'the *Grey* and of his Nature'. 'Once in the year they *farrow* as the fox' (MG.), and Gaston adds: 'and they *farrow* their pigs in their burrows as does the fox'.

'A *Badger*', says Cox (1697), 'is called by several Names, *viz.* a *Gray*, *Brock*, *Boreson*, or *Bauson*, and in French *Tausson*. The Male is called a *Badger* or *Boar-pig*; and the Female is called a *Sow*. These Beasts are plentiful in Naples, Sicily, Lucane, and in the Alpine and Helvetian Coasts; so are they also here in England.'

To-day the badger is generally known as The *Brock* to country folk; many place-names have this prefix, showing its ancient origin. Though unprotected, he has survived without difficulty. The modern term *to badger* reminds us of the old-time hunting of this stout animal by a pack of dogs. Some *stopping* was done, and sacks fastened with draw-strings placed in the *Holes* left open. If he was chased before he could reach his earth, he would 'stand at bay like a *Boar*, and make most incomparable sport'. (Cox.)

'It is the beast of the world that gathereth the most *grease* within....' (MG.)

Topsell, in his *Historie of All Foure-Footed Beastes* (1674), gives some picturesque, though inaccurate, details of the badger's domestic habits; Cox, who was no naturalist, copies them:

'There are two kinds of this Beast (saith *Gesner*), one resembling a Dog in his Feet, and the other a Hog in his cloven Hoof: they differ too in their snout and colour; for the one resembles the snout of a Dog, the other of a Swine: the one hath a greyer coat, or whiter coat than the other, and goeth farther out in seeking of its prey. They differ also in their meat, the one eating Flesh and Carrion like a Dog, the other Roots and Fruits like a Hog: both these kinds have been found in Normandy, France, and Sicily.

'Mr *Turbervil* makes mention of two sorts of *Badgers* likewise, but in a different manner: *For the one* (saith he) *casteth his Fiaunts long like a* Fox, *and have their residence in Rocks, making their Burrows very deep. The other sort make their Burrows in light ground, and have more variety of Cells and Chambers than the former.* The one of these is called the *Badger-pig*, and the other the *Badger-whelp*; or call one *Canine*, and the other *Swinish*. The first hath his Nose, Throat, and Ears yellowish like a *Martern's* Throat; and are much blacker, and higher legg'd than the *Badger-whelp*. Both sorts live upon all Flesh, hunting greedily after Carrion....

'*Badgers* when they Earth, after by digging they have entred a good depth, for the clearing of the Earth out, one of them falleth on the back, and the other layeth Earth on the belly, and so taking his hinder feet in his mouth, draweth the belly-laden *Badger* out of the Hole or Cave; and having disburdened her self, re-enters, and doth the like till all be finished.

'He hath very sharp Teeth, and therefore is accounted a deep biting Beast: his Back is broad, and his Legs are longer on the right side than the left, and therefore he runneth best when he gets on the side of an Hill, or a Cartroad way....

'In *Italy* they eat the Flesh of *Badgers*, and so they do in *Germany*, boiling it with Pears....

'They live long, and by meer age will grow blind ...' (Italics are those of NC.)

Pennant (1776) gives the names *Brock*, *Gray* and *Pate*, and he says that between the tail and the anus 'exudes a white substance of a very foetid smell; this seems peculiar to the badger and the Hyaena'.

MODERN

Brock is a great digger, with short legs and powerful claws to excavate his *sett.* [There is a country fable that his front legs are longer than the back, so he can go down hill faster than up; and Osbaldiston wrote: 'Their legs are longer on their right side than on their left!'] He has a 'fighting' jaw. His *sett* contains a mass of underground passages known as *pipes.* (See Chapter XXIV, No. 104.) The chambers connecting these tunnels are called *ovens* in Devonshire. Unlike the fox, he is spotlessly clean.

The female is called *sow*, and the young *cubs.* The footprint is a *padmark.* He has a queer *yickering* call, which may be heard at nights during the mating season. His relatives are wolverine, otter, skunk, ratel, marten, polecat and weasel.

Badger-Digging.

This is NOT badger-baiting (or badgering), which were prohibited in England in the middle of last century; in *digging* the hunter does not kill the hunted. When caught, he is *bagged* and taken to a place where he can do less harm. Dachshunds (=badge hound in German) are not employed in England, but a Jack Russel type of terrier, to locate and *hold.* The Staffordshire Bull terrier is the only breed which will *close with* and draw out a badger. When the badger rushes out, the Master (called the *Gaffer*) either grabs him in special *tongs*, or *tails* him, i.e. seizes him by the tail and swings him up into the air.

BEAVER

'A *Beaver* differeth but a little from an *Otter* but in his Tail. . . . There is plenty of them in the River *Pontus*, whence the *Beaver* by some is called *Canis Ponticus*: They are also bred in *Spain*, some few in *France*, *Germany*, *Polonia*, *Sclavonia*, *Russia*, *Prussia*, *Lithuania*; and abundance of them in *New England*

'Their fore-feet are like Dogs, and their hinder like Geese . . . their teeth very long . . . (they) will gnaw in sunder trees as big as a man's thigh . . . but the tail of this Beast is most strange of all, being without Hair, and covered over with a Skin like the Scales of a Fish, it being like a Soal, and for the most part six fingers broad, and half a foot long.

'They are accounted a very delicate Dish . . . they must be food that is very sweet, since this Proverb proceedeth from them: *Sweet is that Fish which is no Fish at all.*

'As for the wonderful manner of their Building, I shall let that alone, since it is at large described by *Gesner* in his *History of Beasts.*

'There is nothing so valuable in this Beast as his Stones. . . . They are taken for their Skins, Tails, and Cods. . . . Those skins are best which are blackest.' (N.C) (The italics are *his.*)

Lodge - - -	his house or den.
Kittens - -	the young of a beaver.
Colony - -	a group of beaver families.

(Grey Owl.)

THE WILD CAT

This animal was at one time a beast of the chase. From the thirteenth to the seventeenth century licences were issued to various individuals to hunt the cat and other vermin.

The wild cat was probably hunted chiefly for its fur. There was an old proverb: 'You can have nothing of a cat but her skin.'

The author of *The Master of Game* concludes his short chapter on The Cat: 'One thing I dare well say that if any beast hath the devil's spirit in him without doubt it is the cat, both the wild and the tame.'

The wild cat is believed now to be extinct in the British Isles, except in Scotland, where its stronghold is the Grampians.

These animals, says Pennant, 'may be called the *British* tiger . . . and were formerly reckoned among the beasts of the chace.' (See Chapter XXIV, No. 111.)

The Civet cat is said to produce a scent like musk.

Mole. Izaac Walton called this animal the *Mouldwarp* (from A.S. *Molde*=dust, and *Weorpan*, to cast) (Verstegan); Pennant, the *Mold-warp* or *Want.* Other local names are: *Vuz-peg* (Devon); *Oont* and *Ount* (Welsh). His tail used sometimes to be called the *penny* (the price paid for his destruction).

Hedgehog. This was known as the *Urchin* (Pennant). The term *Want* was also applied to the hedgehog. It is a destroyer of the eggs of game birds.

Topsell, quoting Gesner, describes many curious animals, among others the *Zibeth* or *Sivet-cat*, the *Zebel* or *Sable*, and the Gennet-Cat, called *Genetta.*

PART II

PECULIAR TERMS

'One should make a serious study of a pastime.'

ALEXANDER THE GREAT

CHAPTER X

THE PROPERTIES

OF A YOUNG GENTLEMAN

THE EGERTON MS. begins thus:

> Note ye the properteys
> that longythe to a yonge gentylle
> man to haue knowynge of suche
> thyngys that longythe vnto hym
> that he fayle not in hys propyr
> termys that longythe vnto hym
> as hyt shalle folowe hereynne
> wrytynge &c.

OF ANIMALS

Dame Juliana directs:

Ye shall saye thus;

An Harte *herbouryth*
A Bucke *lodgyth*
An Esquyre *Lodgyth*
A Koo *beddyth*

A Yoman *beddyth*
An Haare in her *fourme sholde rynge* or *lenynge*
A Cony *syttynge*
A Wodcocke *brekynge*. (St. A.)

In the MS. Harl. 2, we are told that:

A har is *formyd schulderyng* or *leneyng*
A boye is *beddyd* brawlyng
A Cony *Syttyth*
A percar *walkyth*
A perterych *lythe*
A fesawnte *stalkyth*
A Crane *stalkyth*
A heyron *stalkyth*.

On the last printed page of Caxton's list at the end of *The Hors, the Shepe—the Ghoos* (S.) is found a miscellany of terms, among which are:

Yf an herte stande he *stalleth*.
Yf a bucke stande he *herkenyth*.
Yf a roo stande he *fereth*

. . . . .

A herte yf he be chasid he will desire to have a river
Assone as he teketh the River he *suleth*, yf he take over the ryver he *crossith*
Yf he retorne he *recrosseth*
And yf he take with the streme he *fleteth*
Yf he take agayn(st) the streme he *beteth* or els *breketh*
Yf he take the londe he *fleeth*.

Explicit.

OF A HOUND

'A hound is of great understanding and of great knowledge, a hound hath great strength and great goodness, a hound is a wise beast and a kind(one). A hound has a great memory and great smelling, a hound has great diligence and great might, a hound is of great worthiness and of great subtlety, a hound is of great lightness and of great perception, a hound is of good obedience, for he will learn as a man all that a man will teach him. A hound is full of good sport.' (MG.)

POINTS OF A GREYHOUND

'A greyhound should have a long head and somewhat large made, resembling the making of a pike. A good large mouth and good seizers the one against the other, so that the nether jaw pass not the upper, nor that the upper pass not the nether. Their eyes are red or black as those of a sparrow hawk, the ears small and high in the manner of a serpent, the neck great and long bowed like a swan's neck, his chest great and open, the hair under his chin hanging down in the manner of a lion. His shoulders as a roebuck, the forelegs straight and great enough and not too high in the legs, the feet straight and round as a cat, great claws, long head as a cow hanging down (probably a mistake in transcription; Gaston has 'the sides long as a hind, and hanging down well').

'The bones and joints of the chine great and hard like the chine of a hart . . . straight near the back as a lamprey, the thighs great and straight as a hare, the hocks straight and not bent as of an ox, a cat's tail making a ring at the end and not too high . . .' (MG.)

The Condyscyons of A grehounde ande of hys propyrteys.

Thy grehounde moste be heddyd lyke a snake
y neckyd lyke a drake
y brestyde lyke a lyon
y sydyd lyke a noynon
y fotyde lyke a catte
y taylyd lyke a ratte
Then ys the grehounde welle y schapte.

(Eg.)

Head like a Snake,
Neck'd like a Drake:
Back'd like a Beam,
Sided like a Bream,
Tailed like a Rat,
And footed like a Cat.

(Quoted in St. A.: also by Daniel as an old couplet.)

OF A HORSE

Round-hoof'd, short-jointed, fetlocks shag and long,
Broad breast, full eye, small head and nostril wide,
High crest, short ears, straight legs and passing strong;
Thin mane, thick tail, broad buttock, tender hide.

(Shakespeare.)

YOUTH AND HUNTING

Sir Thomas Cockaine, in his *Short Treatise of Hunting*, writes 'To the Gentlemen *Readers*':

'It hath bin long received for a truth, that Sir *Tristram*, one of King *Arthures* Knights, was the first writer and (as it were) the founder of the exact knowledge of the honourable and delightful sport of hunting; where tearmes in Hunting, Hawking, and measures of blowing, I hold to be the best and fittest to be used.'

The beasts of the forest and chase have always had their peculiar attributes. Nicholas Cox, in his Introduction to *The Gentleman's Recreation*, says:

'*Hunting* trains up Youth to the use of manly Exercises in their riper Age, being encouraged thereto by the pleasure they take in hunting the *Stately Stag*, the *Generous Buck*, the *Wild Boar*, the *Cunning Otter*, the *Crafty Fox*, and the *Fearful Hare*; also the catching of Vermin by Engines, as the *Fitchet*, the *Fulimart*, the *Ferret*, the *Polecate*, the *Moldwarp*, and the like.' (See Chapter IX.)

He concludes: 'No Musick can be more ravishingly delightful than a Pack of Hounds in full Cry, to such a Man whose Heart and Ears are so happy to be set to the tune of such charming Instruments.'

What quotation could be more delightful than this, as an introduction to the next Chapter?

CHAPTER XI

THE MUSIC OF THE CHASE

[The author has been greatly helped in the MODERN sections of these notes by the clear explanation of 'music' in the Chapter 'What Was That' of D. E. W. Brock's *The Foxhunter's Week-End Book.* The author is most grateful for permission to consult this work. A description of Mr. Brock's book will be found in Chapter XXVI.]

'WHO CAN hear the cheer of the huntsman, added to the cry of the hounds and the blowing of the horn, without being inspired?' (Thomas Smith.)

A. THE VOICE OF THE HUNTSMAN

ANCIENT

'I know also it is impossible for those who see a course to avoid hollowing, without any advice being given for it, since it would almost make a dumb person speak, as is related of the son of Croesus.

'It is proper sometimes to speak to the dogs, for they rejoice to hear the voice of their master, and it is a kind of encouragement to them to know that he is present and a witness of the excellence of their running.' (Blaine.) Thus wrote Arrian, the old Greek hare-courser.

HUNTING CRIES

In the days of *The Master of Game* the hunting cries and 'hound language' were still very much what the Normans had brought over. Those for stag-hunting are covered in Chapter II (e.g. *Cy va! Ho may!*). But hare-hunting provided most of the 'fayre wordes of venery', some of which are given below:

Hoo arere: 'Back there', when hounds come too hastily out of the kennel.

Avaunt: 'Forward'.

Swef, mon ami: 'Gently, my friend'. (Swef, from Lat. *suavis*).

Oyez: 'Hark'.

Illoeques: 'Here' (from Lat. *illo loco*). It has been suggested that the word is the origin of our modern *Yoicks.*

La douce: 'Softly'.

Le voye: 'The view'.

Sohowe (shahou): A term of encouragement, when picking up a line. (See also Chapter V.)

It is from the Norman and appears unlikely to have any connection with 'See! Hie!' The word was *saho*, where *sa* was the Norman form of the mod. Fr. *ca*. The cry, therefore, means 'Come hither, ho!' (Twici, MG., and St. A.)

The fashionable hunters of Elizabeth's day were perhaps the greatest connoisseurs of 'music'. Cockaine and Turberville agree that the correct cry in hunting at that time was:

For deer: *How, how, that's he, that's he.*
For hare: *How, how, that, that.*

Here are some more examples of hound language:

Lyst hallow, hike hallow! hike! (Turberville.)
Ware, ware that! (Cockaine.)
Hey! Silver, there it goes . . . there Tyrant, there! hark! hark!
(*The Tempest*)

The cries of wolf-hunting (e.g. *harlou loulou*) are given in Chapter III.

MODERN

The huntsman may use his voice in many ways, as for example, to encourage his hounds, or to rejoice with them (as at the *kill*); to soothe them (as at a *check*); to scold them (as for *riot*); or again to make much of them.

Foxhunters should be able to recognise the various *cheers* from the examples given below:

Leu-in: Eleu in there[1]	To put hounds into covert.
Leu-try, Leu-try there, *Leu-try in that,* *Try-over, Yoi-try,* *Yoi-ote, Yoi-yo-ote,* *Yoi-rouse 'im, Yoi wind 'im,* *Heu-in and try,* *Try-over-r-r,* *Edawick, Ehre, Edoick:*	Huntsman's cheers to encourage hounds when drawing.

[1] Probably from Norman wolf-hunting (leu = *loup*, a wolf). (See Chapter III.)

Hark, cry hark, *Huic, huic, huic,* *Hark forrard to,* *Try (Lope) forrard:*	To get the pack on to a reliable hound who has *opened* in covert.
Yo-oi, Forrard on, *Forra-r-r-rd,*	Cheer when hounds are running.
Cope-forrard,[1] *Get away together, Hark,*	Cheers of whipper-in
Come away, Cope, *Cope-'e-Cope, Hu-eye,* *Hu-eye-eee,* *Elope:*	Cheers of whipper-in.
Yut-Yut-Yut, Try, *Yo-hote:*	By the huntsman at a *check*, to catch hold of leading hounds and swing them.
Yogueote:	(For 'you go o'er it') used when hounds have gone beyond the scent.
Whoop! Wind-'imm!	When marking to ground.
Eloo at him, Eleew:	When hounds are near the fox.
Who-whoop! Whoop, *Split 'im up!* *Le-leu, Le-leu-eu:*	When breaking up a fox.

H'lope:	Signal from whipper-in in rear to huntsman when hound requires to vomit, etc. Means 'Hold up'.
Get-on-tweem:	Command to hounds to get nearer the huntsman.
Run along, *Get on, leave it,* *Have a care:*	A gentle rate.

Yu-bike:	To put stray hounds back into covert.
Yoi-over, Try-back:	By the huntsman only, when drawing back.
Tally Ho-over! *Yu-Tally-over-r-r!*	Used when the fox has been seen to cross a ride.
Tally Ho-back:	Used mainly in cub-hunting, when a fox heads back.

[1] Also used by huntsman to inform whippers-in that hounds are all on.

Holloa!	Used only by one who has viewed the hunted fox. (See *View Holloa* in Chapter IV.)
Huic Holloa!	A cheer to 'relay' a holloa.

Tally ho: Our modern cry of 'Tallyho' does not appear to have been used by the old English hunters, but it is probably derived from *Ty a hillaut* and other similar cries in the early hunting days in France. It was used when the huntsman was sure the right stag had gone away; also to call up hounds, and at the end of the *curée.*

Another possible derivation is from *Il est hault, il est hault* (he is off), pronounced with a liaison between the final 't' of *hault* and the *il.* According to Lady Apsley (*Bridleways through History,* 1936) Tally-ho! may possibly be derived from the Syriac *Taleb-yon!* (There's the fox!).

Alternately, the cry may come from the Syrian shepherd's call *T'alla hôu* (meaning 'Come hither') and have been brought back to this country by the Crusaders.

The Norman *Taillis au* (To the coppice) is still another suggestion.

It is curious that the word is not found in any of the sporting writers until the eighteenth century. From Twici to Nicholas Cox, a period covering nearly four centuries, there is no mention of it.

Blaine gives an example: '*H-o-u-y, h-o-u-y, h-o-u-y! t-a-ll-y-ho, t-a-ll-y-ho, t-a-ll-y-ho! g-o-n-e-a-w-a-y, g-o-n-e-a-w-a-y, g-o-n-e-a-w-a-y!* The first *hallou* is for the hounds, the last for the gentlemen, for all the field likes to get away with the hounds'. (Groom's Guide, p. 71.) It is interesting to note that he emphasises the 'bad effect of *hallooing* too much, and equally of doing it at a wrong time'.

Soho!: The modern form of *Sohowe* (q.v.), used in hare-hunting and coursing. *Toho!* is now only employed for shooting dogs, to check them.

Yoiyeot: Cheer to soothe harriers striving to work out a puzzle. (Watson.)

Some hunting cries used in Otter Hunting:

Ol-ol-ol-ol-ol-ol-over! Get on to'm! (for encouragement)

Co-o-o-o-orn-yer! W-wor! W-wor! (for endearment)

Yaa-aa-ee-io! Leu-in-on 'm! (for encouragement)
(See also *Heu Gaze*, *Down-water*, *Up-water*, Chapter V.)

RIOT

The proper words for *rating* foxhounds when they are *rioting* are as follows:

On deer - - - -	*Ware*[1] *haunch*
On rabbits and hares - -	*Ware hare* (or *Ware riot*)
On birds - - - -	*Ware wing*

Other *rates* are:

When hounds are running *heelway* (q.v.) - - -	*Ware heel* (see also 'A gentle rate', p. 131)
To warn the field to keep off crops - - -	*Ware wheat*
Warning against wire -	*Ware wire*

But—'Those *Raches*[2] that run to a coney at any time ought to be rated saying to them loud, "*ware Riot, ware*", for no other wild beast in England is called *riot* save the coney only.' (MG.) (*Ryote* was the Old English name for a rabbit; hence, some say, is derived the expression 'to run riot'.)

B. THE SOUND OF THE HORN

ANCIENT

In Saxon times horns were used solely to frighten game. But by the Middle Ages their purpose was both to give information and to call hounds; and, later, to celebrate (especially in France) with gay *fanfares*.

The French were always fonder of the music of the chase than were the English, and they inherited their love for the *winding* of the horn, with the *holloas* of the huntsmen added to the melody of hounds, from the ancient Gauls. But the early English hunting had its music too, and it was much more elaborate than that of the present day. Then every man seems to have carried a horn, and known the proper call. Dryden paints the picture well: 'The possibility of exercising this science of hunting-music, in which our forefathers so much delighted, decreased as the science of hunting itself improved; and at the present day (1843), three or four blasts are all that are heard from the meet to the death.'

[1] Pronounced 'War'. [2] See Chapter IV.

A *Moot* (or Mote) was a single note (long or short). Two were blown after the *unharbouring*. 'The *mote* should never be blown before the *recheating*, unless a man seeth what he hunteth for.' (MG.)

The *Recheat* was originally used for calling hounds back and putting them right; later, simply to call hounds. It may be written ◡◡◡—. Later still the Recheats acquired a variety of meanings and were the favourite blowings. There was 'The double recheat', 'Sir Hewit's recheat', 'Recheat at the unkennelling of a fox', 'Recheat at the *rouseing* of a buck', etc.

The *Forlange* was the signal that the hart was far ahead, and that the hounds had *tailed*. (— — — —/◡◡— —/—)

The *Perfect* (parfit) was a note only sounded when hounds were hunting the right line. (—/—◡◡/— —/—◡◡—◡◡—◡◡/ — —/—◡◡◡)

The *Prise* (or Prize) was blown at the *taking* of the hart, four moots.

The *Menée* could be blown 'for an hert, the boor, the wolf'h male, and alle so the wolf'h female, as wel as to here husbond' (Twici). 'In the French, the *menée* (hark forward) is to be blown at the hall door for the hart, and the *prize* for the buck; but in the old English, the *pryse* is to be blown for both.' (Dryden's Notes.)

The *Mort* was blown at the death of a stag. 'A treble mort' followed by 'a whole *recheat*'. 'The death of a Bucke with Hounds: Two long notes and the *rechate*.' (CK.); but with Bowe or Greyhounds, 'One long' only.

The *Stroke* was a term often used for 'blow the horn', i.e. there were: 'the *stroakes* to call y*e* company to y*e* field', etc.

The *Veline* (—◡◡◡◡◡). See Chapter V, under Glossary of Otter Hunting Terms.

There were two obscure words, *Gibbet* and *Jeopard*, both used for blowing a call on the horn. (Cockaine.) To *blow a Seeke* was to sound a horn.

The original hunting horn (Charlemagne's) was called *Oliphant* (made from elephants' tusk). By the sixteenth century 'the old *cornes* had been given up and all *veneurs* now carried, slung round them from their shoulders, the new type of long metal horns called *trompes*'. By the time of Nicholas Cox a horn 'was *blown*, occasionally *sounded*, and never *winded*—as in the time of Venerie'. (Ap.)

The curved horn, adapted from those of Royal France, was

carried till late in the seventeenth century, when the 'straight' was introduced. The parts were termed 'mouthpiece', 'ferrule' and 'bell'. The sling for the horn was called a *baldrick*. 'A point's a point, if ye can hang a baldrick or your spur on it.' (G. Paget.)

MODERN

Most of the ancient calls have fallen into disuse. There are no standard sounds, but, generally speaking, the horn can be used as follows:

(i) One or more toots, as a signal; e.g. (one toot) to let hounds and the Field know where the huntsman is.

(ii) Long-drawn out notes; e.g. to indicate a blank covert, a lost fox, or 'Home'.

(iii) A succession of lively notes, as in *doubling* the horn (q.v., Chapter IV); e.g. on *viewing* the fox, when blowing hounds away on to the line, or at a *kill*.

Some examples:

— A single long note: = Moving off to a fresh covert.

⏑⏑/⏑⏑: = Whippers-in to put hounds on to the huntsman.

⏑⏑⏑/⏑⏑⏑: = All hounds are on.

— — — — — —: = Summonning lost hounds.

⏑⏑/⏑⏑⏑/⏑ . . . . . ⏑: = Cheering the pack on to the line of a fox in covert.

⏑⏑⏑—/⏑⏑⏑—/⏑⏑⏑—: = Blowing the pack out of covert on the line of a fox. (*Gone away!*)

⏑— —/⏑— —/⏑— — —/⏑⏑—: = Going home.

—⏑⏑⏑⏑/—⏑⏑⏑⏑: = The *Veline*; the *Gone away!* in Otter hunting.

NOTE: The sound of the horn is sometimes known as the *weep* of the horn.

To *touch* or to *wind* the horn is to blow it.

In Otter hunting the sound of the horn at a kill is termed *Rattle*.

C. THE CRY OF HOUNDS

ANCIENT

To an Elizabethan 'the pleasure of hunting was an aesthetic one, to get on some eminence within the park and listen to the *cry* of hounds, enhanced if possible by a natural echo'. (Ap.)

Abbaye: The *baying* of the hounds.

Hue: Originally a French word describing the cheering on hounds. Hence comes our expression *hue and cry*.

MODERN

Hounds may *speak* (or *throw the tongue*) with:

(i) A single cry (may be just a whimper or a sharp squeak); e.g. on first finding a fox.

(ii) Many cries: e.g. on *hitting off* the line on a *screaming scent* (a *crash*). This is more like a 'muffled roar' (BR); a 'deep *baying*' might describe hounds *marking to ground*.

(iii) Angry cries: e.g. when *chopping* their fox.

(iv) Squeaks: e.g. when *rioting*.

(See *cry*, Chapter IV.)

CHAPTER XII

MALE AND FEMALE

(i) BIRDS

NAME	MALE	FEMALE
Black Game	*Black Cock*	*Grey-hen*
Duck	see Wild Duck	
Goose	*Gander*	*Dame*
Hawk	see Chapter VIII	
Peafowl	*Peacock*	*Peahen*
Pheasant	*Cock*[1]	*Hen*[1]
Ruff	*Stag* (mod. the *Ruff*)	*Reeve*
Swan	*Cob*	*Pen*
Wild Duck or Mallard	*Drake*	*Duck*

Comments:

1. The terms *Cock* and *Hen* are applied to the male and female of the majority of birds, and of fishes.

(ii) ANIMALS

NAME	MALE	FEMALE
Ass	*Jackass* (see App. III)	*She-ass*
Badger	*Boar*	*Sow*
Boar	see Wild Boar	
Buffalo	*Bull*	*Cow*
Camel	*Bull*	*Cow*
Cat	*Tomcat*	*Quean* (O.E.)
Deer[1]: Red	*Stag*, or *Hart*	*Hind*
Fallow	*Buck*	*Doe*
Roe	*Roe-Buck*	*Doe*
Ferret[2]	*Dog*	*Bitch*
Fox	*Dog-fox*	*Vixen*
Goat[3]	*Billy-goat*	*Nanny-goat*
Hare[4]	*Buck*	*Doe*
Horse[5]	*Horse*	*Mare*
Hound	*Dog*	*Bitch*

Leopard	*Leopard*	*Leopardess*
Lion	*Lion*	*Lioness*
Otter	*Dog*	*Bitch*
Pig	*Boar*	*Sow*
Polecat	*Hob*	*Jill*
Rabbit	*Buck*	*Doe*
Rat	*Buck*	*Doe*
Seal		
Sheep	*Ram*[6]	*Ewe*
Tiger	*Tiger*	*Tigress*
Whale	*Bull*	*Cow*
Wild Boar	*Boar*	*Sow*

Comments:

1. For the terms for 'All Maner Dere' at various ages, see Chapter II.
2. Ferret: Also (for Male) *Buck*, *Jack* or *Hob*; (for Female) *Doe* or *Jill.*
3. For *Geats*, see Chapter XXIV, No. 126, Notes.
4. Hare: Sometimes (for Male), *Jack-Hare*: (for Female) *Puss.* (*Puss* is also a general term for the Hare of either sex: see App. III.)
5. Horse: For 'Sex and Age', see Chapter XXII.
6. *Wether*: A Ram castrated.

CHAPTER XIII

THE YOUNG OF ANIMALS

(i) BIRDS

The young of

Birds are called	*Poots* (O.E.)
Ducks (tame)	*Ducklings*
(wild)	see Wild Fowl
Eagles	*Eaglets*
Game Birds	*Cheepers*
Geese	*Goslings*
Grouse	*Cheepers* (later, *Poults*)
Hawks	*Eyesses*
Partridges	*Squeakers*
Pigeons	*Squabs*
Swans	*Cygnets*
Wild Fowl	*Flappers* (alt. *Flacker*; from dial. Eng. *flacker* =to flutter, as a bird)

The following company terms represent the young of birds:

Of Chickens, Hens, etc.	a *Brood*
Coots	*Covert*
Ducks	*Team*
Grouse, Partridges	*Covey*
Pheasants	*Nye*

(See Chapter XXIII.)

(ii) ANIMALS

The young of

Badgers are called	*Cubs* (*Pigs* (Os.))
Bears	*Cubs*
Beavers	*Kittens*
Boars	*Squeakers*
Buffaloes	*Calves*
Camels	*Calves*

Cats - - - - -	*Kittens*
Coneys - - - - -	*Rabbits* (see Note below)[1]
Cows - - - - -	*Heifers*
Deer: Red - - - -	*Calves*
Fallow - - - -	*Fawns*
Roe - - - -	*Kids* (or *Fawns*)
Elephants - - - -	*Calves*
Foxes - - - - -	*Cubs*
Goats - - - - -	*Kids*
Hares - - - - -	*Leverets*
Horses - - - - -	*Foals* (see Note below)[2]
Hounds - - - - -	*Puppies*
Leopards - - - -	*Cubs*
Lions - - - - -	*Cubs*
Martens - - - -	*Kittens* (or *Cubs*)
Otters - - - - -	*Cubs* (O.E. *Whelps*)
Pigs - - - - -	*Farrow* (O.E.)
Rabbits - - - - -	*Bunnies* (Gael. *bun*, a stump) (see Note below)[1]
Seals - - - - -	*Cubs* (or *Pups*)
Sheep - - - - -	*Lambs*[3]
Squirrels - - - -	*Drays* (see Note below)[4]
Swine (tame) - - - -	*Shoots* (Os.)
Tigers - - - - -	*Cubs*
Whales - - - - -	*Calves*
Wolves - - - - -	*Cubs*

Comments:

1. In old days a rabbit was called *ryote*; *rabbit* was applied only to the little ones.

2. Horses: For definition of *Yearling*, *Colt*, *Filly*, etc., see Chapter XXII.

3. *Hog:* Sheep or bullock of 1 year old.
Hogget: Sheep of 2 years old.
or Colt of 1 year old.
or Boar of 2nd year.
Hogsteer: Wild Boar of 3 years old.

4. Squirrels: The earliest meaning of *draye* (or *drey*) was a nest. (See Chapter XXIV, Notes.)

The following company terms represent the young of animals:

Of Cats - - - - a *Kindle*
Cubs, Whelps - - - *Litter*
Rabbits - - - - *Nest*

(See Chapter XXIV.)

CHAPTER XIV

FOOTPRINTS

ANCIENT

For the footing and treading:

Of a Hart	the *slot*
Of a Buck, and all Fallow Deer	*view*
Of all Deer, if on the grass and scarce visible	*foiling*
Of a Fox	*print*
Of other like vermin	*footing*
Of an Otter	*mark*[1] (or *marches*)
Of a Boar	*track*

The Hare, when in open field, is said to *sore*:

when she winds about to deceive the hounds, she *doubles*;
when she beats on the hard highway, and her footing comes to be perceived, she *pricketh*:
in snow it is called the *trace* of the hare. (Os.)

(A similar list is given by NC.)

Trace. This was the original term for the track of deer. Roy Modus says: 'of stags, of black beasts, and wolves, the *trace*; and of other beasts the *foot*', and Gaston that the term for the footprint of the deer should be *voyes* or *pies* (view or foot). At the time of *The Master of Game* 'trace' was the proper sporting term in England, and it was used variously for the track of stag, wild boar and other game. The trace of deer on hard grass was called the *foil*.

Slot. This word had become, by the beginning of the seventeenth century, the proper term for the footprint of deer, 'the rounded track, the blunted toe print, the widespread mark, the fresh *slot* in short of a stag.' (Dr. Collyns.)

[1] The Otter. Daniel says: 'The Otter has no *heel*, but a round ball under the sole of the foot, by which its track in the mud is easily distinguished, and is termed the *seal*.'

The old harbourers considered that any *slot* into which four fingers could be placed (i.e. one about three inches wide) belonged to a *warrantable* stag. To-day the Devonshire hunters are satisfied, it is believed, with two and a half inches.

An old stag walks more evenly than a hind; the latter is said very often to *misprint*. Gaston says that if a stag is tired the toes will be widespread, but when going fast his claws will be closed; and in Roy Modus it is stated that the print of the two bones (*dew-claws*) in hard earth is a sign that the stag is in full flight.

Os is the false toe, or *dew-claw*, of the hart and hind.

Argos (in English, *Ergots*) is proper only of the boar, buck and doe. 'The old hart's hind-foot doth never over-reach the fore-foot; that of the young ones does.' (Os.)

Sarbote was an old term meaning 'to become footsore'.

Piste. The tread or track made by a horse.

Strutt tells us that the Buck and Doe were beasts of Sweet *flight*; and the Fox, Marten, Otter, Badger were beasts of stinking *flight*. He appears to have got muddled over the word *fute:* it is the foot which leaves some of the scent. But the oldest lists are the most interesting:

BEASTS OF 'SWETE FEWTE'

Buck, Doo, Beere, Reynd der, Elke, Spycard (St. A. adds: Otre and Martwn) (from Harl. 2 and St. A.).

BEASTS OF 'STINKING FEWTE'

Roobucke, Roo, *Fulmard*, *Fyches* (Fechewe), *Bauw* (Cat?), *Gray*, Fox, Squirrel, *Whitecat*, Otyr, *Stot*, *Pulcatt* (Harl. 2 adds: Wesyll and Marteron) (St.A.).

It is curious to find the otter and marten classed under both heads; 'stinking' would seem to be their appropriate and correct description.

MODERN

Spoor: A comprehensive term for the *track* or *trail* of wild animals pursued as game. It is used, as a rule, collectively, e.g. the spoor of lions, elephants, etc.

Generally, the terms given at the head of this chapter may be used, except:

Seal: This is the more usual term for the footprint of the otter.

Pug: The footprint of a beast, e.g. of a lion, tiger, boar. Also used in the sense: to track a beast by its footprints.

Sign, *Trail:* Terms used, especially in America, for the tracks by which a quarry may be followed. (To *trail* = to *Pug*.)

Pad: To track a fox is to 'pad' him.

Trod: The track of a hare.

CHAPTER XV

ANIMALS RETIRING TO REST

ANCIENT

The proper terms are:

For their lodging—

A Hart	*harbours*[1]	A Fox	*kennels*
Buck	*lodges*[1]	Marten	*trees*
Roe	*beds*[1]	Otter	*watches*
Hare	*seats* or *forms*	Badger	*earths*
Coney	*sits*	Boar	*couches*

(Os.)

The list given by GM. agrees with the above, except for his rendering: 'An Otter *kenelleth*.' (This is probably a mistake.) He omits hart, marten, badger and boar.

A similar list is contained in RS. and NC.

Dryden's table (from his Notes on Twici) gives the same terms, but for Coney his term is *Burroweth*, and he adds Wolf *Traineth*.

Hunting term used of a hare when she is lurking or squatting . . . *Tapassant*. (Os.) Daniel talks of hares '*quatting* in their forms'.

Osbaldiston also defines *Burrows* as holes in a warren, serving as a covert for hares, rabbits, etc.

'Without mentioning the miraculous stories which are and have been long recited of the Hare's craftiness when hunted, they will certainly when hard pressed go to *Vault*; that is, take the ground like a Rabbit.' (RS.)

Daniel says: 'If an Otter was not found soon by the river side, it was imagined that he had gone to *couch* more inland . . .' He also states that an Otter '*vented*, or came to the surface of the water to breathe'. (See Chapter V.)

'The hare *squats*; the fox *lies down*; a fox is *recovered*; a deer is *fresh found*.' (Blaine.)

[1] Also given in St. A.

Tappy. 'To lie hid as a deer may do.' (Os.)

The bed of harts, bucks and roebucks is called *lair* (or *ligging*),
hare is called *form*,
fox is called *earth* or *kennel*,
badger is called *earth*,
coney is called *burrow*.

(Dryden.)

MODERN

The terms given at the head of this chapter may be used, with the exception of the following:

The best term for a

	may be	
Hare		*squats*
Rabbit	- - - -	*sits* (above ground)
		burrows (below ground)
Fox	- - - -	*kennels* (above ground)
		goes to earth (below ground)
Otter	- - - -	*goes to couch*

and for their 'bed', as given by Dryden above, adding for the

Otter	- - - -	*Couch* (for its litter)
		Hide (temporary retreat)
		Holt (its lair by day)
Boar	- - - -	*Den*
Mole	- - - -	*Fortress*

CHAPTER XVI

THE DISLODGMENT OF ANIMALS

ANCIENT

To EXPRESS their dislodging, they say,

Unharbour the hart		*Untree* the marten	
Rouse	buck	*Vent*	otter
Start	hare	*Dig*	badger
Bolt	coney	*Rear*	boar
Unkennel	fox		

(A similar list is given by Daniel (RS.)) (Os.)

Note the differences in GM.'s list:

We say *dislodge* the Bucke
Start the Hare
Vnkennell the Foxe
Rowze the Hart
Bolt the Conie

[NOTE.—Osbaldiston's list was compiled nearly two hundred years later than that of Gervase Markham.]

Dryden gives :

Dislodge or *rouse* the buck		*Dig* or *find* the badger	
Start or *move*	hare	*Raise*	wolf
Find or *unkennel*	fox	*Find*	roebuck or roe
Bay	marten		

NOTE.—*Imprime* was a term sometimes used for unharbouring the hart.

QUESTING

The harbourer *sued* or *sewed* (Fr. *suivre*) with the *lymer* for a hart and buck.

A Huntsman was said to *quest* or *seek* for a hare.
draw for a fox.
quere and *quete* for a wolf (in France).

MODERN

The correct terms for Deer appear to be:

Dislodge (or *Rouse*) a buck
Unharbour hart
Seek & find the roe (as given by AM.)

For the remainder, the terms given by Osbaldiston may be used, except that the modern term for Otter appears to be *unkennel*.

CHAPTER XVII

ORDURE OR EXCREMENT

ANCIENT

THERE WAS a proper term for the dung of every kind of beast; in some cases there were several terms, and several ways of spelling the same term. But 'it does not appear that the English were ever so precise in the names for the different kinds of ordure of the hart as the French'. (Dryden.)

In his *Notes on Twici* Dryden gives the following table:

Hart & Hind:	*Fues* *Fewmets* *Fewmishing*	Fox:	*Waggying* *Billetings* *Fiants* *Fuants*
Hare:	*Croteys* *Crotels* *Crotisings*	Marten:	*Dirt* *Fiants* *Fuants*
Boar:	*Freyn* *Fiants* *Lesses*	Roe Buck & Roe:	*Cotying* *Fewmets* *Fewmishing*
Wolf:	*Freyn* *Lesses* *Fiants* *Fuants*	Otter:	*Spraits, Spraints*
		Badger:	*Werdrobe* *Fiants* *Fuants*
Buck & Doe:	*Cotying* *Fewmets* *Fewmishings*	Coney:	*Crotels* or *Croteys* *Crotisings*

Comments:

The Master of Game says that the droppings of a Hart only are to be called *fumes*; of buck and roebuck, *croties*. For 'stinking beasts' he gives the term *drift*. He is the only authority to give the term *waggying* for the *billets* of a fox, and *werdrobe* for the *fuants* of a badger.

For the hare, Halliwell gives *Buttons*.

Twici is the only authority for the term *fiants* for a wolf.

Later a more exact use was made of the terms, and they became simpler:

Of a Hart and all deer is called	*fewmets* or *fewmishing*.
Hare	*crotiles* or *crotising*.
Boar	*lesses*
Fox	*billitting*
Other the like vermin	*fuants*
Otter	*spraints*

(NC. and Os.)

Comments:

The term *Lesses* was used for the dung of a wild boar, bear or wolf.

In *The Sportsman's Dictionary*, 1807, the term *blittering* appears for the fox. This is probably a copying error.

For the Otter, Daniel says it 'is very cleanly, depositing its excrements or *spraints* in only one place'. Cockaine gives another term, *swaging*.

Of the Beare—the *Track* or *Treading*. (Guillim.)

'*Mute*, or ordure, dung, more especially of birds. . . . ,
(See p. 110)

'*Tuel*, the fundament of any wild beast.' (Os.)

MODERN

SUGGESTED CORRECT TERMS NOW TO BE USED

Red Deer	*Fumes*	Fox	*Billiting*, or *Billet*
Fallow Deer, Roe Deer	*Croties*	Otter	*Spraints*, or *Wedging*
Hare, Rabbit	*Crotiles*	Boar	*Lesses*
		Badger	*Fuants*

Vermin (general term) *Fuants*

Horses	*Droppings* (*dung*)
Hounds	*Puer*
Hawks	*Mutes*

CHAPTER XVIII

TAILS OF ANIMALS

ANCIENT

THE TAIL of a

Hart, Buck or other Deer is called the	*single* (or *sengill*)
Boar	*wreath*
Fox	*brush* or *drag*
Fox, the tip at the end	*chape*
Wolf (or Greyhound)	*stern*
Hare and Coney	*scut*

(NC. and Os.)

Comments:

AM. says: 'The tail of a hart hath no other appellation; but that of a buck, roe, or any other deer, is called the *single*.'

The Master of Game says of the roe-deer that 'their hinder parts were called *Target*'.

'*Chape*, among hunters, means the tip at the end of a fox's tail; so called, as the tail itself is termed *breech*, or *drag*.' (Os.) 'Terms of the *Tayle*: That of a Fox is termed his *Bush*, or *holy water sprinkler*.' (Guillim.)

'To *stern* the young is to take off a small portion of the tail of each.' (Blaine.)

MODERN

The tail of a Fox-hound is known as the	*stern*
an Otter	*rudder*
a Fox	*brush* (the tip = *tag*)
a Hare, Rabbit	*scut*
Deer	*single*
Hawk	*trains*

CHAPTER XIX

CRIES OF ANIMALS

ANCIENT

(At rutting time):	A Hart	*belleth*
	Buck	*groans* or *troats* (hoots)
	Roe	*bellows*
	Hare	*beats* or *taps*
	An Otter	*whines*
	A Boar	*freams*
	Fox	*barks*
	Badger	*shrieks*
	Wolf	*howls*
	Goat	*Rattles*

(Os.)

Comments:

N. Cox says of Stags that 'the Males in their raging desired Lust have a peculiar noise, which the *French* called *Reeve*'.

Blaine says the hare 'and rabbit' *beats* or *taps*.

Blaine also gives 'the badger *yells*', and he adds, 'the polecat, stoat, and ferret, *chatter*'. (*An Encyclopaedia of Rural Sports*, 1840.)

(Of Birds):	A Bittern	*lows* (RS.)
	Partridge	*jucks**
	Pheasant	*cocketts* (see Chapter XXIII, No. 37, Notes)

[*Note: The calling of partridges when they settle down for the night was termed *jucking*. (Blaine.) *Jucking-time* was the season for listening to the calling of the cock-partridge. (Os.)]

Tiger: The voice of this beast was called *Ranking*, according to this verse:

Tigrides indomitae rancant, rugiuntque Leones.

Beagles: Were said to *yearn* (i.e. bark at their prey). (Os.)

Harper Cory writes: 'Every species of animal has a series of noises which form the language of that particular unit of the animal world. For instance, the grey squirrel has fifty major and minor noises, and apparently every grey squirrel understands them. Black bears have a small code of sounds, and though I have never discovered which is the sound for cake, it must be a well known one, for if cake is given to a bear to-day, he will return at the head of many friends to-morrow, and the entire company will want cake.

'Grey Owl and Anahareo . . . learned to distinguish the inflexions of the beaver language until they knew when the animals were happy or sad, angry or uneasy, hungry or satisfied, and so forth. The noises of animals are strange languages to us until we have patience to study them.'

For some seventy amusing examples of the noises of animals, the reader is referred to an *Extract from Rabelais' Works* in Appendix I, B (4).

MODERN

The ancient terms given above are generally (or should be) used (except for the Bittern (q.v.)). For the rest, some examples are given below:

We say:	An Ass	*brays*
	A Barking deer	*barks*
	Bear	*growls*
	Bull	*bellows*
	Cat	*mews*
	Cattle	*low*
	A Chital	*whistles*
	Dog	*barks, growls, snarls*
	Donkey	(See Ass)
	An Elephant	*trumpets*
	A Frog	*croaks* (bull frog *trumps*)
	Horse	*neighs, whinnies*
	Hound	*bays, gives tongue* (see Chapters IV and XI)
	Hyaena (striped)	*laughs*
	Jackal	*howls*
	Lion	*roars*
	Monkey	*chatters*
	Mouse	*squeaks*
	Panther	*saws*

	Pig	*grunts*
	Sambhur	*bells*
	Seal	*barks*[1]
	Sheep	*bleats*
	Stag	*roars* (end of Sept., when the rut follows)
	Tiger	*growls*

(Of Birds):	A Bittern	*booms*
	Chicken	*peeps*
	Cock	*crows*
	Crane	*trumpets*
	Crow, rook	*caws* (see Chapter XXIII, No. 45, Notes)
	Dove, pigeon	*coos*
	Duck[2]	*quacks*
	Eagle	*screams*
	Geese (wild)	*honk, honk*[3]
	A Hen	*cackles* or *clucks*
	Nightingale	*sings*
	Ostrich	*wails*
	Owl	*hoots*
	Pheasant	*crows*
	Raven	*croaks*
	Swan (wild)	*trumpets* (see Chapter XXIII, No. 52, Notes)
	Turkey	*gobbles*
	Woodpecker (green)	*yaffles* (laughs)

Many of these words are onomatopaeic, e.g. the *sawing* of panthers, the *neighing* of horses, the *booming* of bitterns, etc.

[1] Bulls are sometimes said to *bellow,* the cows to *bleat,* and the Bachelor seals to *whistle.*

[2] For the cries of Wigeon, see Chapter XXIII, No. 57, Notes.

[3] Mr. J. Farmer writes of 'that most exciting and romantic of all wildfowl voices. It is often likened to the sound of hounds giving tongue on some distant line, but it always reminds me of the voices of school-children playing in a village school court-yard; a musical babbling that comes on the gusts of wind and fades again without revealing its origin'.

Song-birds	*pipe*, *trill* or *churr*
Insects	*buzz*

NOTE: A giraffe neither roars nor whispers; it is voiceless.

* * *

PECULIAR CRIES

Apart from the general terms, there are certain descriptive expressions which seek to convey the actual song, cry or noise made. Owing to lack of space only a few examples can be given:

Tiger: (questing note) *Aungh-ha.*
Langur: (curse) *Ugha-ugh-a.*
Peacock: (at dawn) *Mia-a-oo!*
(alarmed) *Tok-tok.*
Quail: '*Wet-my-lips* (or *feet*).' (see App. III.)
Canada Goose: *Aah-oook! Aah-oook!*

The subject is a fascinating one.

* * *

THE LANGUAGE OF THE FEET

Some animals make curious thudding sounds with their feet to intimidate foes or as an alarm. Sheep (particularly), rabbits, kangaroos and llamas, for example, often employ this method.

CHAPTER XX

THE MATING OF ANIMALS

ANCIENT

MALE:	A Hart or Buck	*goes to rut*
	Roe	*tourn*
	Boar	*brim*
	Hare or Coney	*buck*
	Fox	*clickitting*
	Wolf	*match* or *make*
	An Otter	*hunteth for his kind*

(NC. and Os.)

Comments:

Cox speaks of the Hart or Buck 'when they *go to Rut*, and make their *Vaut*'. *Rutting* season is, usually, mid Sept. to end October.

Daniel says: 'Foxes go to *clicket* in the Winter.'

'An Otter and Ferret *grow salt* much about the same time.'

(NC.)

Blissom: The act of a ram when *coupling* with an ewe.

(Os.)

Ryding Time: Rutting season.

FEMALE

'*The appetency*', says Blaine (1840), '*of the mare is vulgarly called horsing*, the bitch goes to *heat*, the cow to *bull*, the fox and the hare *clicket*, the doe *ruts*, the wolf goes to *match* or *mate*, the wild boar and sow, and in some countries the badger also, *brims*, the rabbit goes to *buck*, the hare the same, or it *clickets*, &c.'

Daniel uses the expression 'to *kindle*', i.e. to bring forth young, for the *doe* both of the hare and rabbit. The term first appears in MG. for the hare. (See Chapter XXIV, No. 116, Notes.)

Farrow (noun): An O.E. term for a young pig.
Farrow (verb): Of sows, to give birth to a litter.

MODERN

The terms given above may be used.

For the act of coition the general terms are:

For Birds - - -	*Tread*	also *Couple, Pair*
Animals - - -	*Cover*	
Fish - - -	*Spawn*	

Comments:

For Hawks the term is *cawk*.

'Let the Dog that *lines* her be of good fair breed.' (Cox.)

For Deer, one speaks of the *rutting season*.

Pair: Cf. *Pairing-Time* (p. 77).

CHAPTER XXI

BREAKING AND DRESSING

ANCIENT

THE PROPER terms (according to Dryden, in his Notes on Twici) for skinning the different animals, and for their integuments and fat, are the following:

	Skinning	Integument	Fat
Hart and Hind:	*Flean, Flayed*	*Leather, Hide*	*Tallow, Suet*
Hare:	*Stripped, Cased*	*Skin*	*Grease, Tallow*
Boar:	*Stripped*	*Pyles, Leather, Hide, Skin*	*Grease*
Wolf:	*Stripped*	*Pyles, Skin*	*Grease*
Buck and Doe:	*Skinned*	*Skin, Leather, Hide*	*Tallow, Suet*
Fox:	*Cased*	*Pyles, Skin*	*Grease*
Marten:	*Cased*	*Pyles, Skin*	*Grease*
Roebuck and Roe:	*Skinned*	*Leather, Hide*	*Bevy Grease*
Otter: / Badger: / Coney:	*Cased*	*Pyles, Skin*	*Grease*

All the beasts which carried *suet* and *fewmets* were *flayed*, and all the beasts which carried *grease* and *fiants* were *torn* (i.e. *cased*). (Twici.) But, *flayed* was proper only of the hart; *skinned* of the buck and roebuck.

(For *fewmets* and *fiants*, see Chapter XVII, Ordure.)

NOTE: 'You shall say—a Fox *uncased*.' (Guillim.)

BREAKING

To cut open a deer the proper term was to *undo*.

,, up ,, ,, ,, ,, ,, *break up* or *brittle*.

The Roebuck was taken to the kitchen entire.

Hardel: Besides meaning 'coupling hounds together', this was the O.E. term for binding together the four legs of the roe-buck, head between the forelegs, ready for carrying him whole to the kitchen. (O.F. *hardelle* = a cord.) From *hardeled* comes, evidently, the modern term—*Hurdle a roe*. (Appendix to MG.)

'The dressing of the Roe is termed the *herdlenge*.' (Blome.)

Twici says that the boar was 'undone with the hide on'. The *undoing* of a boar was the *dressing* of it.

Margaret of Austria, Regent of the Netherlands, could *undo* a boar or *brittle* a stag singlehanded.

From *The Ancient Ballad of Chevy-Chase* comes this verse:

The blewe a mort uppone the bent,
The semblyd on sydis shear:
To the quyrry then the Persè went
To se the *bryttlyng* off the deare.

'A huntsman is now said to *break up* his fox, when he cuts off the head and brush and gives the carcase to the hounds.' (Dryden.)

'The death of the Stag is the *breaking up*; or, in still more modern language, the *take*; that of the fox is to be *worried*; and *whoo whoop* is the death cry of both fox and hare.' (Blaine.)

GREASE

The fat of all sorts of deer (except roe deer) is called *suet* (sometimes *tallow*); of roe deer *bevy grease*; of all other beasts *grease*. The hare and rabbit have very little fat, but what there is of it is *grease*.

Although the fat of deer is suet, yet it was sometimes said that 'this deer was a *high deer of grease*' (i.e. that he was very fat.) 'In the *pride of his grease*' was the same as saying 'in the fattest time of year'.

The season of the hart and buck was called *grease time*, because that was the season when they were fat and fit for killing (July and August). Strutt called it *Grace* or *Grass* time, and this error was copied by others.

[NOTE: Deer's grease is very good for dressing shooting boots, etc., and dry-fly fishers commonly use it for their reel lines.]

Snet (sic!): 'The fat of all sorts of deer.' (Os.)

Taking Assaye: This 'was an entirely English practice, and meant taking the measure of, or testing the depth of, fat or grease, on the death of a stag'. (Lady Apsley.)

DRESSING

There followe the dewe termys to speke of brekynge or dressynge of dyvers beestis & foules, etc.

A Dere *broken*
A Gose *reryd*
A pygge *hedyd* & *sided*
A Capon *sawcyd*
A Chekyn *trusshyd*
A Cony *unlacyd*
A Crane *dysplayed*
A Curlewe *unjoyntyd*
A Fesaunt *alet*
A Quayle *wynggyd*
A Plover *myncyd*
A Pegeon *thyghed*
A Swanne *lyfte*
A Lambe *sholderyd*
A Kydde *sholderyd*
An Henne *spoyllyd*
A Malarde *unbracyd*
An Heron *dysmembryd*
A Pecock *dysfygured*
A Byttoure *untachyd*
A Partryche *alet*
A Raale *brestyd*
A Wodcocke *thyghed*

(St. A.)

It is interesting to compare the above list with that given over 300 years later by Daniel, who says:

'Such was the pointed Attention to the *Minutiae* of the Table that a *Boke of Kervinge* was printed, which proves that the pleasures of good Eating must have been highly valued. *Carving*, indeed, was, in the Feudal Times, an Art in which the superior Ranks of Men were instructed. Before a person could receive the Honour of *Knighthood*, it was necessary for him to fill several subordinate Stations: among the rest, part of his *Noviciate* was passed as a *Carving Esquire*. The Terms of a *Kerver*, as taken from the above-mentioned Book, printed by *Wynkyn de Words*, are as here followeth.' (The italics are those of RS.)

This is his list:

Breke that Deer.
Lesche that Brawn.
Rere that Goose.
Lyste that Salmon.
Sauce that Capon.
Spoyle that Hen.
Fruche that Cheken.
Unbrace that Mallard.
Unlace that Conye.
Dismembre that Heron.
Display that Crane.
Dysfygure that Pecocke.
Unjoint that Bitture.
Untache that Curlewe.
Thye that Woodcocke.
Thye all manner smalle Byrdes.
Tymbre that Fyer.
Tyere that Egge.
Chynne that Samon.
Strynge that Lampreye.
Splat that Pyke.
Sauce that Plaice.
Sauce that Tench.
Splay that Breme.
Syde that Haddock.
Tuske that Barbel.
Culpon that Troute.
Fyne that Chevin. (i.e. Chub.)

Alay that Fesande.
Wynge that Partryche.
Wynge that Quaile.
Mynce that Plover.
Thye that Pygyon.
Border that Pastie.
Trassene that Ele.
Trance that Sturgeon.
Undertrounch that Porpus.
Tayme that Crabbe.
Barbe that Lopster.

Here endeth the goodlye terms of Kervynge. (RS.)

Barbecue: This was the roasting whole of a large ox or fine hog; it might then be stuffed with spice and basted with madeira.

MODERN

We talk now of:

Cleaning - - -	birds, or fishes
Gralloching - - -	stags (see Deerstalking, Chapter II)
Breaking up	the fox (i.e. cutting off the *brush*, *mask* and *pads*)
Skinning - - -	other animals

CHAPTER XXII

THE HORSE

ANCIENT

The colour of Greek horses was often referred to as *xanthos* (=golden-haired); they were probably a *dun* colour, like the Celtic horses of the Northern (or Asiatic) type. The other main breed, the Arabian, was noted for its bright *bays* with white *marks*. According to Professor Ridgeway (author of the *Origin of the Thoroughbred Horse*), the first crossing of these two types resulted in *whites* and *greys*—colours which have been rightly prized from very early times.

By the 18th century a great variety of colours were recognized, for example:

'Colours of a Horse: the terms by which we call a horse's coat or outward appearance, in England; and they are these following, with the explanation of such as seem obscure.

1. *White*, 2. *black*, 3. sad *iron-grey*, which is black, with the tips of the hairs whitish; 4. *grey*, which is darkish white; 5. dark, or *black-grey*, that is, a deep-coloured brownish red, a chestnut-colour; 6. *bay*, i.e. a light whitish-brown red; 7. *flea-bitten*, that is, white, spotted all over with sad reddish spots; grey flea-bitten; 8. *dapple-grey*, that is, a light-grey, spotted, or shaded with a deeper grey; 9. *dapple-bay*, spotted with a deeper colour; 10. *dun*, a light-hair colour, next unto white; 11. *mouse-dun*, a mouse colour; 12. *sorrel*, lighter than a light-bay, inclining to a yellow; 13. *bright-sorrel*, lighter than the former; 14. *rount*, a kind of flesh-colour, or a bay intermixed with white and grey, a roan colour; 15. *grizzle*, a light rount, or light flesh-colour; 16. *pye-bald*, that is, a horse of two colours, as some part of him white, and the other parts bay, iron-grey, or dun-colour.' (Os.) (The italics are the author's.)

Osbaldiston then goes on to expound what the French say on this subject. He gives a list of 31 colours, which comprise:

6 *Sorrels* (including 'The flaming-sorrel').
1 *Dapple*, 1 *White*, 1 *Starling*, 1 *Tiger*.

4 *Bays* (including 'The gilded-bay . . . has more choler, which animates him').

6 *Greys* (including 'Fire-brand grey; . . . horses of this colour are very nimble and active').

1 *Isabella:* 'a colour that denotes a good horse'. *Isabels* were cream-coloured horses—(from a colour favoured by Queen Isabella of Spain).

1 *Wolf-colour*, 1 *Black*, 1 *Mouse-colour*.

3 *Pyed:* 'those which have the least white, are the most coveted . . .'.

1 *Porcelaine*; '. . . white bodies mixed with red spots'.

2 *Roans* (including 'The vinous roan').

1 *Rubican:* 'grey, sorrel or black, with a little grey or white upon the flanks . . . horses of this colour are very mettlesome'.

And he adds to each colour a short and amusing description.

The modern terms for colours are, luckily, somewhat easier to understand.

Arzel: 'A horse that has a white mark upon his far foot behind.' (Os.)

Pomeled: Applied to a flea-bitten or dappled horse. (=spotted, like a *chital*.)

Seeling: A horse was said to *seel* when white hairs began to grow in his eye-brows.

Tramelled: Of a horse 'that has blazes upon the fore and hind feet on one side'. (Os.)

Zain: 'A horse of a dark colour, neither grey nor white, and without any white spot or mark upon him.' (Os.)

MODERN

COLOURS

Custom has ordained that only certain descriptive terms should be used:

Bay: This may vary from light gold to a dark brown. In between is the bright blood mahogany, the commonest colour for a horse. They may be termed *light*, *bright* or *dark* bay. The *bay* is distinguished from the *chestnut* by having a black mane and tail, and, nearly always, some black on the legs. A bay with *black points* (i.e. when the hair on the lower part of the leg is black) is considered a hardy colour.

Black: This needs no description.

Brown: A very dark colour, sometimes almost indistinguishable from bay or black.

Chestnut: A reddish-brown. There are three kinds:

Bright: almost 'ginger'.
Liver: deep, inclining to purple.
Washy: pale and yellowish.

Cream: This colour is not common.

Dun: A fulvous brown (or fawn); varies from a mouse colour (i.e. *Blue dun*) to a yellow dun. Horses of this colour often have *zebra* markings, and are common in India.

Grey: There are three kinds:

Dappled: a mottled effect.
Flea-bitten: coloured with small reddish-brown spots (tufts of hair).
Iron: a hard, lead colour.
(A grey horse tends to go white with age.)

Piebald: Patches of two different colours (black and white).

Roan: There are three kinds:

Blue: the colour is produced by a mingling of black, white and yellow hairs.
Red: with red, white and yellow hairs. The red roan is sometimes called *Sorrel.*
Strawberry: red and white hairs. Occasionally a *chestnut roan* may be met.

In the *Blue* and *Red Roan* (but not the *Strawberry*) the legs are black.

Skewbald: Large patches of white and any colours other than black. Sometimes the term *Odd coloured* is used when the patches are of more than two colours.

Sorrel: A yellowish brown colour. See *Red Roan.*

White: This needs no description.

If in doubt as to the colour, look at the fine hair on the muzzle.

The Royal College of Veterinary Surgeons has issued a list of colours recommended by them. It includes all the above colours, with the addition of:

Black-brown
Bay-brown
Mealy-bay (a variety of the *light bay*).

It omits *White*.

The varieties of *Chestnut* are given as:

> *Bright*, *Golden* and *Red*, *Dark* (covering *Liver* or *Mahogany*), and *Light*.

Sorrel is classified under *Light chestnut* (instead of under *Rea roan*).

THE 'MARKS'

Star: A small patch of white in the centre of the forehead.

Blaze: A white marking spread over the forehead, and sometimes down the whole width of the face. An exaggerated blaze is called 'white face'.

Race (or Stripe): A white marking running down the nose in a thin line.

Snip: A white or pink patch on either nostril or lip.

Stocking: White on the leg, extending from the coronet to the knee or hock.

Sock: So termed when the white extends upwards for a short way only.

Upperlip: / *Underlip:* Terms denoting white skin at the edges of the lips.

List (or Ray): The dark lines seen along the back of some horses, all donkeys, and many mules.

Zebra Marks: Any striping on limbs or body. Often seen in mules and donkeys, but not common in horses.

Flesh marks: Patches of skin with no colouring matter.

The colour of a horse is that of its coat. Northern horses are white-skinned, whereas the true Arabian invariably has a black skin. White-haired, black-skinned horses thrive best in the tropics.

In describing a horse, the word 'white' is usually omitted (when referring to the white hairs on the legs), and the following order should be adhered to: colour, country, sex, age, height, markings: e.g. *grey Arab gelding, 7 years, 15·2½, sock forelegs, off hind fetlock partly.*

WARRANTIES AT A RECOGNISED SALE

(See Catalogue descriptions)

Good Hunter (a complete warranty): Sound in wind, eyes and action; quiet to ride and capable of being hunted.

Good Performer: As above, but admits of an inherent weakness which may develop later.

Hunter: As for Good Hunter, less 'action'.

Hack: Quiet to ride, sound in action.

Regularly ridden: Quiet.

Believed to be sound: A warranty of soundness. Such warranties take precedence over a Veterinary Surgeon's certificate.

Faults/Vices which must be mentioned:

Crib-biting, windsucking, tubing, etc.

SEX AND AGE

Foal: Either sex, under one year old.

Yearling: Either sex, one year old.

Colt: Young unbroken male (loose term). Young stallion up to three years (race-horses).

Filly: Female, up to three years. Thus: *colt foal, filly foal, yearling colt* and *yearling filly* are the terms used.

Gelding: Castrated male.

Stallion:
Entire: } Uncastrated male.

Mare: Female, three years and over.

Rig: Male, with only one testicle removed. (Old term *Ridgeling*; mod. *Ridgel.*)

Pony: Up to 14 hands; or rather larger (applied to polo or pony-racing).

Cob: A thick-set type, not exceeding 15 hands.

Galloway: A trotting horse, the product (probably) of fell pony and Cleveland. The breed is extinct.

A *Tit* is a little horse. 'Some call a horse of a middle-size a double-Tit.' (Os.)

In breeding, the father is called the *sire,* and the mother the *dam.*

Aged: Seven years old and over.

Rising; off: A horse that is nearly three years old is said to be *rising three,* while one that is just over three years would be *three off.*

A horse's age may be told from his teeth.

Mule: The result of a cross between a jackass and a mare. (See Chapter XXIV, No. 140, Notes, and App. III.)

Jennet (or *hinny*): The offspring of a horse and a she-ass.

Jumart: The offspring of a bull and a mare.

Hack: This may mean a horse kept for hire, or for general purposes, or one worn out with hard work. *Hackney* or *Hack* derives from the Andalusian *jaca* (='the horse of the country').

Brumby: An Australian wild horse.

A GLOSSARY

Back: A horse which is very sensitive to a cold saddle is said to have a *cold back.*

To *back a horse* is to ride it for the first time.

A *hollow-* or *saddle*-back is one in which the line from withers to loins is decidedly concave; the opposite to *roach.*

A horse is said to be *dipped* in the back when the withers slope deeply.

A *razor* back: where the backbone is particularly prominent.

Bars: (i) Of the mouth—the bare portions of the gums of the lower jaw. (ii) Of the hoof—the portions of the wall of the hoof which are turned inwards at the heels.

Bishoping: The practice of rasping the incisor teeth to make an old mouth look young.

Bone: A horse (or hound) with good measurement below the knee is said to have *plenty of bone.*

Boring: Leaning the weight of the head and neck on the bit.

Brisket: The lower portion of the horse's chest.

Brushing: Striking the inside of the fetlock by the toe of the opposite hoof, usually at the trot. At the gallop—the point struck is just below the knee, and the term is then *speedy cutting.* (See also *Cutting.*)

Cannon (shank or shin): The bone (q.v.) from knee to fetlock.

Chestnuts (or *Castors*): Horny growths above the knees, and just below the hocks, on the inside of the legs.

Colic: Equine indigestion; may be *spasmodic* or *flatulent.*

Coronet: The region round the top of the hoof, below the pastern.

Crest: The upper part of the neck (from which the mane springs), from the withers to the poll.

Crib-biter: A horse that catches hold of the manger with its teeth, at the same time swallowing air. It grunts as it gulps. (Cf. *Windsucker.*) A stable vice.

Croup: The upper portion of the body between the loins and the tail.

Curb: (i) A bony enlargement at the back of the hock. (ii) Short for *curb-bit* = a bit having the action of a lever.

Curry-comb: A metal scraper for cleaning the body brush.

Curtal: A horse (or dog) with a *docked* tail.

Cutting: A form of *Brushing* (q.v.) where the point struck is the inside of the coronet.

Dishing: A horse *dishes* with a foreleg when he throws the foot outwards as he raises it off the ground.

Dock: The root of the tail. A *docked* horse is one which has part of the bone of the tail removed.

Drench: Liquid medicine. To *drench* a horse is to pour the liquid down its throat.

Dumping (or *Stumping up*): Shortening the toe by rasping the front of the wall of the hoof.

Ergot: A small horny growth, in a tuft of hair, behind the fetlock.

Eye: When the eye is small and sunken it is known as *pig-eye*; a prominent eye is called *buck-eye*. A *wall eye* is one which has a bluish-white appearance, due to lack of colouring matter.

Fetlock: (i) The joint between the cannon-bone and the pastern. (ii) The tuft of hair that grows behind this joint. (Orig.: *feetlock*.)

Flat-catcher: A horse that, superficially, looks 'a good 'un', but is not.

Forearm: Reaches from the elbow to the knee.

Forehand: Includes head, neck and fore-limbs.

Forging: Striking the inside of the fore shoe with outside of hind shoe.

Foxy oats: Oats that, due to insufficient drying, have become heated and discoloured, and give off an acrid smell.

Frog: The thick V-shaped horny buffer between the angle of the heels. It has a depression in the centre called the *cleft*.

Fullering: A groove on the ground surface of the shoe, in which the nails are sunk.

Gaskin (or second thigh): Prominent bunch of muscles between the thigh and the point of the hock.

Goose rump: A pronounced slant from croup to dock. A horse with such drooping quarters is said to be *goose-rumped*.

Gummy legs: i.e. not *clean*; where the lines of the tendons are not well defined.

Hands: (i) A horseman is said to have *good hands* when he has a light and sensitive feeling on the reins, and rides his horse with sympathy and the minimum of interference with its mouth.

(ii) Horses are measured by *hands* (the invention of Leonardo da Vinci); a hand is four inches. The height is taken from the highest point of the withers to the ground.

Heels: Cracked or *greasy* heels are usually due to washing and not thoroughly drying the heels, causing a chapping of the surface.

Herring gutted: Term denoting a light or weedy body, running up fine; (*tucked up*)—opposite to *well ribbed up*.

Hidebound: A condition of the skin when it loses its mobility. The coat is said to *stare* when it has a dull look and does not lie flat.

Hips: Prominent hips, with their *points* wide apart, are termed *ragged*.

Hocks: The large joints between the gaskin and the hind cannon-bone. *Cow-hocks* have their *points* turned in (seen from behind)—like a cow. *Sickle-hocks* are those which are exceptionally bent (seen from the side). Hocks are termed *well let down* when they are long, low and *straight-dropped*.

Hogging: Clipping the bristles of the mane flush with the crest.

Irons: Stirrup-irons.

Jowl: The space, in front of the throat, between the branches of the jaw.

Knees: When the width (from front to rear) of the cannon just below the knee is small, the term is *tied in below* or *tied at* the knee. *Calf knees* (=*Back at the knee*, a fault) are those which (viewed in profile) tend to show rather a concave line—opposite to *Over at the knee* (a grave defect in jumping). *Well let down*—see under *Hocks*.

For Good measurement below the knee, see under *Bone*.

Broken knees cover a variety of injuries when the skin of the knee is broken. (Old term—horse was said to be *crowned* when, from a wound, the hair on the knees would not grow again.)

Laminitis: Fever in the feet.

Lampas: Inflammation of the gums behind the incisor teeth of the upper jaw.

Loins: Extend from the end of the back to the croup. A horse with weak loins (not *well ribbed up*) is said to be *slack in the loins*. In this condition the last rib is short and a considerable distance from the point of the hip.

Lop-ears: Ears which are set on in a pendulous manner.

Lymphangitis ('Monday morning disease'): A swollen condition of the hind legs.

Martingale: A strap fastened to the horse's girth to hold his head down. There are two main kinds:

(i) A *standing* m.—attached to the bit or noseband.

(ii) A *running* m.—with rings, for attachment to the curb-reins.

There is also an *Irish* m., which is not really a martingale at all. It consists of a short strap, about 6 inches long, with rings through which the reins pass.

Mud fever: A scabby condition affecting the abdomen and hind legs; due to not drying the parts thoroughly. (Cf. *Cracked heels.*)

Neck: A *Ewe neck* is a thin neck with a concave arch. When convex, it is called *high-crested.*

A *swan-necked* horse is one which has a neck like a fowl (i.e. the curve tends to become ewe-necked at its lower end).

A short, thick and rather stiff neck is termed *bull neck.*

Over-reach: Wound caused by a foreleg being struck by a hind foot (e.g. in landing over a jump). They may be *high* or *low.*

Pastern: Is situated between the fetlock and the hoof.

Pelham: A *snaffle* and *curb* combined, with one mouthpiece only.

Poll: The part immediately between and behind the ears.

Quarters: Short, narrow quarters, lacking muscle between the thighs, are termed *split-up*. (See *Goose rump.*)

Rein: A horse is said to have a *good rein* when he has a good sloping shoulder, a long neck and a well set on head.

Ribs: For *Well ribbed up* see under *Loin.*

Roller: A surcingle, to keep the horse-rug in place.

Roman nosed: When the line of the face (viewed from the side) is convex. In the Arab, the line is generally straight or concave (*dished*).

Rubber: A cloth, generally used to give the coat a polish.

Screw: A cheap, ill-bred horse; probably, also, an unsound one.

Snaffle: A form of bit consisting of a single mouthpiece (or *bar*) which may be either jointed or unjointed. The jointed should not be used with a martingale. The unjointed may have a straight or curved (½-moon or *mullen*) bar.

The *gag* is an efficient and humane form of snaffle for raising the head.

A *snaffle-mouthed horse* is one which will bend at the poll and flex its lower jaw on the feel of a snaffle only.

Spavin: Bog spavin—a distension of the joint oil-bag of the inner and upper part of the hock.

Bone spavin—a growing together of the inner and lower part of the hock.

Speedy cutting: See *Brushing*.

Splint: A bony growth on the cannon bone.

Star gazer: A horse with an *ewe neck* is liable to poke out its muzzle and look upwards.

Stifle: The large joint of the hind leg behind the lower part of the flank.

Tail: Banging a tail is to cut its hairs level.

Docked—see *Dock*.

Thoroughpin: An enlargement of the hock—just in front of and above it.

Thrush: Inflammation of the fleshy *frog*: caused by dirt. It has an unpleasant smell.

Tush: A permanent tooth, which appears in the male at about five years, behind the corner teeth on each side in both jaws.

Weaving: A nervous habit of rocking from side to side in the stall. The horse at the same time places its weight alternately on each fore-foot. A stable vice.

Wind: An affection of the lungs, making expiration difficult, is termed *Broken wind*, or *Gone in the wind*.

Windgall: A soft swelling above the fetlocks, being a distension of the joint oil-bags.

Wind-sucker: A horse that arches its neck and swallows air by giving a gulp. Another stable vice. (Cf. *Crib-biter*.)

Wisp: A pad of twisted hay or straw; used for massaging the coat to improve condition.

Withers: The bony ridge between crest and back, above the shoulder-blade.

PART III

GROUP TERMS

'He (the hunter) must be active and quick eyed, well advised of speech and of his terms, and ever glad to learn, and that he be no boaster or jangler.'

The Master of Game

PART III

Sir John Buttesthorn, the Knight of Dupplin, was head huntsman to the King and famous through all England for his knowledge of venery. To him 'came the young gallants of the country . . . to learn from him that lore of the forest and the chase which none could teach so well as he'.

To him came also Nigel. 'And straightway the old knight began a long and weary lecture upon the times of grace[1] and when each beast and bird was seasonable, with many anecdotes, illustrations, warnings and exceptions, drawn from his own great experience. He spoke also of the several ranks and grades of the chase: how the hare, hart, and boar must ever take precedence over the buck, the doe, the fox, the marten and the roe, even as a knight banneret does over a knight, while these in turn are of a higher class to the badger, the wildcat, or the otter, who are but the common populace of the world of beasts. Of bloodstains also he spoke—how the skilled hunter may see at a glance if blood be dark and frothy, which means a mortal hurt, or thin and clear, which means that the arrow has struck a bone.

' "By such signs", said he, "you will surely know whether to lay on the hounds and cast down the *blinks* which hinder the stricken deer in its flight. But above all I pray you, Nigel, to have a care in the use of the terms of the craft, lest you should make some blunder at table, so that those who are wiser may have the laugh of you, and we who love you may be shamed."

' "Nay, Sir John," said Nigel. "I think that after your teaching I can hold my place with the others."

'The old knight shook his white head doubtfully. "There is so much to be learned that there is no one who can be said to know it all," said he. "For example, Nigel, it is sooth that for every collection of beasts of the forest, and for every gathering of birds of the air, there is their own private name so that none may be confused with another."

' "I know it, fair sir."

' "You know it, Nigel, but you do not know each separate name, else you are a wiser man than I had thought you. In truth

[1] = *Grease*. (See Chapter XXI.)

none can say that they know all, though I have myself pricked off eighty and six for a wager at court, and it is said that the chief huntsman of the Duke of Burgundy has counted over a hundred—but it is in my mind that he may have found them as lad, he went, for there was none to say him nay. Answer me now, how would you say if you saw ten badgers together in the forest?"

' "A *cete* of badgers, fair sir."

' "Good, Nigel—good, by my faith! And if you walk in Woolmer Forest and see a swarm of foxes, how would you call it?"

' "A *skulk* of foxes."

' "And if they be lions?"

' "Nay, fair sir, I am not like to meet several lions in Woolmer Forest."

' "Ay, lad, but there are other forests besides Woolmer, and other lands besides England, and who can tell how far afield such a knight-errant as Nigel of Tilford may go, when he sees worship to be won? We will say that you were in the deserts of Nubia, and that afterward at the court of the great Sultan you wished to say that you had seen several lions, which is the first beast of the chase, being the king of all animals. How then would you say it?"

'Nigel scratched his head. "Surely, fair sir, I would be content to say that I had seen a number of lions, if indeed I could say ought after so wondrous an adventure."

' "Nay, Nigel, a huntsman would have said that he had seen a *pride* of lions, and so proved that he knew the language of the chase. Now, had it been boars instead of lions?"

' "One says a *singular* of boars."

' "And if they be swine?"

' "Surely it is a herd of swine."

' "Nay, nay, lad, it is indeed sad to see how little you know. Your hands, Nigel, were always better than your head. No man of gentle birth would speak of a herd of swine; that is the peasant speech. If you drive them it is a *herd*. If you hunt them it is other. . . . You can tell us, Mary?"

' "Surely, sweet sir, one talks of a *sounder* of swine."

'The old Knight laughed exultantly. . . .

' "Hark ye! only last week that jack-fool, the young Lord of Brocas, was here talking of having seen a covey of pheasants in the wood. One such speech would have been the ruin of a young squire at the court. How would you have said it, Nigel?"

' "Surely, fair sir, it should be a *nye* of pheasants."

' "Good, Nigel—a *nye* of pheasants, even as it is a *gaggle* of geese or a *badling* of ducks, a *fall* of woodcock or a *wisp* of snipe. But a covey of pheasants! What sort of talk is that? I made him sit even where you are sitting, Nigel, and I saw the bottom of two pots of Rhenish ere I let him up." '

(From *Sir Nigel*, by Conan Doyle.)

NOTE. In each chapter in this Part the third column contains the old term in its original spelling: its equivalent modern spelling is shown in the second column. The last column gives the source of origin. For the key to the abbreviations see Chapter XXVI.

In the second column, the suggested correct modern term is indicated by *italics*: the remaining terms are in roman type.

CHAPTER XXIII

BIRDS

True Company Terms - - - - -	*
Terms which represent the young or progeny - -	†
Terms which represent characteristics - - -	‡
Terms which represent noises or cries - - -	§
Suggested correct modern term - - - -	*italics*

NAME	GROUP TERM		AUTHORITY
	Modern	Original	
1. Birds (small)	a‡*dissimulation* of	Dyssymylacyon Dissimulacion	Eg. St. A.
Birds	**flock* or *congregation: ‡flight: volery aviary		N. G.T.
2. Bitterns (Bitournys)	‡*siege*	Sege	Eg., St. A.
3. Bustards	**flock*		Os.
4. Capercailzies	*tok*		N.
5. Chickens	§*peep*	Pype	Eg.

		Pepe	St. A.
	†brood		N.
6. Choughs	§*clattering*	Chaterynge	Eg. (only)
		Clateryng	St. A.
7. Coots	†*covert*	Couerete	Eg.
		Couert	St. A.
(mudhen)	fleet		PS.
8. Cormorants	‡*flight*	fflyȝt	P.
9. Cranes	**herd*	Herde	Eg., St. A.
10. Crows	§*murder*	Mursher	Eg.
11. Curlews	**herd*	Herde	Eg., St. A.
12. Dotterel	**trip*		Os.
13. Doves	‡*flight*	fflyght	Eg.
		fflight	St. A.
(turtle)	‡pitying	Pyttyvsnys	P.
	‡true love	Treweloue	Harl. 1
	‡*dule*	Duell	St. A.
14. Ducks			
(on the water)	‡*paddling*	Padelynge	Eg.
		badelyng	St. A.
(in flight)	†*team*	Teme	Harl. 1, F.
(two)	*brace*		G. T.
	sore or safe		RH.
15. Dunbirds. See Pochard.			
16. Dunlin			
(Sandpiper)	‡*flight*		N.
17. Eagles	convocation		ISDN.
18. Finches	§*charm*	chyrme	S.
19. Fowls	§*scry*	scrye	Sk.
20. Geese	§*gaggle*	Gagelynge	Eg.
(on the water)		Gagle	St. A.
	*flock		Os.
(on the wing)	*skein*		F., ISDN., N.
21. Goldfinches	§*charm* (chirp)	Chyrme	Eg.
		Cherme	St. A.
	§trimming or trembling	Tremynge	Harl. 1 (only)
22. Grouse			
(a single family)	†*covey*		ISDN.
(larger bands)	**pack*		Os., ISDN.
	pack or brood		RJN.
23. Gulls.	colony		N.
24. Hawks			
(of 2 of the tower)	*cast*	Caste	Eg.
		cast	St. A.
(of 3 of the tower)	*leash*	Lece	St. A.
merlin	leash	lesshe	Harl. 1
goshawk	‡*flight*	fflyght	Eg.
		Flight	St. A.

25. Hens	†*brood*	Broode	Eg.
		Brode	St. A.
26. Herons	‡*siege*	Sege	Eg., St. A.
	sedge		F., PS.
27. Jays	*band		PS.
28. Lapwings	‡*deceit*	Dyssayte	Eg.
		Desserte	St. A.
29. Larks	‡exaltation	Exaltacyon	Eg.
		Exaltyng	St. A.
	‡*flight*	flyght	Harl. 1
	*bevy	Beuye	S. (only)
30. Magpies	§*tidings*	Tydynge	Eg.
		Titengis	St. A.
31. Mallard	‡flush	fflushe	Eg.
	‡*sord* or sute	Sort	P.
		Soorde	Harl. 1
		Sorde or Sute	St. A.
	puddling		PS.
32. Nightingales	‡*watch*	Waycche	Eg.
		Wache	St. A.
		watching	All. and RH. only
33. Oxbirds	fling		F., ISDN.
34. Parrots	**flock*		GT.
35. Partridges	†*covey*	Couaye	Eg.
		Couy	St. A.
(two)	*brace*		GT.
36. Peacocks	‡*muster*	Monstyr	Eg.
		Mustre	St. A.
	‡ostentation		ISDN. (only)
	‡pride		GT. (only)
37. Pheasants	†*nye*	Ny	Eg.
		Nye	St. A.
	nide, nie or nye		AM.
(a family)	†brood		ISDN.
	bouquet, brace		GT.
38. Pigeons	‡*flight*		ISDN.
	*flock		GT.
39. Plovers	**congregation*	Congregacyon	Eg.
		Congregacion	St. A.
	‡flight		PS.
	wing		Os, ISDN.
	stand		RJN.
	leashe		GT.
40. Pochard	‡*rush* or flight		F.
	‡knob or rush		CW.
(Dun-birds)	‡rush		ISDN.
(Atteal or attile)	‡diving	Dyuyng	Harl. 1.
41. Poultry	run		N.

42. Quails	**bevy*	Beuy	Eg., St. A.
43. Ravens	‡*unkindness*	Unkyndenys	Eg.
		vnkyndenes	St. A.
44. Redwings	crowd		PS. (only)
45. Rooks	‡*building*	Byldynge	Eg.
		beldyng	St. A.
	clamour		GT., CW.
46. Ruffs	*hill*		F., ISDN., N.
47. Sheldrakes	‡*dopping*	Doppyng	Harl. 1.
48. Snipe	‡*walk*	Walke	Eg., St. A.
	wisp or whisp		Os.
(dead)	*couple*, leash		GT.
49. Sparrows	**host*	Oste	Eg.
		Ost	St. A.
	tribe		PS. (only)
50. Starlings	§chattering	Clatering	Harl. 1
		Chatteryng	Harl. 2
	§*murmuration*	Murmuracyon	Eg.
		Murmuracion	St. A.
51. Swallows	‡*flight*	fflyght	Eg.
		Flight	St. A.
52. Swans	**herd*	Herde	Eg., St. A.
	†team	Teme	Harl. 1
	bank		PS. (only)
	wedge		RJN.
	herd or bevy		N.
53. Swifts	**flock*		N.
54. Teal	‡*spring*	Sprynge	Eg., St. A.
	coil		PS. (only)
	bunch, knob or spring		N.
55. Thrush	‡*mutation*	Mutacyoñ	P. (only)
56. Turkeys	rafter		PS. (only)
57. Widgeon	**company*		F.
	bunch		PS.
(in the air)	*flight*		N.
(on the water)	bunch, company or knob		N.
58. Wildfowl	*trip*		F.
	trip or plump		RJN.
	plump, sord or sute		N.
59. Woodcock	‡*fall*	ffalle	Eg.
		fall	St. A.
	flight		Os. (only)
60. Woodpeckers	‡*descent*	discēcion	S. (only)
61. Wrens	**herd*	Herd	P.
		Herde	St. A.
62. Fieldfares	**flock*		RS.
63. Ptarmigan. See Grouse			
64. Storks	mustering		'Field'
65. Penguins			

NOTES (BIRDS)

1. BIRDS.

Dissimulation. This refers to the habits of flocks of small birds of distracting the attention of unwelcome visitors. '. . . the Larke, which everflyes from-ward her nest, when she sees any body eyes her.' (Cotgrave, 1650.) Cf. Notes, 28. Lapwings.

Volery. A flight of birds. (N.)

Aviary. A place for keeping birds. Evidently not a group term. A young bird may be called a *flapper.* (See 58. Wild fowl.)

2. BITTERNS.

Siege. See 26. Herons.

Osbaldiston gives as alternative names for this bird *butterdump* and *miredrum.* Hawker gives two more: *Bogbumper* and *Bitterbum*; and Pennant *Myredromble.*

3. BUSTARDS.

Flock. 'In Hungary this bird is so common as sometimes to be seen four or five hundred in a *Flock.*' (RS.) It is now extinct in England.

4. CAPERCAILZIES.

Tok. A nesting-place, or an assembly of capercailzies. (N.)

This bird is also known as *Cock of the Wood* or *Wood* (or *Giant*) *Grouse.*

The correct spelling would appear to be 'Capercaillie'. Its passionate spring love-song is known as the *lek* or *spel,* though *lek* is proper only to black game.

5. CHICKENS.

Peep. The proper term for the noise made by chickens. Cf. 'The Chicken peepeth' from Hoole's edition of *Commenius,* 1672, and 'a *Peep* or *Flock* of Chickens'. (RH.)

Brood. See 25. Brood of Hens.

(NOTE: *Chickens* is really a double plural. *Chicken* is the true plural of *chick.*)

6. CHOUGHS.

Clattering. Given in nine lists. (See 50. Starlings.)

It is said that all true Celts await the return of King Arthur, whose spirit, they affirm, lives now in the form of that beautiful bird—the Cornish Chough.

7. COOTS.

Covert. Hodgkin suggests that *Couert* is derived from the French *couvert* denoting a hatch of young coots, 'that which was covered', rather than from 'covert' = a secure hiding-place. The coots' nests are large and clumsy, and Colonel Hawker says; 'The reason that all wild-fowl seek the company of coots is because these birds are such good sentries, to give the alarm by day, when the fowl generally sleep.'

Fleet. The origin of this term is obscure, unless it derives from the A.S. *fleot* = a number of ships.

From a white mark on its forehead, the bird is sometimes known as the 'bald coot'.

8. CORMORANTS.

Flight. 'Not a numerical or company term.' (PT.)

Cormorants were used for fishing, and were *flown* or *lett fli* at the fish. However it was no doubt used to describe a number of these birds. Cf. 24. Goshawk. (The term only occurs in P. and S.)

These birds were hood-winked, according to Willoughby, in the manner of the Falcons till they were let off to fish. Whitlock tells us 'That he had a *Cast* of Corvorants, *manned* like Hawks, which would come to Hand'.

An 'absurd' name for this bird was '*Isle of Wight Parson*' (Hawker). Hawker also gives 'The common Great Black one, alias Corvorant, or *Cole goose*; the *Green*, *Shag*, *Scarfe* or *Scart*; and the Crested Corvorant.'

9. CRANES.

Herd. The proper term for a flock of cranes. N. adds the terms *sedge* or *siege*, for which there appears to be no authority.

10. CROWS.

Murder. This word is possibly intended to represent the noise of crows. P. gives *Morther*, and S. *Murther*.

Rev. Daniel, referring to the *Royston*, or hooded Crow, says that 'They are gregarious, but in the breeding Season separate into pairs, build in Trees, lay six eggs, and are much attached to their Offspring: after that period they again unite in bands, and are often seen in small flocks near London . . .'

11. CURLEWS.

Herd. The proper term for a flock of curlews.

The flesh of the curlew was thought by some to be very good; the old proverb:

> A *Curlew*, be she white, or be she black,
> She carries twelve-pence on her back,

favours this presumption. It is when the curlew returns to the sea shore that they acquire an unpleasant fishy taste.

The little Curlew was known as the *Whimbrel*, and 'by some called *Curlew Jacks*' (Blaine). The stone Curlew is a land bird, and called the *Great* or *Norfolk Plover*, and *thick-kneed bustard*. (Hawker.)

12. DOTTEREL.

Trip. An accepted company term. (See 126. Goats.)

The dotterel is a species of plover, esteemed for its flesh, and so called from its seeming stupidity in allowing itself to be easily taken. 'It has become proverbial to speak of a foolish or dull person as a "silly dotterel." ' (F.)

The Ring Dotterel = *Ring Plover* or *Sea Lark* (Hawker). *Turnstone* is a Sea Dottrell (Pennant).

13. Doves.

Flight. The term probably refers to their characteristic sudden flight after settling.

The three terms given for the turtle-dove all express the same notion, i.e. the bereaved dove mourning for 'the dear departed'. The fidelity of the dove was proverbial: if she were bereft of her mate she sat alone for ever after, being a strict monogamist.

Chaucer says:

'Soul as the turtil that hath lost hir make';

and Shakespeare:

'As true as steel, as plantage to the moon,
As sun to day, as turtle to her make.'
(Troilus and Cressida, Act III, Sc. 2.)

Dule = the French *deuil* = mourning. Some writers have misquoted 'duet'.

It is interesting to note that several have mistaken the word *turtil* for 'turtle' (i.e. tortoise), and, in one case, for 'turkey'. (RS. gives 'a dule of Turkies'.)

14. Ducks.

Paddling. The Egerton MS. gives the correct spelling: 'a *Padelynge* of Dookysse.' As one duck can paddle, this cannot be a true company term.

Team. 'Teem' = a brood of young ducks. The A.S. word *team* = offspring. Cf. the modern expression 'teeming with'. '. . . it would be said . . . of ducks, a "*short*" or "*long team*".' (F.)

RH. gives 'A *Sore*, or *Safe* of Ducks and Mallards, or a *Team* of Ducks'. (See 31. Mallards, and 58. Wildfowl. (See Chapter VI, under Wildfowl.)

In Somersetshire the rising of the decoy in the eve was called *rodding*. (Cf. *Roding*, p. 72.)

15. Dunbirds. (See 40. Pochard, and 58. Wildfowl, and Chapter VI, Wildfowl.)

16. Dunlin. (See 33. Oxbird.) 'A *trip* of dunlins', *Word Lore*, vol. iii, 1928.

17. Eagles.

Convocation. There appears to be no other authority for this majestic and suitable term. It is not often that more than one eagle is seen at a time.

Blaine mentions the Golden eagle; the Great Sea-eagle, also known as the *Erne*, or white-tailed Sea-eagle; and the Fishing eagle (Sea-eagle), Osprey or Fishing hawk.

18. Finches. (See 21. Goldfinches.)

19. Fowls.

Scry. This term is not in the St. Albans list, though it occurs in another part of that book. It refers to the screaming of wildfowl. (Cf. the German *Schreyen*, and our provincial *skreek*.)

20. Geese.

Gaggle. NED. states that it is 'One of the many artificial terms invented in the 15th century as distinctive collectives . . . but unlike most of the others, it seems to have been actually adopted in use.' This may be so, but the word relates to, and is the proper term for, the peculiar noise of the goose. (Cf. Appendix I, 'A *gaggle* of gossips'.)

'The Goose *gaggleth*.'

(Hoole's *Commenius*, 1672. The lively and vocal alphabet.)

(See also the quotation under 43. Ravens (Notes).)

'It would be said . . . of geese a "little *gaggle*" or a "small *skein*".' (F.) (See Folkard's remarks under 58. Wildfowl.)

Hesketh Prichard, describing the bernicles in his *Sport in Wildest Britain*, speaks of the *gaggles* which, when disturbed, seek safety on the wide strands of estuaries.

Skein. A descriptive term; lit. a measure of thread, yarn or silk. (N.)

The *Grey Lag* is the origin of the domestic goose, which is of vast longevity. Nor would it appear that this attribute is confined to the tame, since the Germans have a proverb, 'Older than a wild goose'.

A Solan Goose = Gannet (or *Gan* (Welsh)). (*Solan* is an Irish word meaning 'quick sight'.)

Daniel (RS.) refers to Brent geese (in *Ireland* they are called *Bernacles*'); he says that they fly in the shape of a wedge, with great clamour, and that they are easily tamed. (See quotation under 52. Swans, and Chapter VI.) ('A *Lag* of geese', *Word Lore*, vol. iii, 1928.)

Whiffling: 'that hurtling acrobatic dive' (Peter Scott) as they plane downwards.

21. Goldfinches.

Charm. The word is the old English *cirm* (a loud noise), and has many variants; *chirm*, *chyrme*, *chern*, *chirk*, *chirp*, *chirrup*. It refers to the noises of these birds and not to their congregation, but is probably the most commonly quoted term of all supposed collectives. (See under 57. Widgeon.)

The local name for goldfinch in many countries was *Proud Tailor*. 'A Proude shewyng of taloris' (Chapter XXVII)—due to the gay colour of their liveries.

22. Grouse.

Pack. The following quotations are given to show the early use of the word 'pack':

'a *Pack* of Grous, or Heath-cocks.' (RH.)
'a *Pack* of grouse.' (Shooter's *Guide*, 1816.)

Covey. In practice, *covey* is generally used to denote a single family, and *pack* for the larger bands which form later on in the season. This view is confirmed in N. Some sportsmen insist that only *pack* is correct; the debate continues.

Rev. Daniel gives the following notes (RS.);

Black Grous, *Black Cock*, or *Black Game* (or *Heathcock* (Os.)); their *Broods* are not found in tall ling, but chiefly in marshy ground.

Red Grous, *Moorcock*, or *Red Game* (or *Gor-cock*. (Os.)); they pair in the Spring. The young Brood (which at the first are called *Poults*) follow the *Hen* during the whole summer; in winter they join in *Flocks* of forty or fifty which are termed *Packs* . . .

White Grous, *White Game*, or *Ptarmigan:* They seldom make long flights, but fly taking a small circle like pigeons. In summer they keep in small *packs*; never, like the *Grous*, take shelter in the heath, but beneath loose stones. In winter the *Ptarmigans* assemble, and fly in *Flocks*, still preserving their stupid tameness. In Nova Scotia they are called *Birch Partridges*.

There is also the *Hudson's Bay Ptarmigan*, or *White* Partridge. *Flocks* of two hundred, or more, of these assemble in October and live much among the willows, the tops of which they eat, and thence take the name of *Willow Partridges*.

(Colonel Thornton, in *A Sporting Tour*, spells their name *Ptarmigants*.) This is the only bird in the British Isles to change its plumage in winter (cf. the stoat and mountain hare). It has a harsh guttural croak. (See Chapter VI.)

23. Gulls.

Hawker refers to 'Gulls, *terns*, or sea swallows', and says they are called *Kipps* near Lydd. The common gull was called the *seamew*.

24. Hawks.

Cast. The number of hawks cast off at a time: a couple: also of other birds. (NED.) (See Chapter VIII for the use and origin of *Cast*.)

Leash. A set of three (NED.)

Cast and *leash* were applied to two and three hawks of the tower, just as *brace* and *leash* were applied to greyhounds.

The hawk of the tower belonged to the upper classes, the *marlion* (*merlin*) being for a lady's use.

Flight. The goshawk (for a yeoman) was '*lett fli*' and not *cast*.

RH. gives (incorrectly); 'An *Eirey* of Hawks; two a *lease* of Hawks, and three a *staff* of Hawks.' Daniel mentions the 'common Buzzard or *Puttock*' (a kite) as making 'great havoc among the *Leverets*'.

See Chapter VIII, Hawking.

25. Hens.

Brood. Hodgkin says; 'The term ranks in the same category as a "*covey* of partridges", "*nye* of fesants", etc., all meaning "a brood, a family of young hatched out at once, a hatch", but each bird mentioned has its specific term for its hatch.'

'A *Broud* of Cocks and Hens.' (RH.)

26. HERONS.

Siege. The Egerton MS. has these three terms:

'a *Sege* of Betowrys/
a *Sege* of Hayrynnys/
a *Sege* vnto a Castelle/'

Just as a commander sits down and lays siege to a castle, so does the patient heron stand in the water waiting to pounce on the unwary fish. This is borne out by definitions in *Gentleman's Recreation* (NC.). Herons do not sit on the ground in company; occasionally a pair may be seen flying overhead with their young.

RH. gives two incorrect spellings: 'a *Seigh* of Bitters', and '*a Shegh* of Herons'. Bibbesworth uses the term *bevy*.

Osbaldiston defines 'a Heron *at siege*, is a heron standing at the waterside, and watching for prey', and '*Heronry*—a place where herons breed'.

Heron Hawking used to be a favourite sport. 'Not to know the *Hawk* from the *Heronshaw*, was an old Proverb, taken originally from this Amusement; but in course of time it was absurdly corrupted to, "He does not know a *Hawk* from a *Hand-saw*," and served to express great Ignorance in any Science.' (RS.) In E. Anglia this bird is known as *Hanser*.

27. JAYS.

Band. This term is generally used for armed men, musicians, etc.

28. LAPWINGS.

Deceit (*Desert*). An alleged name for a covey of Lapwings. (NED.)

The word is misprinted in St. A., and in all the authorities that followed. The term refers to the habit of the bird during the nesting season and after.

Swainson describes this habit as follows: 'During the season of incubation the cock bird tires to draw pursuers from the nest by wheeling round them, crying and screaming to divert their attention . . . whilst the female sits close on the nest till disturbed, when she runs off, feigning lameness, or flaps about near the ground as if she had a broken wing.'

The word is mentioned in fifteen lists, of which the first eight give the correct form; variations are *dyssayt*, *Disseit*, *disceite*, etc. Chaucer refers to 'The false Lapwing, ful of trecherie' (*The Assembly of Fowls*), and Shakespeare: 'Far from his nest the lapwing screams away' (*Comedy of Errors*, Act IV, Sc. 2).

It is possible that in *deceit* a *double entendre* is intended. The word *desert* is now so commonly applied to a flock of lapwings that custom may be said to have sanctioned its use. (See 39. Plovers.)

The old name for this bird was *wipe*, and it is still called *wipa* in Sweden.

29. LARKS.

Exaltation (or *Exalting*). A fanciful name for a flight of larks.

(NED.) This is not a company term. It refers only to, and is the proper term for, a lark which soars into the sky and sings.

Flight. The proper term for a large assembly of larks, and refers to their characteristic rushes when disturbed. Cf. 13. Doves.

Bevy. This may be a mistake of an early scribe. It is a company term—and larks do assemble in large numbers.

'A *Said* of larks', *Word Lore*, vol. iii, 1928.

30. MAGPIES.

Tidings. This word has been sadly mangled on its journey through the lists, eight in all, in which it appears. Two examples are given above; other variations are: *Tythingys*, *Tygendis*, *atygendes*, *tygendes*, *tygenes*. The word means 'news' (tythyng), and refers to the superstition, for good or bad luck for the future, according to the number of *pyes* seen.

Halliwell gives *tithing*, a company of magpies. R. Bosworth Smith in his *Bird Life and Bird Lore* (1905) talks of a *Convocation* of Magpies. There is a French expression, *bavarde comme un pie*, applicable to over-talkative women.

The (so-called) Australian magpie is also termed piping crow or *organ bird*.

31. MALLARD.

Flush. The word is onomatopoeic and refers to the manner in which these male wild duck rise from the water. So also *Sord*, *Sourde*, etc., derived from the Latin *surgere* = to rise. The term has been misspelt by several authorities: *sore*, *suce* (All.) and *sore* or *safe* (RH.). It was used in a passage in St. A. to mean a company, but its original meaning is quite clear, i.e. the uprising of 'duck' when *flushed*. (See Chapter VI, under Wildfowl.)

Cf. *diving* of atteals (pochard), *dopping* of herles (sheldrakes), *spring* of teals, etc.

Harl. 2 gives 'it spryngyth or *sordyth* up sodēly be hym'.

Puddling. Cf. *Paddling*.

32. NIGHTINGALES.

Watch. This is the proper term for the nocturnal singing of nightingales. They do not sing in company.

Swainson says: 'The nightingale and the blind worm had only one eye apiece. Having been invited to the wren's wedding the former was ashamed to show herself in such a condition. So one day she surprised the snake while asleep, and stole his eye. On discovering his loss he said, "When I catch you asleep I will get it back!" "Will you?" was the bird's reply: "I will take care never to go asleep again." And so, ever since, from fear of being caught, the nightingale continues singing both by day and night.'

This simple and very beautiful legend explains the true significance of 'watch'.

33. Oxbirds.

Fling. This may be a descriptive term: more probably it is a misprint for *flight*, which is the term given for the Dunlin (No. 16).

There is an African Oxbird (or Ox-pecker), but it is more likely that the Dunlin or Sandpiper is intended. Folkard refers to the annual visant, 'the Dunlin, Oxbird or *Stint*'.

Hawker gives Oxbird, *Purre*, or *Stint*, and says they belong 'to the tribe of sandpipers'.

35. Partridges.

Covey. i.e. a brood. The old French *Couvée* . . . 'as many as come of one sitting'. (Cotgrave.) Blome describes a *Covey* of Partridges as 'a *Brood* that always accompany together with the old ones until paring time'.

'And ye schall say I have fonde a *Couey* of pertrich, a *beuey* of quayles, and *eye* of fesauntes.' (Harl. 2.)

Sometimes partridges, after being paired, if the weather be extremely severe, 'all gather together, and again form the *Covey*, and are then said to *pack*.' 'In two points the *red* differ from the common Partridges, in being found in *Flocks;* whereas, among the latter, only those belonging to the same Covey herd together; the *red* are also observed to *perch* on Trees, etc.' (RS.)

There is an old proverb:

> If the partridge had but the woodcock's thigh
> 'Twould be the best bird that e'er did fly.

(See Chapter VI.)

36. Peacocks.

Muster. Alleged term for a company of peacocks (the notion is that of sense 1, show, display). (NED.)

RH. misspells *Mustet*. The word (from the French) refers to the habit of this bird of 'showing', i.e. spreading its magnificent *fan*. The true tail is hidden. The correct term for the display of its upper tail coverts is the *train*.

Holland (*Plinie* 6, c. 20) gives a fine description: 'The peacocke farre surpasseth all the rest in this kind, as well as for beautie as also for the wit and understanding that he hath; but principally for the pride and glorie that he taketh in himself. For perceiving at any time that he is praised, and well liked, he spreadeth his taile round, *shewing* and setting out his colours to the most, which shine again like precious stones.'

37. Pheasants.

Nye. There are many variations in the spelling of this word. Besides those given above, the following forms occur: *Ye*, *Jye*, *Je*, *Neye*, *Any*, *Eye*. (See the quotation from Harl. 2 under 35. Partridges.) It means a hatch, i.e. the young brood which accompany the parent birds until the mating season.

Rev. Daniel mentions that he once killed a brace of Cocks of the same *nide* as that which contained a hen pheasant with the plumage of the male.

M. Temple (ISDN.), referring to the word *Nye*, says; 'Webster, who is usually very accurate in these matters, gives it without any indication that it is now obsolete, so that I cannot help suspecting that it must still be in use somewhere. Whether obsolete or not, it is almost certainly incorrect in the form in which the old books give it. It should not be a A *Nye* but An *Eye*, Eye being an old English word which signifies a brood.' (See also Chapter XXVI, No. 34.)

This view is strengthened by the quotation from Harl. 2 and the spelling *ye* (Harl. 1), though in the Egerton list the spelling is *Ny*, and in the Harl. 2 list *nye*. (Cf. an adder for *a nadder*, and an umpire for *a numpire*.)

'At sunset', says Alex. Mackintosh, '(they) fly up into the long branches of oak trees, in order to roost all night,' and then they 'invariably make a noise, which is called *cocketting*. . . .' (Mod. *cocking*.)

In his Spring display the cock pheasant stands high on his feet with the tail on the ground, *crows* and then beats his wings vigorously. This is called *drumming*.

(See Chapter VI.)

Bouquet. This term is also used by 'Middle Wallop' (Leslie Sprake).

38. Pigeons.

Flight. Cf. 13. Doves. M. Temple (ISDN.) says; 'It is still obligatory to speak of A *Flight* of Pigeons and A *Bevy* of Quails, as it has been ever since Englishmen used crossbow bolts against the one and nets against the other.'

Flock. 'In the beginning of Winter they' (the Ring-doves or Wood-pigeons) 'assemble in large *Flocks*, and leave off their Plaintive *Cooing*, which they commence in March, when they pair.' (RS.)

Pigeons have the various names expressive of their several properties, such as *carriers*, *tumblers*, *powters*, *horsemen*, *croppers*, *jacobines*, *owls*, *nuns*, *runts*, *turbits*, *barbs*, *helmets*, *trumpeters*, *dragoons*, *finnikins*, &c, all birds that at first might have accidentally varied from the stock-dove. (Os.)

'Of *wild* pigeons, or (more properly speaking) doves', says Hawker, 'there are three kinds: the *Stock*, or Wild Pigeon; the *Ring*, *Cushat* or *Queest*, and the *Turtle*'. The *Ring* is the Wood-pigeon. When there are immense numbers of wood-pigeon in the country, a disease, sometimes called *acorn disease*, breaks out.

39. Plovers.

Congregation. A true company term. Plovers assemble in flocks. (Technically of plovers.) (NED.)

Wing. This term appears to have fallen out of use.

No confirmation can be discovered for the other terms.

'a *Desart* of Lapwings and Plover' (RH.)

The following notes are from RS.:

The *Golden Plover* is the size of the *Turtle* (i.e. the turtle-dove). It wants the back toe, by which it is distinguished from other birds of its kind.

The *Grey Plover* generally comes in small flocks about October. Having fed, they fly to some splash of water to wash their beaks and feet; a habit which is also common to Woodcocks, Lapwings, Curlews, and many other birds which feed on worms.

The *Lapwing*, *Peewit*, or *Bastard Plover* is everywhere well known by its loud and incessant cries whilst on the wing, whence, in most languages, a name has been given to it as imitative of the sound. It is the one famous for its eggs.

In *Lorraine* there is an old proverb, 'Qui n'a pas mangé de Vanneau, ne sait pas ce que gibier vaut' . . .

For the *Norfolk Plover* see No. 11. Curlew.

(See also No. 12. Dotterel.)

40. Pochard.

Rush, *flight*, etc. Folkard is the best authority on wild fowl. (See 57 and 58.) N. gives '*flight*, *rush*, *bunch* or *knob*'.

Diving. The term refers to the bird's action in the water.

The Pochard, Red-headed Wigeon, or Dun Bird.

'They have a hissing Voice,' says Daniel; 'their flight is more rapid than that of the Wild Duck, and the noise made by their Wings is quite different; The Flocks observe no particular shape in flying, as the Duck in Triangles, but form a close body. . . . These birds are eagerly bought by the London Poulterers, under the name of *Dun Birds*.'

(See Chapter VI, under Wildfowl.)

The Pochard used to be known in Roxburgh as the *diver* or *doucker*, and in the Orkney Isles as the *atteal* or *attile* duck.

41. Poultry.

Run. This may refer to the enclosed ground where poultry can wander and peck.

42. Quails.

Bevy. The proper term for a company of quails. (NED.) A true company term. (See 29. Larks, and Chapter VI.)

The following notes are taken from RS. :

Quails have but *one brood* in a year, and never breed in a state of confinement.

Such intimate relation has by some been supposed to exist between the partridge and the quail, that they have called the latter the *dwarf partridge*.

43. Ravens.

Unkindness. An extract from SW. explains this term:

'Ancient writers held the opinion that the raven was utterly wanting in parental care, expelling its young ones from the nest, and leaving them prematurely to shift for themselves, until it saw what colour they would be, during which time they were nourished with dew from heaven. . . . However, this unkindness on the part of the parents was repaid, for when "they be old, and have their bills overgrown, they die of famine, not sharpning their bills again by beating them on a stone, as the eagle doth. Neither will their young ones help them, but rather set upon them when they are not able to resist" (Swan's *Speculum Mundi*, p. 389).'

Their 'unkindness' may rather be due, however, to their ferocity in defence: for they 'will scarcely suffer any Bird whatever to come within a quarter of a Mile of (their) *Nest*, . . .: besides the *Raven* seizes the young *Rooks* from their Nests to feed its own'. (RS.). If this is so, though still 'black' as their plumage, their 'unkindness' assumes a different quality.

> Anger the Rauen, he will flye about,
> As though his meaning were to seize vpon thee;
> The goose will *gaggle*, and the Cocke crie out,
> And euery other bird call shame vpon thee:
> Annoy the Larke, and he will hang the wing,
> Trouble the Nightingale, she leaues to sing;
> Onely the Cuckoe, which surmounts them all,
> She still chaunts Cuckoe, whatsoere befall.
>
> (Pasquil's *Night-cap*, 1612)

44. Redwings.

Redwings appear in England 'in vast flocks' about the same time as the Fieldfares. 'When the *Redwing* appears in Autumn, on the *Suffolk* Coast, the *Woodcocks* are certainly *at hand*; when the *Royston Crow*, they are *come*.' (RS.)

Redwing, *Swinepipe* or *Wind Thrush* (Hawker).

45. Rooks.

Building. A company (of rooks); a rookery. (NED.)

This was the correct term for a 'yonge gentylman' to use when speaking of rooks nesting. Rooks make a great fuss over the 'building' of their nests.

'And we shall say that hawkys doon draw when they bere tymbering to their nestes and nott they *beld* ne make their nestes.' (*The Boke of Hawkynge*, p. 1, St. A.)

Clamour. A descriptive term for their cawing.

Gilpin says: 'Among all the Sounds of Animal Nature, few are more pleasing than the *Cawing* of Rooks. The Rook has but Two or three Notes, and when he attempts a Solo we cannot praise his Song; but when he performs in *Concert*, which is his chief delight, these Notes . . . become harmonious. . . . You have this Music in perfection when the whole *Colony* is raised by the discharge of a Gun.'

The term *colony* is also used by Washington Irving in his *Bracebridge Hall*, where, referring to rook shooting, he says 'that a lamentable havoc takes place in the *colony* about the old church'.

The modern accepted rook term is believed to be *parliament*, but no authority for this can be traced.

Rooks, according to Daniel, may always be known from the *Carrion Crow* by their being in *Flocks*, whereas the *Crows* go only in *Pairs*

46. RUFFS.

Hill. A good descriptive term which deserves to be brought back into use.

The *Reeve* is the female of the Ruff. Daniel says that the latter 'are entitled to the Appellation of *Combatants*, given them by Buffon, who notes, they not only contend with each other in single Rencounters, but they advance in order of Battle; and that these hostile Armies are composed entirely of the *Males*, which . . . are much more numerous than the *Females*. Love is the Source of these Contentions. . . . Soon, after their arrival, the Ruffs begin to *Hill*, that is, to collect on some dry Bank near a splash of Water, in expectation of the *Reeves*, which resort to them.'

The Ruff is so called from the circle of feathers on the neck, which appear in the spring. This remarkable ornament, like the ruff worn by our ancestors, drops off when the bird moults, in June.

The male birds of the first year were called *stags*; until the second season, and also from the end of June until the breeding time commences, the plumage of both sexes is similar.

47. SHELDRAKES.

Dopping. The full term from Harl. 1 is a '*Doppyng* of *herles*'. It is also given in Harl. 2, 'a *doppyng* of Scheldrakys', and by Strutt. ISDN. writes 'dropping', but this is probably a misprint.

The word *dop* was used in East Anglia to denote a short quick curtsey.

Hodgkin says; 'The term "*dopping*" is probably equally applicable to either bird in its sudden disappearance under the water when disturbed.' (See Chapter VI, under Wildfowl.)

The red-breasted merganser = diving goose, known in the Orkney and Shetland Isles as the *harle duck*, or *herald duck* (from the Icelandic *hareld*). The goosander was sometimes known as the shell duck.

48. SNIPE (OR SNITE).

Walk. The term refers to their characteristic mode of progression. Similar terms occur in Harl. 2:

A percar *walkyth*,
a perterych *lythe*,
a fesawnte *stalkyth*,
a crane *stalkyth*,
a heyron *stalkyth*.

Wisp. Probably refers to their swift zig-zag motion in flight. (See Chapter VI.)

49. SPARROWS.

Host. A name for a 'company' of sparrows. (NED.)

This is a true company term. 'There is the notion of an army or hostile force, and not without cause, from their destructive habits.' (Hodgkin.)

50. STARLINGS.

Chattering. This would seem to be the correct spelling of the term when applied to '*starys*', and *clattering* for Choughs, *q.v.*, No. 6. But the more usual term is

Murmuration. An alleged name for a flock of starlings. (NED.)

Both terms are intended to describe the noise made by these birds.

RH. incorrectly gives a 'flight' of stares! (See Chapter XXVI, No. 15).

51. SWALLOWS.

Flight. Probably refers to their swift skimming flight.

The same term, with slightly different meanings, is applied to Goshawks, Doves, Pigeons, Larks and Swallows.

52. SWANS.

Herd. This is the proper term for a company of swans. The term is also applied to Cranes, Curlews and Wrens, to 'all man̄ dere' (St. A.), and to Harlots (*q.v.* App. I).

'Of swans it would be said, a "small *herd*".' (F.)

Team. 'This may mean a *brood* of young swans.' (PT.) (See 14. Ducks.)

Wedge. This obviously refers to their wedge-shaped manner of flight. In a poem by W. G. M. Dobie the term is applied to geese:

'Had I not seen, against the glowing light
Of dusk, a *wedge* of wild geese in their flight,
And heard their *clamour*—Ah, that magic cry!'
(*The Field*, 25 Jan., 1923)

The Wild Swan is generally known as the *Whooper* or *Whistling* Swan, and is smaller than the *Mute* or Tame. The latter have not the remarkable formation of the windpipe that occurs in the wild swan, and the utmost noise they can make is a mere hiss. On its bill is a prominent black knob. It has now generally reverted to a wild state; its chief note is a hiss. There is also Bewick's Swan.

Swanneries. Area where swans are kept.

Swan-upping. The marking of swans on their beaks.

'Wild Swan, *Elk* or *Hooper*' (Pennant).

'A *game* of Swans' (*Word Lore*, vol. iii, 1928).

Rev. Daniel employs many terms for a number of wild swans: 'small flocks', 'immense throngs', 'prodigious Multitudes', and *trips*. 'In their Flight the Swans follow so closely that the *Bill* of the one lies upon the *Tail* of the other.'

Like the Rook, their cry is more pleasing when they fly in company than when heard solo. It has been variously compared to the notes of a violin, the sound of a clarionet; Charles St. John says there is 'a wild harmony in their bugle cry' (*A Tour in Sutherland*). From the ancients came the fable of the swan being endowed with the powers of melody, and it has been asserted that the swans whistle or sing before they die. Others have likened their note to the words 'Whoogh, Whoogh', but the usual term is *trumpeting*, and the largest swans are often called *Trumpeters*. Poets, says Plato, turn at death into swans.

The swan's fighting attitude is called *busking*.

53. Swifts.

Flock. It is curious that there should be no special term for these swiftest of all birds. It is said that they can hardly walk, or 'take off' from level ground.

Swifts are sometimes called *Black Martins*.

54. Teal.

Spring. This term is given in sixteen lists, and refers to their characteristic action when *flushed*.

Bunch. Knob. (See under 58. Wildfowl, also Chapter VI, under Wildfowl.)

Garganey were called *summer teal* (Hawker), (*cricket teal* in Hampshire). 'Of all the prizes that a wildfowl shooter could wish to meet with, a *flock* of teal is the very first . . . I have seen teal "*duck the flash*". . . . If you *spring* a teal, he will not soar up like a wild duck.' (Hawker.)

55. Thrushes.

Mutation. The full term 'a *Mutacyoñ* of threstyllys' occurs only in P., and it helps to explain the isolated term 'a *Mutacion*' in the Hors, Shepe, & Ghoos list. (S.)

According to an old legend the thrush had a 'mutation' of old legs for new.

It is possible that the term was also used to describe the moulting of birds. (Alexander Neckham's *De Naturis Rerum*, 1863.)

57. Widgeon.

For notes on the terms see under 58. Wildfowl.

'A shrill clear *pipe* denotes a single cock wigeon, as does a long "*purre*" a hen; but when the call of the cock is one short soft note, and not so often repeated, you may expect to find a company. If so, you will probably soon hear the birds "*all in a charm*" (that is, in full chorus). . . . When wigeons are "in a *charm*", they are *not minding you*.'

The above remarks are by Colonel Peter Hawker in his *Instructions to Young Sportsmen*. He corroborates the use of the term *company* for widgeon, but it is doubtful whether 'charm' is here correctly employed in the sense intended. (See 21. Goldfinches, and Chapter VI, under Wildfowl.)

58. Wildfowl.

Trip. Daniel, in his account of *Old Merry's* fowling skill, says 'At *Wild-Fowl*, either singly or in *Trips*, he was a fatal shot,' and Folkard explains: 'A small number of wild-fowl, as ducks and geese (about thirty or forty), is termed a "*trip*". The same of widgeon, dunbirds, or teal, is termed a "*bunch*"; and a smaller number (from ten to twenty) is called a "*little knob*".'

Daniel also speaks of the *Punter*, who lies upon his belly and gets 'near the *Rout* of fowl'.

Gilpin has given us an interesting description of wildfowl shooting in the Hampshire coast. Here is one of his vivid pictures: 'Sea fowl usually feed by Night, when in all their multitudes they come down to graze on the Savannahs of the Shore. As the sonorous Cloud advances (for their noise in the Air resembles a pack of Hounds in full cry), the attentive *Fowler* listens which way they bend their course . . .' (See Chapter VI, under Wildfowl.)

A *flapper* is the name for a 'young wild-duck in a state of immaturity, partly fledged, and consequently unable to soar in the air or to fly any distance.' (F.) In France called *balbrans*, from the German.

59. Woodcock.

Fall. An alleged name for a covey or flight of woodcocks. (NED.)

The following is a quotation from a tract by Charles Morton, reprinted in the *Harleian Miscellany*, ii, 583: 'Consider their coming, which is so sudden (as to divers of the kinds) that it is as if they dropped down on us from above. In woodcocks, especially it is remarkable that upon a change of the wind to the east, about Alhallows-tide, they will seem to have come all in a night; for though the former day none are to be found, yet the next morning they will be in every bush: I speak of the West of England, where they are most plentiful.'

Hodgkin remarks that 'This sudden appearance of the birds is what is meant by "a *ffalle* of Woodecockys", and the phenomenon is metaphorically comparable to a *fall* of snow.' Support for this view is given by these extracts from RS.: 'Upon the *Sussex* Coast *Woodcocks* have been seen at their first dropping . . .' and 'At their first Arrival, they drop in *hedge rows* . . .' It is, however, possible that the term may be derived, not from their sudden appearance, but from a peculiarity of their flight: 'The Woodcock, though its flight for the time is *rapid*, is yet seldom long supported; it stops with such promptness as to fall apparently like a dead weight; . . .' (RS.) Probably there is a combination of both meanings. (See Chapter VI.)

In Barbary, where they are found in plenty during the winter, the Africans called them the *Ass of the Partridge*.

60. Woodpeckers.

Descent. The alleged term for a flight of *woodwales*. (NED.)

This seems to be the proper term for the peculiar flight of the *woodwale* or green woodpecker. It only occurs in this list (S.), and comes next to 'an *Exaltation* of Larkes', to which it forms a pretty contrast. Woodpeckers are generally solitary in their habits and do not move in 'flights'.

Yarrel (*Hist. Brit. Birds*, 1876-82) says: 'It frequents woody districts, and is commonly seen passing with an easy and undulating flight from one tree to another, nearly always alighting after a deeper sweep than the preceding, on the lower side of a bough or near the bottom of the trunk, often but a foot from the ground, whence it climbs upwards in an oblique direction, partly supporting itself by the stiff pointed feathers of its tail, moving by starts, and if possible keeping the tree between the observer and itself. Arrived near the top, it will fly off, either returning to the lower part of the same tree by a short circuit, or settling upon another, but in either case to renew its movements in the same way.' He adds: 'Selby says he had repeatedly seen it descend trees by moving backward. The editor has not been so fortunate. . . .'

The green woodpecker is called *Yaffle* from its laughter.

61. WRENS.

Herd. (See 52. Swans (herd).) Hodgkin says: 'The wren probably was allowed the proper term of "*herd*"—the word applied to harts—because it was the king of birds. Swainson refers to the migration of the wren in such numbers that at Caistor they have been observed to be like a *swarm* of bees on the hedges.'

There is a fascinating legend telling how the wren became king. The bird we now call 'The Royal Wren', 'The King of Birds', is really the goldcrest or firecrest, belonging to the family *regulidae* (Regulus regulus), to which our wren does not.

However, he is now king *de facto*—on our farthings.

62. FIELDFARES.

Flock. 'The *Fieldfare* is, like the *Redwing*, only a Visitant, making its appearance about the beginning of *October* . . . (from the) *North*, from whence it sometimes comes into *England* in prodigious *flocks*.' (RS.)

63. PTARMIGAN. See 22. Grouse.

64. STORKS.

Mustering. There is a migration of storks from Asia Minor via Cyprus every September. D. Forbes writes of his observation from near Aleppo: 'Just after dawn, storks began to appear from the Northern horizon to what looked like a pre-arranged meeting-place, first in twos and threes, gradually increasing in numbers till the air was full of them. Noisily in hundreds they circled with tremendous chattering as if discussing their plans. Suddenly after about a couple of hours a party broke away in regular formation, followed in sections by the others, until, within half an hour, not a stork was to be seen.'

N. Bagshawe writes: 'At Kyrenia we could hear their faint "*honk! honk!*" far out to sea; then they would appear, flying in the formation of the letter Y, two or three leaders, and then two long branching tails in echelon. . . . What intelligence and instinct! This was more than eighteen years ago. Habits do not change!' (*The Field*, May, June, 1937.)

65. PENGUINS.

In the Dassen Is. (near Cape of Good Hope) the penguins (black-footed) are dubbed *Jack-asses* because their cry resembles the bray of a donkey. Their nesting ground is termed a *rookery*.

NOTE ON THE WORD 'BIRD'.

It is derived from the O.E. *brid*, and its earliest meaning was 'nestlings'. Later it came to be applied to the smaller, as was *fowl* to the larger, species. In modern usage, 'fowl' is confined to wild or water-fowl and to domestic poultry.

CHAPTER XXIV

ANIMALS

TRUE Company Terms	- - - - - -	*
Terms which represent the young or progeny	- -	†
Terms which represent characteristics	- - -	‡
Terms which represent noises or cries	- - -	§
Suggested correct modern term	- - - -	*italics*

NAME	GROUP TERM Modern	GROUP TERM Original	AUTHORITY
100. Animals	a menagerie of		GT.
101. Antelopes	**herd*		N.
102. Apes	‡*shrewdness*	Schrewdenys	Eg.
		Shrewdenes	St. A.
103. Asses	*pace*	Passe	Eg.
		Pase	St. A.
	pace or herd		N.
	*drove		RJN.
104. Badgers (Grays)	*cete* (set)	Syght	Eg.
		Cete	St. A.

105. Bears	‡*sloth*	Slouthe	Eg.
		Sleuth	St. A., N.
106. Beasts	**drove*		Dig.
	*flock		GT. (1440)
107. Boars	‡singular	Synguler	Eg., St. A.
	**sounder*		N.
108. Bucks	**herd*	heerde	Harl. 1
	brace or leash		N., GT.
109. Buffaloes	**herd*		N.
110. Camels	*flock		GT.
111. Cats	**clowder*	Cloudyr	Eg.
(tame)	cluster		S.
	‡glaring	Gloryng	Harl. 1
(wild)	dout	Dovt	P.
(wild)	destruction		S.
(young)	†*kindle*	Kyndyll	St. A.
112. Cattle (Nete)	**drove*	Droffe	Eg.
		Droue	St. A.
	*drove or herd		N.
	herd or mob (Australian)		GT.
113. Chamois	**herd*		GT.
114. Colts	*rag*	Rage	Eg.
		Ragg or Rake	St. A.
115. Conies	bury	Bery	Eg., St. A.
116. Cubs (at birth)	†*litter*		GM.
117. Curs	‡*cowardice*	Cowardenys	Eg.
		Cowardnes	St. A.
118. Deer (all sorts)	**herd*	Herde	Eg., St. A.
119. Dogs	kennel		GT.
120. Elephants	**herd*		GT.
121. Elk	gang		RJN., N.
122. Ferrets	‡*business*	Besynys	Eg.
		Besynes	St. A.
123. Foxes	earth	Nerthe	Eg.
	‡*skulk*	Skolke	P.
		Skulke or Sculke	St. A.
124. Geldings	brace		GT.
125. Giraffes	**herd*		N.
126. Goats	**trip*	Tryppe	Eg.
		Trippe	St. A.
	herd or tribe		N.
	flock		GT.
127. Hares	*drove or husk	Droue or huske	Eg.
	husk or down	huske or downe	Harl. 2
	trace	Trace	P.
	**trip*	Tryppe	P.
		Trippe	St. A.
(of 2, 3,)	brace, leash		GT.
128. Harts	**herd*	Herde	Eg., St. A

129. Horses (stud)	*harras*	Harrys	Eg.
		Harasse	St. A.
	stable		CW.
130. Hounds	brace	Brasse	Eg.
	mute	Mute.	St. A.
Grey-hounds (of 2)	*brace*	Brace	St. A.
,, (of 3)	*leash*	Lesse	Eg.
		Lece	St. A.
Running Hounds (of 2)	*couple*	Couple	St. A.
Bloodhounds	*sute*	Sute	S., St. A.
Raches	kennel	Kenelle	Eg.
		Kenell	St. A.
	pack		NED., GT.
131. Kangaroos	troop		N.
132. Kine (Nete). See 112. Cattle.			
133. Leopards	‡*leap*	Lepe	Eg., St. A.
134. Lions	‡sault	Sawt	P.
	‡sowse	Sowse	Eg.
	‡*pride*	Pryde	Eg.
		Pride	St. A.
	troop or pride		N.
	*flock		GT.
135. Mares	**stud*	Stoode	Eg.
		stode	St. A.
136. Martens	‡*richness*	Riches	St. A.
137. Mice	nest		GT.
138. Moles	‡*labour*	Labyr	Eg.
		Labor	St. A.
139. Monkeys	*troup*		RJN.
		troop	N., CW.
	cartload		GT.
140. Mules	*barren*	Burdynne	Eg.
		Barrē	P.
		Baren	St. A.
	rake		GT.
141. Oxen	**team*	Teme	Harl. 1
	yoke, drove, team or herd		N.
142. Pigs	litter		CW.
143. Pups	litter		N.
144. Rabbits	†*nest*	neste	Eg.
		Nest	St. A.
145. Racehorses	field or string		N.
146. Rhinoceros	‡crash		Kenya Game Reports (modern)
147. Roes	**bevy*	Beuy	Eg., St. A.
148. Sheep	*flock*	fflocke	Eg., St. A.
	hurtle		GT.

149. Shorthorns	**herd*		GT.
150. Spaniels (of 2)	*couple*	Copylle	Eg.
		Coupull	St. A.
151. Squirrels	*dray*	Dray	NC.
152. Swine (wild)	**sounder*	Sundyr	Eg.
		Soundre	St. A.
(tame)	**drift*	Dryfte	Eg.
		Dryft	St. A.
,,	trip	trippe	MS. Digby, 182
	doylt or herd		RJN.
153. Toads	knot		GT., N.
154. Trotters (pigs)	nest, set		GT.
155. Whelps	†*litter*	Lyttur	Eg.
		Litter	St. A.
156. Wolves (wild)	**route*	Rowte	Eg.
		Route	St. A.
	pack, rout or herd		N.
157. Frogs	army		Craven Glos. 1828
158. Stoats	pack		J. W. Day
159. Tiger			
160. Otter			
161. Weasels	pack		R. Jefferies

NOTES (ANIMALS)

101. ANTELOPE.

Herd. This is the 'company' term for 'all maner der'. (See 108 and 118.)

102. APES.

Shrewdness. The word is included in seven lists, also mentioned by Randle Holme, who spells it *Swrednes*. It means wanton mischief.

Jesters, says Plato, turn at death into apes.

103. ASSES.

Pace. A company or herd of asses. (NED.)

Osbaldiston, believing it to be a company term, defines: '*Pace*, of asses, a herd or company of those beasts.' The word, actually, refers to the path or track made by asses to and from their pasturage. Cf. 114. *Rag* of colts. Hodgkin says: 'There has been more trouble in arriving at what appears to me to be the true and satisfactory explanation of this pair of terms than with any other in the series.' The original term was *Passe* (Eg.) = Passus, the place gone through. From Cotgrave we get:

> 'Les passées d'un Cerf, *His rack, or passages;*
> *the places which he has gone through or by.*'

Thus the two terms are practically synonymous, and 'probably refer to the "track" or "walk" of these particular quadrupeds to their feeding-grounds.' (PT.)

For definition of Mule and Jennet, see Chapter XXII.

104. BADGERS.

Cete (Set). The meaning of this term is doubtful. It is not a company term, as the badger is not gregarious, so that it is unlikely that the word is derived from Coetus = a meeting or assembly. Neither has the badger particularly good sight, so that the reading *syght* (Eg.) is probably an error. It is possible that the term may be the old Chaucerian word for 'city'.

Eric Parker, in *Game Pie*, refers to a *colony* of badgers and to their *set*, or underground home. This latter is probably the correct modern term, from the original *cete*. (A company of badgers. NED.)

The badger's hair, next the root, is of a dirty yellowish white, the middle is black, and the extremity grey, hence arose the old saying: 'as grey as a Badger'. In all the lists (nine) in which he appears, he is called a *Gray*, e.g. 'a *Cety* of *greyes*' (S.).

The badger was once divided by naturalists into the Swine-badger and the Dog-badger, but Buffon remarks that the badger not only admits of no varieties, but does not even approach to any other species. (See Chapter IX. Vermin.)

105. BEARS.

Sloth. This word, spelt in many ways (e.g. *Slothe* (P.), *Slewthe* (St. A., 1496), *Slouth*, etc.), comes from the A.S., means 'slowness', and refers to their characteristic amble. It has nothing to do with 'sleuth' (Ice., *sloth*, a trail), as applied to hounds. Osbaldiston defines '*Slought, hunting term*, a herd, or company, of some sort of wild beasts, as a slought of bears'. This is the only reference to *slought*, and it looks as if he has muddled the word with the original *Slouthe*. (See Chapter III.)

106. BEASTS.

Flock. The popular company term, generally used for Sheep.

107. BOARS.

Singular.

'And when he is of .iiij. yere . . .
From the *Sounder* of the swyne then dep*ar*trith he.
A *synguler* is he so: for a lone will he go.' (St. A.)

From this it is evident that a singular is one boar, upwards of four years old, and the expression seems to be incorrect, though given by twelve authorities. The proper company term is *sounder*. (See 152. Swine, and Chapter III.)

Sounder. (See 152. Swine.)

108. BUCKS.

Herd. The term Herd is applied to Deer, All Manner of Deer, Bucks, Harts; to Cranes, Curlews, Swans and Wrens; and to Harlots. For definition of *Herds*, *Bevies*, etc., see Chapter II; the names for different-sized herds are also given in Chapter II. (See also 118. Deer.)

111. CATS.

Clouder. Obs. var. *Cludder*, a crowd, heap, cluster. (NED.)

'*Clouder* is probably the same word as *clutter*, and is evidently the proper term to be used for "a lot of cats".' (PT.) Eg., after 'a *Cloudyr* of Cattys', adds 'non dicitur a *clouster*' (or cluster); this latter variation is only given in the 'S.' list.

Glaring. 'This is evidently the proper term to use of a cat's eyes shining in the dark.' (PT.)

Dovt. = Do-out, and means a 'destruction'.

Kindle. A *brood* or *litter* of kittens. (NED.)

Randle Holme, wrongly, gives: 'a *Kindle*, or a Wauling of Cats', and Strutt, for some reason, has altered the word to *kendel*. (For Wild Cat, see Chapter IX, Vermin.) (See also Chapter XXVI, No. 34.)

112. CATTLE.

Drove. A number of animals, driven or moving along in a body (s.v. Drift). (NED.)

114. COLTS.

Rag. An alleged name for a 'company of colts', from Ragged, A. 1. (NED.)

Os. gives '*Rag* or *Rake*, a company or herd of young colts'. The word does not appear to have anything to do with 'ragged', nor with the A.N. *ragerie* = wantonness (from which 'a *rage* of Maydenys' is derived). The alternative form was *Rake*, 'the extent of a walk or course' (Brockett's *Glossary*, 1829), and the modern spelling might be *Rack*, expressing the same meaning as the word *Pace* for asses. (See 103, and Chapter XXII.)

115. CONIES.

Bury. Hodgkin says: 'A *bury* or *burrow* of conies, i.e. a rabbit's burrow. It does not mean a herd of conies (Halliwell) or a company of rabbits (NED.). It is the proper term for its dwelling-place or home.'

'Two Conies are called a *couple*, and three are called a *couple & a halfe* of Conies. If they be many feeding out togethers, we say it is a *fayre game* of Conies.' (T.) RH. gives the same information—'. . . if more a *Game* of Conyes.'

Originally a *Coney* was the name for a full-grown rabbit. (See 144. Rabbits.)

116. CUBS.

Litter. The whole number of young brought forth at a birth. (NED.)

The only other list which contains this phrase is given in *The Gentleman's Recreation* (NC.). G. Turberville says that 'For Fox, Badgerd and other such vermine . . . their encrease is called A *lytter*'.

'Just as the term "*kindle*" was also applied to hares and rabbits (which are also called "*puss*") so the term "*litter*" was applied to the young of the fox, of which the male is known as the *dog-fox*.' (PT.) (See Chapter XX. Mating.)

117. CURS.

Cowardice. Applied to a company of curs. (NED.)

This term refers literally to their chief characteristic.

118. Deer.

Herd. A company of animals of any kind, feeding or travelling in company. (NED.)

'A *Herd* of all maner der' is the earliest example, and a similar expression is given in some thirteen lists. E.g. 'A *Heard* . . . of all other sorts of Deer' (NC.). (See 108. Bucks.)

In modern times the term *herd* is applied to many other companies of beasts, as: antelopes, buffaloes, cattle, chamois, elephants, giraffes, swine. (See Chapter II, 'All Maenr Dere'.)

119. Dogs.

Kennel. A *pack* of hounds, or of dogs of any kind. (NED.)

(See 130. Raches, and Chapter IV.)

Dingo. Australian wild dog.

120. Elephants.

Herd. (See 118. Deer.)

122. Ferrets.

Business. A company of ferrets. (NED.)

The term obviously describes the ferret's relentless method of work. Two misprints are interesting:

fesynes (Str.);
fesnyng (N.).

Coping a ferret = Tying string round its mouth so that it cannot bite and kill the rabbit. A ferret is said to *lay-up* when it remains a long time in a hole.

(Terms for Male and Female are given in Chapter XII.)

123. Foxes.

Earth. The hole or hiding-place of a burrowing animal, as a badger or fox, etc. Also fig. (NED.)

This word only appears in the Eg. and Pork. MSS., and the 'S.' list, the spelling in the last two cases being *erthe*. Here is the origin of our correct term for a fox's hole.

Skulk. In the Pork. MS. the following three terms occur together:

'a *Skolke* of freris/
a *Skolke* of thewys/
a *Skolke* of foxys/'

It is clear, therefore, that the word is not a company term, and refers to Reynard's stealthy prowling around the hen-roosts. The fox is not a gregarious animal.

'2 a *Brase*, 3 a *Lease*, more a *Litter* or *Stalke*.' (RH.)

The latter word, of course, is quite incorrect; 'stalk' is applied to Foresters.

'When a fox has young ones in her, they say she is *with cub*.' (*The Sportsman's Dictionary*, by H. J. Pyc, 1807.)

(See 116. Cubs, and Chapter IV.)

In the North a fox was called *Tod*.

124. GELDINGS.

Brace. A pair; a couple; a. orig. of dogs. (NED.) (See Chapter XXII.)

126. GOATS.

Trip. This term is given by no less than eighteen authorities. The word, a true company term, is also used for hares, swine (two MSS. only) and sheep (Ray), *q.v.* Its origin is doubtful: various suggestions have been made, e.g. from Icel. *thyrpa* or *thrypa*, from *tyrfa* = a flock, or it may be a corruption of 'tribe', which rendering is given by Strutt. Cf. 148. Sheep. RH. gives both 'a *Tripp* of Goates' and 'Wilde Goates an *Heard*'. (See also Chapter XXVI, No. 34.)

There is a great variety in the spelling of the word for goats; *gete*, *geete*, *geates*, *gayte*, *gait*, *goete*, *gotes* and *goates*. 'As a matter of fact, *geet* is the plural of *goat*, as teeth of tooth' (PT.), and Turberville further explains: 'Then the Goats part from the female (which are called *Geats*, and the buckes *Goats*) and the Geats draw neare to some little brooke or water to fawne, & to abide there all the somer.' (*The Book of Hunting*, 1611.)

Flock. Now commonly used, but *Trip* (or perhaps *Tribe*) appears to be the proper term.

127. HARES.

Husk. According to Strutt, an old name for a company of hares. (NED.)

Down. Hodgkin says: 'There seems to be some confusion in these terms: *a Drove* might refer to a company of hares when "driven", for this form of hunting was in vogue at this period; of *huske* nothing can be said with certainty—Dr. Bradley suspects some scribal error, which the later lists have copied. *Dunne*, *downe*, or *don* suggest comparison with the word *donie*, a hare, which Jamieson gives, which is possibly from the adj. *dun*.'

Trace. Found, besides, only in the 'S.' list, where it is spelt *Trase*. The word refers to the hare's footprint in the snow: 'Also in time of snow we say the *trace* of an Hare.' (Turberville, 1611.) *Trace* was later used as an active verb (e.g. in 'The Mourning of the Hare', Pork. MS., *temp*. Edward IV). (See Chapter XIV, Footprints.)

Trip. A herd or company of hares. (PT.) (See 126. Goats.)

R. Holme gives 'an *Herd* of Hares', but he has merely copied misprints for Herd of Hartes in two lists.

Brace, *Leash*. '2 a *Brase*, 3 a *Lease*, or *Brase & halfe*' (RH.), which agrees with Turberville's directions. (See 116. Cubs, and Chapter I, III and V.)

An interesting note (by AM.) states that when there are several *leverets* at a birth, they are invariably marked with a star on the forehead, and when there is but one it never has this mark.

129. HORSES.

Harras. An enclosure or establishment in which horses and mares are kept for breeding: hence a stud breed, or race of horses. (NED.)

Hara (Latin) was originally a pigsty. The word has been spelt in a variety of ways, mostly with two 'r's'.

In the Eg. MS. occurs: 'a *Stalyn* of olde Hors'. The word seems to be a variation of the old word *stalon* or *stalan* for 'stallion', and 'is a proper term to be used when speaking of an *olde Hors*. This seems to me to be a preferable interpretation to the participle of the verb "to stale", which applies as much to young horses as to old.' (PT.).

For the Colours and Descriptions of Horses and Glossary of Connected Terms, see Chapter XXII.

130. Hounds.

Brace. This term was originally used of dogs.

Leash. A set of three. (NED.)

Spelt in many different ways in the lists: *Lesse*, *Leys*, *Lees*, *Lece*, *Lese*, *Lease*.

Couple. A *brace* of dogs used for hunting, especially harriers or spaniels. (NED.)

Turberville lays down 'The difference betweene hounds and Greyhoundes for termes', i.e.

Greyhounds: 2 = a *brace*, 3 = a *leash*.
Hounds: 2 = a *couple*, 3 = a *couple and a half*.

The full quotation is given in Chapter IV, *q.v.*

RH. adds; '16 a *Kennell* of Hounds, or a *Mute*:
20 a large *Kennell*.'

Mute. A pack of hounds (quotes St. A. and RH. (as above)). (NED.) Strutt says; 'a *mute* of hounds for a number'.

(See also under Kennel.) (O. Fr. *meute* = pack or kennel.)

'. . . mute de chiens est quant il ya douze chiens courans et ung limier et se moyns en ya elle nest pas dite mute . . .' (*Le Roy Modus*, by A. Neyret, 1486.)

Kennel. A pack of hounds, or of dogs of any kind. (NED.)

Sherwood (1650) says; 'A *kennell* of hounds. Meute de chiens, mute de chiens,' and the *Boke of Hunting* (1611) gives 'The *Kennell* or lodging for the hounds'.

The term evidently came to be, 'in a metaphorical sense, used for the pack of hounds itself.' (Os.) 'In true sporting phraseology it is a *kennel* of foxhounds—a *pack* being thought more appropriate to harriers.' (Blaine.)

Sute. The full expression is a '*sute* of a *lyam*', which Hodgkin says means the 'following' (*suite*) of a led hound.

'Hounde made to the *suyte*, called a bloude-hounde, *odorator*, odoriferous.' (Huloet, 1552.)

'*Limiers*. Chiens qui ne parlent point.' (*La Venerie de Iaque du Foüilloux*, 1561.)

A *liam* was a rope made of silk or leather by which hounds were led.

Two items from the *Book of Hunting* (1611) give further light on the phrase:

'And to every one of these you may give two couples of hounds to lead in *lyames*.'

'Then take my Hound, in *liam* me behind.'
(The Blazon pronounced by the Huntsman.)
Pack. The modern company term for *mute* or *kennell.*
(For Hounds, see Chapter IV.)

131. KANGAROOS.

Troop. Used also, sometimes, for Lions and Monkeys.

133. LEOPARDS.

Leap. An alleged name for a company of leopards. (NED.)

This term, and the *sawt* and *sowse* of a 'lyon', 'are only specific variations for the same thing, namely, jumping on to the prey by these animals. The *leap* is probably only inserted here for the sake of the alliteration.' (PT.)

Topsell quotes: 'Panther, commonly called a *Pardal*, a Leopard, and a *Libbard.*' (See App. III.)

The Jaguar (as opposed to a leopard) has a central black dot in the rosette-shaped spots.

134. LIONS.

Sawt. Only given in the Pork. MS. It is the same word as the 'sault' (Old French = leap) in 'assault', Fr. *sauter*, Lat. *saltare.* (See 133. Leopards.)

Sowse. Only found in the Eg. MS. 'To leape or seaze greedily upon, to *souze* doune as a hauke' (Florio, 1611).

It is the same word as the hawking term (at) *souce* or *souse.*

Pride. Supposed to be the chief attribute of lions:

'lyons orgueilleux . . .' (Phoebus).

'Many desire to foote it with a grace,
Or Lion-like to walke maiesticall.'

(J. Lane, *Tom Tel-Troths Message*, 1600)

Pride would appear to be the usual, and best, term.

135. MARES.

Stud. Admittedly a collective term. In Danish the word is *stot.* A collection of mares for breeding purposes. (See Chapters XXII, and XXVI, No. 34.) Hence our *stud farms.*

136. MARTENS.

Richness. This is probably an allusion to the marten's valuable skin: 'the *firre-Martin* is most excellent, for princes and great Nobles are clothed therwith . . . the saying of *Martiall, Venator capta Marte superbus adest*, Heere commeth the proud hunter that hath killed a Martin . . .' (Topsell, *Fourefooted Beasts*, 1607.)

'There are three kinds of vermin in law: a marten; a beaver; and an *ermine.*' (Old Welsh Laws, tenth century.) (See Chapter IX, Vermin.)

There is a great variety of spelling for both *rychesse* and *martrones.* Allde misprints 'a Riches of Matrons', copied by Helme (1614), which 'shows how little the meanings of phrases were grasped'. (PT.) Strutt gives 'a richess of martins', which may be the origin of a later confusion by some writers who referred the term to the bird 'martin', instead of the animal 'marten'.

138. Moles.

Labour. An alleged term for a company of moles. (NED.)

The term refers to their characteristic industry:

> 'The field-mouse builds her garner under ground,
> For gather'd grain the blind *laborious mole*
> In winding mazes works her hidden hole.'
>
> (Dryden's Virgil, *Georgics*, Bk. i)

(See Chapter IX, Vermin.) '*Moeles*, a *Labour*.' (RH.)

140. Mules.

Barren. Specific term for a drove of mules. (NED.)

(The word is spelt with only one 'r' in all but one list.)

Halliwell in his dictionary says; '*Barren*, a company of mules.'

'The Egerton MS. has the probable original reading, "a *Burdynne* of Mulysse", and as mules are not infrequently described as burthen-bearing ("No burthen-bearing mules", Peacham's *Compleat Gentleman*, 1634 . . . Repr., 1906), it is possible that *barren* or *baren* may be a corruption of the word *berynge* (bearing), with a *double entendre*, suggested by the *barrenness* of mules. The word *burdynne* itself may, indeed, have a quasi-punning reference to the Latin word *burdo*, which is the name of the offspring of a horse and a she-ass, whereas a *mule* proper is derived from a jackass and a mare.' (PT.) (See Chapter XXII.)

Rake. Only given by GT. It is properly applied to colts, *q.v.* 114.

141. Oxen.

Team. Hodgkin says: 'A *team* of horses (or oxen) is properly a string of horses drawing a plough or wagon. For Statute-duty, in a team two oxen or horned cattle were to be considered as equal to one horse. (See *Farmer's Lawyer*, 1774.)'

Yoke. A piece of timber, hollowed or made curving near each end, and fitted with bows for receiving the necks of oxen, by means of which two are connected for drawing; a pair that work together. (N.)

2 a *Yoke*, 3 a *Yoke & a halfe*. Some say a *pair* of Oxen or *Bullocks*. *Cows*, & *Oxen*, a *Drove*.' (RH.)

A strip of ox-hide rendered pliable is called a *Reim*. An old name for the wild ox was *bugle*.

142. Pigs.

Farrow. An O.E. term for a *litter* of pigs. (See Chapter XX.)

144. Rabbits.

Nest. A number of birds, insects, or other animals occupying the same habitation. A brood, swarm, colony. (NED.)

'The nest refers to the comfortable place the doe has prepared for her young in the burrow.

'Formerly a *rabet* was called such until a year old, when it became a *coning* or *coney*. This distinction is now lost.' (PT.)

The nest burrow is now often termed the *stop*.

Harling a rabbit 'is done by passing the blade of the knife between the bone of the thigh and the great sinew—where there is nothing but skin—and then thrusting the other foot through the hole thus made. The hare or rabbit can then be conveniently . . . slung on a stick.' (Richard Jefferies.)

'The doe', says Osbaldiston, 'goes with young 30 days, and then she *kindles*; and if she take not buck presently she loses her month, or at least a fortnight, and often kills her young and eats them. . . . The does cannot suckle their young till they have been *at buck* again.' (See Coney, 115.)

'Four kinds are acknowledged among dealers and fanciers—*warreners*, *packers*, *hedgehogs*, and *sweethearts*. The latter are the tame varieties.' (Blaine.)

Rabbits are born undergound, naked and blind; *leverets* at birth are laid in a *form*, are clothed in fur, and their eyes are open.

145. Racehorses.

Field. The horses in a race other than the favourite. (N.)

Though this may be technically correct, the term is commonly used to mean *all* the horses in a race.

String. Probably from the meaning 'a line of things'.

147. Roes.

Bevy. The proper term for a company of maidens, or ladies, of roes, of quails, or of larks. (NED.)

Found in twenty-one lists, but it should be noted that there is no mention in any of them of a '*bevy* of maidens', the old term for whom is *rage*. (See Appendix I.) This is a true company term. Its derivation is uncertain. (Perhaps from the Italian *bevere* = drinking?) (See Chapter II.)

148. Sheep.

Flock. A company term. Ray (1674) gives 'A *Trip* of Sheep, i.e. a few sheep (*Norf.*).' (Cf. 126. Goats.)

150. Spaniels.

Couple. (See 130. Hounds, and Chapter IV.) Strutt gives: 'a *couple* of Spaniels or harriers'.

151. Squirrels.

Dray. Given by Os. and NC. = the young of squirrels, but earlier authorities use the term as meaning 'nest'. 'A *Draye* or *Drey* of Squirrels.' (Topsell's *Foure-footed Beastes*, 1607), and 'A Squirrels *Dray*'. (NC.)

'In the summer time they build them nests (which in our countrey are called *Drayes*) in the tops of the Trees, very artificially of stickes and mosse, and such other things as woods do affoord them.' (Topsell.)

Daniel, describing the pine 'Martin', says 'in Scotland it is the only kind of Martin, wher it inhabits the Fir forests, frequently usurping the *Drays* or nest of the Squirrel . . .'

The squirrel derives its name from the form of its tail, which serves as an umbrella (*okia*, a shade).

152. SWINE.

Sounder. This word is the O.E. *sunor* = herd; adopted into Norman French it became *soundre*. Norman French is the main source of our old hunting terms.

The term was not originally restricted to wild swine, but as it 'became obsolete except as a hunter's word, it came to mean a herd of wild and not tame swine' (PT.). (See also Chapter XXVI, No. 34.)

'*Swine*. 12 makes an *Heard*, or a *Sounder*, a *Scoure*, or a *Singuler*.' (RH.) (Cf. 107. Boars, and Chapter III.)

Drift. (See NED., definition under 112. Drove.)

DRYFTE, or *drywynge* of bestys. . . . (Wright's *Voc.*, 1857). In *Bishop Hall's Contemplations* the term is applied to birds as well as to cattle: 'he that brought *armies* of frogs and caterpillars to Egypt can as well bring whole *drifts* of birds and beasts to the desart.' (Craven, *Glossary*, 1828.)

Trip. See 126. Goats.

153. TOADS.

Knot. A cluster; a collection. (N.)

156. WOLVES.

Route. This term is included in twenty lists, the earliest (Eg.) giving 'a *Rowte* of wylde wolfys'.

> 'And a *Rowte* of wolues where thay passin inne
> So shall ye hem call as many as thay bene.' (St. A.)

G. Turberville in his *Boke of Hunting*, 1575, says that 'the same number (as of Swyne) serueth for a *route* of Wolues'; 'but this', says Hodgkin, 'is only because he has misread the passage in *The Booke of St. Albans*, which defines subsequently the sizes of Sounders . . . "a *Route* of Wolues" is just as many as happen to be in the pack.' '12 makes a *Route*: some say 6 makes a *Rout* or *Rowte*.' (RH.) Sometimes *Route* was used for wolves advancing; *Pack*, when they were running away.

The original meaning of this term is doubtful, but it is probable that it meant 'travelling' and not 'assemblage'.

(See Appendix I, Note 1, and Appendix III.)

For the hunting of the Wolf, see Chapter III.

157. FROGS.

Army. (See quotation from *Bishop Hall's Contemplations*, under 152. Swine (drift).) In New York State a bull-frog is called *Irish nightingale*.

159. TIGERS.

There was no company term for tigers; they do not herd. Derivation is from the archaic Persian word *tigra* = swift as a javelin.

160. OTTER.

The term *bevy* was used by Halliwell. (See Chapter V.)

CHAPTER XXV

FISHES AND INSECTS

True Company Terms - - - - - -	*
Terms which represent the young or progeny - -	†
Terms which represent characteristics - - -	‡
Terms which represent noises or cries - - -	§
Suggested correct modern term - - - - -	*italics*

FISHES
(and all that swim in the sea)

Name		Group Term		Authority
200. Eels	a	**swarm* of		RS.
201. Fishes		*school or *shoal	(Skoue)	P.
			(Scoll)	St. A.
		**shoal* or draught:		
		haul, run or catch:		N.
		aquarium, cran, flock		GT.
(of 3)		*leash*		RS.

202. Herrings	army, *shoal	RS.
	*shoal, glean, *cran*	N.
203. Mackerel	*shoal	
204. Minnows	**shoal*	RS.
205. Perch	pack	GT. (only)
	**shoal*	RS.
206. Pilchards	**shoal*	N., RS.
207. Porpoises[1]	**school*, gam	N.
	*school, herd	GT.
208. Roach	**shoal*	RS.
209. Sardines	family	C.W. (only)
210. Seals[1]	*herd, *pod*	N.
211. Smelts	*quantity*	RS.
212. Sticklebacks	**shoal*	RS.
213. Whales[1]	*school, *gam*, pod	N.
(sperm)	*herd	GT.
214. Whiting	pod	N., CW.
215. Dogfish	*troop*	RS.
216. Jellyfishes	*smuck*	N.
217. Trout	*hover*	See Ch. VII
218. Turtles	bale	*Word Lore*, vol. iii, 1928

NOTES (FISHES)

200. EELS.

Swarm. '. . . immense *swarms* of young Eels . . .' (RS., vol. ii, 1807, p. 546), and, referring to eels (p. 547): '. . . such multitudes of Fishes. . . .'

Eels go to the sea to *spawn*, and their young are known as *fry*. (See Chapter VII, Elver.)

'Give *Eels* and no Wine to your Enemies.' (Italian proverb.)

A *stick* of eels = 25 eels strung on a row, and ten *sticks* make a *bind*.

201. FISHES.

School. Hodgkin writes; 'A *Skoue* is evidently a North Country writing for "*scole*", or "*school*", or "*shoal*". One still speaks of a *school* of porpoises, but a *shoal* of fish, though the words appear to be identical. Possibly this *scole of fysshe* is in the lists as being of the same sound but of different meaning and origin to the *scole of scolers*. Anyway it is a company term.' (See also Chapter XXVI, No. 34.)

Other variations in spelling are: *scull* and *scale*.

Draught. This is simply the quantity of fish taken in a net by drawing.

Haul = what is caught in a net.

Run. Refers probably to the 'flow' of a lot of fishes.

Catch. This term explains itself.

[1] Mammals.

Aquarium. Should only be used to refer to the tank or tanks containing (plants or) fishes.

Cran. A measure for fresh herrings containing 37½ gallons, or about 800 herrings; as many as will fill a barrel (Scots.). (N.)

Flock. Generally only used for an assemblage of birds or small animals (and sheep).

202. HERRINGS.

Army. Rev. Daniel says: 'Herrings are in the greatest abundance in the highest *Northern* latitudes. . . . This mighty *Army* begins to put itself in motion from the Icy sea early in the Spring; this body is distinguished by that name, for the word Herring is derived from the *German Heer*, an Army, to express their number, which is so vast, that were all the Men in the World to be loaded with Herrings, they could not carry the *thousandth* part away.' Cf. also the old Icelandic word *haringr* (= a Troop).

Shoal. 'The Herring is always found in *Shoals* . . .' (RS.)

Glean. This refers to the quantity of fish gathered.

Cran. See 201.

'A *hand* (5) of oranges or herrings' and 'a *mease* of herrings' (*Word Lore*, vol. iii, 1928).

203. MACKEREL.

Shoal. An actual example of the use of the word has not been discovered, but they are described as 'Gregarious fish'. (RS.)

204. MINNOWS.

Shoal. 'This beautiful fish abounds in many of our small gravelly streams, where they keep in *shoals*: it is sometimes called the *Pink* . . .' (RS.)

205. PERCH.

Shoal. They 'have one particularity, which is contrary to the Nature of all fish of Prey in *fresh* water (and they are so voracious as to attack their own kind), that they are gregarious, swimming in *Shoals*'. (RS.)

The Germans have this proverb: More wholesome than a *Perch* of Rhine.

206. PILCHARDS.

Shoal. Rev. Daniel says that 'Of all migrating fish, the *Herring* and the *Pilchard* take the most adventurous Voyages. . . . About the middle of *July*, the *Pilchards* in vast *Shoals* approach the *Cornish* coasts. . . .'

207. PORPOISES.

Gam. This term is more correctly used of whales, *q.v.*

208. ROACH.

Shoal. The roach is a gregarious fish, 'keeping in large shoals. . . . It is so *silly* a fish that it has acquired the name of the *water Sheep*, in contra distinction to the *Carp*, who, for his Subtlety, is termed the *water Fox* (cf. Chapter VII, *River Fox* (= Carp)). The proverb of "*Sound as a Roach*" appears to be not peculiar to this Country; the

French have the same idea, who compare people of strong Health to their *Gardon*, our *Roach*, and yet this fish is not more distinguished for its *vivacity* than many others.' (RS.)

210. Seals.

Pod. A shoal of whales or seals. (N.)

They assemble each year from June to September on two islands in the Bering Sea. The part occupied by the bachelor seals is termed the *hauling ground*.

The Seal was known as the *Sea-calf* or *Seoile* (the *Sea-horse* was the Walrus).

Only two seals breed on the shores of Britain—the Common Seal which breeds in the summer, and the Great Grey or Atlantic Seal which waits for the autumn.

211. Smelts.

Quantity. Walton mentions that, one August, such vast *quantities* of smelts came up the Thames that Women and Children became Anglers for them.

'The smelt derives its name from having, in the opinion of some, the Scent of a *Violet*; of others, that of a *Cucumber*; and so strange is the disagreement respecting the Smell of this fish, that the *Germans* (says Mr. Pennant) distinguish it by the very elegant title of the *Stinck-fish*; the name of *Sparling*, which it bears in Wales, and in the north of England, is taken from the French *Eperlan*.' (RS.)

212. Sticklebacks.

Shoal. '*Banstickle*, or *Sharpling*', says Rev. Daniel, 'is the smallest fish in this Country, and is called by these several names in different parts of it; . . . is obliged to *colonize* . . . there are amazing *shoals*, that come up that River (the Welland) in form of a vast Column.'

213. Whales.

Gam. A school of whales. (N.) Sometimes *pod* is used of a small number; *shool* or *herd* of a large number.

The most important whales now are the blue whale and the fin whale, both harmless. The 'blue' is the largest 'animal' in the world, and when fully grown is about thirty times as heavy as an adult elephant. In the palmy days of whaling the sperm whale or *cachalot* and the whalebone or *baleen* whales were highly esteemed. The *narwhal* is a small whale called the *sea unicorn*. The pilot or *Ca'aing* whales, found near the Shetland Islands, are often termed *black-fish*. (See Chapter VII.)

214. Whiting.

Pod. This term is generally used of seals (or whales).

ADDITIONAL NOTES

Other fishes to which the term *shoal* is applied by Rev. Daniel are: bream, carp, flounders, gugdeon, mullets and sturgeon. He also states that 'Of the *Sea* fishes, the *Cod*, *Ling*, *Haddock*, *Herring*, *Pilchard*,

Sprat, and *Sparling*, or *Smelt*, are the most remarkable for assembling in immense *Shoals*'.

RS. in this section refers to vol. ii (1807) of *Rural Sports*.

For all Fishing Terms see Chapter VII, Fishing.

215. DOGFISH.

Troop. 'The Dog-fish, which in vast *troops* assiduously attend the Herrings wherever they go . . .' (RS.)

Dogfish comprise several species of small sharks, so called from following their prey in packs like dogs. (N.)

216. JELLYFISHES.

Smuck. N. defines this as 'a crowd of jellyfishes'.

218. TURTLES.

Bale. Has this come from 'a *dule* of turtles'? (See Chapter XXIII, No. 13, Doves.)

INSECTS

NAME		GROUP TERM		AUTHORITY
300. BEES	a	*swarm of	Swarme	Eg., St. A., N.
		grist		N. (only)
(around queen)		cluster		GT. (only)
301. Caterpillars		army		Craven Glos.
302. FLIES		‡*business*	Besynes	S. (only)
		business, cloud, *swarm		GT.
		*swarm, grist		N.
303. GNATS		**swarm*, cloud		N.
304. Grasshoppers		cloud		GT.
305. Insects		*swarm		N.
306. Lice		*flock	Flock	S. (only)
307. Locusts		*swarm		RS.
		cloud, plague		GT.
308. Wasps		†*nest*		CW.
309. Snakes (young)		bed		?
310. Ants		†nest		?

NOTES (INSECTS)

300. BEES.

Swarm. 'A *Swearm* Of Bees, Wasps, and such like Insects.' (RH.)

'This may be taken as a company term, for one bee cannot swarm by itself, unless it be like Lord Dundreary, who "flocked in a corner" all by himself.' (PT.)

Grist. Lit = provision (A.S.).

Cluster. It has the same meaning as *bunch*. Applied usually to inanimate objects, e.g. grapes, nuts; but also to 'tame cattes', and to churls. The male of the honey-bee is called a *drone*.

301. Caterpillars.

Army. See the quotation from *Bishop Hall's Contemplations* under No. 152. Drift.

302. Flies.

Business. Hodgkin says 'the term is to be taken literally, as *one* blue-bottle can be quite busy enough without the assistance of any of his fellows'. (Cf. Ferrets, No. 122, Notes.)

Cloud. A great multitude. (N.)

Hatch is used of a swarm of mayfly on the water.

303. Gnats.

Swarm. (See under 300. Bees.)

The word is used for a large number or body of small animals, insects or people, particularly when in motion.

306. Lice.

Flock. The expression only occurs in the same list (S.) as contains 'a *Besynes* of flyes'.

307. Locusts.

Plague. Anything troublesome or vexatious. (N.)

308. Wasps.

Nest. For definition, see 144. Rabbits.

SUMMARY

1. Of the old group terms for Beasts and Birds, Fishes and Insects (but excluding Persons), only the following can be considered to be 'Proper termes when they are in Companyes':

Herd	*Drift*	*Stud*	
Bevy	*Sounder*	*Congregation*	
Trip	*Route*	*Host*	
Drove	*Clowder*	*Swarm*	
Flock	*Pack*	*School* or *Shoal*	(15)

2. In addition, there are some terms which, though they originally had a restricted meaning, may still be classed as true collectives:

Brace (for 2)	*Kennel*	*Brood*	
Lease (for 3)	*Mute*	*Covert*	
Couple (for 2)	*Litter*	*Covey*	
Team	*Kindle*	*Nye*	(12)

3. Two terms were possibly so used:

Gaggle, and *sord* or *sute*. (2)

4. The rest of the old terms were incorrectly interpreted (see Chapter XXVII), though many of them have become 'correct' through long use, e.g. *charm*, *pride*, *wisp*, *drey*, *spring*, etc.

5. Of the more modern terms, some examples are:

Band, *Company*, *Troop*, *Skein*, *Hatch*.

PART IV

BIBLIOGRAPHY

'No one can get the highest enjoyment out of sport unless he can live over again in the library the keen pleasure he experienced in the wilderness.'

THEODORE ROOSEVELT

CHAPTER XXVI

THE AUTHORITIES

THE EARLIEST TREATISES ON THE CHASE

THE CLASSICS of Venery come from France, and are the original authorities on hunting terms and ceremonies. From these famous works authors of many nationalities borrowed freely for several centuries.

1. *Le Art de Venerie.* By William Twici. c. 1323.

This is the oldest-known treatise on hunting in England. Written or dictated in Norman French by King Edward II's huntsman, Master W. Twici (or Twety). Reprinted 1843 by Sir Henry Dryden, whose Notes are most scholarly and instructive.

Twici was in receipt of a daily wage of 7½d.

The names of animals to be pursued he gives as: Beasts for hunting—hare, hart, wolf, wild boar; Beasts of chase—buck, doe, fox, martin, roe; Beasts for 'greate dysporte'—grey or badger, wild-cat, otter. (Cf. Chapter I.)

2. *Le Livre du Roy Modus et de la Royne Racio.* (Author unknown.) 14th century.

Known shortly as *Roy Modus*, it is the earliest prose work on the chase in the French language. The portion on sport was written between 1328 and 1338, and the whole work printed in 1486.

The word Modus means 'method', and Racio 'reason'.

3. *Livre de Chasse.* By Gaston de Foix. 1387.

This work, shortly called *Gaston Phoebus*, is perhaps the most famous hunting book of all times. Gaston copied much from the chapters on stag-hunting in *Roy Modus*.

4. *The Master of Game.* By Edward, Duke of York. *c.* 1410.

This is the oldest work on the chase in the English language. The author was first cousin to Henry IV, at whose court he was Master of Game. All but five of the thirty-six chapters are a translation of *Gaston Phoebus*. The book was published in a beautiful edition in 1904 by Messrs. Baillie-Grohman, with exhaustive notes and a valuable appendix on hunting terms.

(The numbers in brackets refer to the number of company terms given in each list.)

MSS.

5. *Egerton MS.* 1995 (106) c. 1452, Eg.
6. *Porkington MS.* 10 (109) 15th century, P.
7. *Harley MS.* 541 (48) ,, Harl. 1.
8. *Harley MS.* 2340 (45) ,, Harl. 2.
9. *Addl. MS.* 33,994 (10), a fragment ,, Add.
10. *Robert of Gloucester MS.*, College of Arms (50) ,, RG.
11. *Digby MS.* 196, Bodleian Library (50) ,, Dig.

(Of all the seven MSS. shown, the Egerton is probably the oldest.)

PRINTED BOOKS

12. *The Hors, Shepe, & the Ghoos* (Caxton) (106) c. 1476, S.

Reprinted by Sir Mark Masterman Sykes, 1822.

There exists a solitary proof-sheet of the last page of Caxton's edition of *The Book of Curtesye*: this sheet (called the *Lytell John* list (15)) is practically identical with the last fifteen terms in the 'S.' list.

13. *The Book of St. Albans* (164). By Dame Juliana Barnes. 1486, St. A.

Contains a most interesting and comprehensive list; in view of its importance a further note on the Book will be found in Chapter XXVII, together with the full list of the terms.

14. *The Book of Hunting*. By George Turberville. 1575, T.

In spite of his claim to authority, practically the whole of his work is copied from Du Fouilloux's famous *Venerie*, which appeared about fifteen years earlier.

Spelling very inconsistent; 2nd edition printed 1611.

15. *The Book of Hawking, Huntyng, etc.* (159). By Edward Allde. 1586, All.

This is one of the many reprints of *The Book of St. Albans*. Iohn Helme, in his *Ievvell for Gentrie*, 1614, copied Allde's list.

16. *A Short Treatise of Hunting*. By Sir Thomas Cockaine. 1591. CK.

(Recent editions, 1897 and 1932.)

A charming little book, 'compyled for the delight of Noblemen and Gentlemen'; it contains hints from the author's own experience, and does not include any of the copious copyings from previous works, so common among the sporting writers of the Middle Ages.

17. *The Gentleman's Academie* (6). By Gervase Markham. 1595, GM.

'OR *The Booke of S. Albans*: . . . And now reduced into a better method.' (See Chapter XVI.)

18. *The Gentleman's Recreation.* By Nicholas Cox. 1674, NC.

This book was at first a great success. It ran through five more editions in Cox's lifetime, the last appearing in 1721. Richard Blome's folio edition appeared in 1686. The fourth edition (much enlarged) was reprinted in 1928 by the Cresset Press. Cox seems to have been a good sportsman, but a poor naturalist; his popular work, in spite of many 'errours', contains much valuable information, and is very good reading.

19. *The Academy of Armory and Blazon.* By Randle Holme. 1688, RH.

A great deal of information is given, but much of it is inaccurate. 'His supreme effort (is) "a *Flight* of Stares" amongst the birds. He has evidently recalled the expression of "a Flight of *Stairs* or Steps", has confused it with *stares*, starlings, and included it as a company term.' (PT.)

20. *British Sportsmen.* By Osbaldiston. 1785, Os.

A most interesting and detailed work in the form of a dictionary. Under RACING AND HUNTING and SHOOTING TERMS are to be found most of the technical terms applicable to our subject. In 1807 was published *The Sportsman's Dictionary*, by H. J. Pye; in method and scope it is very similar to Osbaldiston's work.

21. *Rural Sports* (58). By Rev. W. B. Daniel. 1801, RS.

Dedicated to Strutt (No. 17). Contents cover most of the beasts of forest and chase, Game Birds, Wild Fowl, Fishing, Shooting and Hunting Terms in general. A standard work that combines 'entertainment with instruction'.

22. *The Sports and Pastimes of the People of England* (58). By Joseph Strutt. 1801, Str.

Strutt was an accomplished engraver, artist, pioneer antiquary, and a distinguished author. He was the foster parent of the Waverley Novels. His book is an able study, full of careful research; was reprinted by W. Hone in 1830, and in 1903 J. C. Cox brought out a new edition.

23. *The Driffield Angler* (13). By Alexander Mackintosh. 1806, AM.

This little work is divided into two parts: Fish, Baits, Flies and Instructions for Shooting.

24. *The Wildfowler* (20). By H. C. Folkard. 1859, F.

An expert on his subject. The book, written in an original yet distinguished style, is 'worthy the pen of a Buffon or Gilbert White'. There is a list of both ancient and modern terms as applied to waterfowl when *congregatus*. He speaks of birds *in charm*, meaning when they are 'talking'. A book full of enthusiasm and sage counsel—one to possess. (See Preface, Chapter VI, and Chapter XXIII, No. 58.)

25. *The Folk Lore and Provincial Names of British Birds*. By Rev. Charles Swainson, M.A. 1885, SW.

Swainson was the Rector of Old Charlton. Many 'terms' owe their origin to folk-lore, and this book, which the author endeavoured to model on M. Rolland's *La Faune Populaire de la France*, is a mine of information on the subject.

26. *Proper Terms*. By John Hodgkin. 1909, PT.

An exhaustive research on the origins of Company Terms. Hodgkin came to the conclusion that what were supposed to be 'artificial terms invented in the fifteenth century as distinctive collectives' were not, in fact, company terms at all. His summing up is masterly. Frequent quotations have inevitably been made from this critical and valuable work. (See Summary at end of Chapter XXV.)

27. *Notes on Sporting Rifles*. By Major Gerald Burrard. 1920, GB.

This is the standard work on the subject. Invaluable for the novice and the old hand alike. Both Hill and Jungle shooting are covered in detail—('There is no such thing as an all-round rifle.'). The chapter on sights and sighting is lucid and exhaustive.

28. *Game Pie*. By Eric Parker. 1925, GP.

An anthology of Shooting by one to whom all sportsmen are indebted for his rich knowledge of field and forest, and of the lore and language of the chase.

29. *Gathered Together*. By Philip and Helen Gosse. 1927, GT.

A slight book containing lists of terms from St. A. and Str., and a long list of modern collective terms. There are many inaccuracies; the book does not pretend to be complete.

30. *Pacific Sportsman*, Vol. 8, No. 3 (17) (San Francisco). 1929, PS.

An American monthly magazine to which Mr. W. W. Richards contributed a note on the correct names for the different gatherings of birds.

31. *A Collection of Terms, denoting Assemblages of Animals, Birds, Human Beings, etc.* By Colonel R. J. Nicol, O.B.E. 1933, RJN.

This attractive book was produced privately, for the author's pleasure and that of his friends. By his help and kindness in presenting a copy of his little book, Col. Nicol rendered much assistance in the early days of research.

32. *Bridleways Through History*. By Lady Apsley. 1936, Ap.

This happy book 'Hunts through History', tracing the ways of horse and man in 'sport' throughout the ages. It deals with the nature and customs of hunting from the time of the Greeks, onwards through Charlemagne, the Normans and Crusaders, the Royal Hounds of France, Shakespeare's England, the Stuarts and the Squires, to the present day.

Lady Apsley has succeeded in the 'mixing of History, Riding and Hunting' in a most fascinating book.

33. *The Foxhunter's Week-end Book*. By D. W. E. Brock. 1939, Br.

A mine of information and entertainment—a book for every mood, with special reference to The Countryside, The Foxhound and The Horse. Valuable instruction is given on a host of subjects from 'Turn-out' to 'taking your own line'; feeding, shoeing, bitting, 'music', scent (among many other matters) are dealt with. There is a grand anthology and a most useful bibliography.

DICTIONARIES AND VARIOUS

34. *Etymologicon Linguae Anglicanae* (25). By Stephen Skinner, M.D. 1671, Sk.

This work is all in Latin. Hodgkin examines Skinner's list of terms (in the fourth section of the dictionary), and comes to the conclusion that 'only the following can be regarded as true collectives: *Kyndyll* of cats, *Nye* of feasants, *Rascall* of boyes, *Scole* of fish, *Sounder* of swine, *Stode* of maarys, *Tryppe* of gete.' Hodgkin adds: 'Of the others, "*Gagle* of geys", "*Sorde* or *Sute* of Mallards", and "*Thrave* of Throsshers" may possibly have been used as collectives: the term *synguler* is correctly explained, and the rest are incorrectly interpreted.'

35. *Nouns of Multitude.* By M. Temple. 1925, ISDN.
An article from *The Illustrated Sporting and Dramatic News.*

36. *The New English Dictionary.* NED.

37. *Nuttal's Dictionary* (Special *Daily Mail* Edition). N.

38. *The Complete Crossword Reference Book.* By C. H. R. Thorn. 1932, CW.

OTHER AUTHORITIES QUOTED OR CONSULTED

39. *Treatise.* By W. de Bibbesworth. *c.* 1300.

40. *Boke of Kerving.* By Wynkyn de Worde. *c.* 1495.

41. *The Book Named the Governour.* By Sir Thomas Elyot. 1531.

42. *La Chasse du Loup.* By Jean de Clamorgan. 1566.

43. *Tom Tel-Troth's Message.* By John Lane. 1600.

44. *Night-cap.* By Pasquil. 1612.

45. *A Display of Heraldrie.* By John Guillim (2nd ed.). 1632.

46. *Compleat Gentleman.* By Peacham. 1634.

47. *Dictionary of French and English Tongues.* By Sherwood. 1650.

48. *French-English Dictionary.* By Cotgrave. *c.* 1650.

49. *Historie of Foure-footed Beastes.* By E. Topsel. 1658.

50. *Commenius.* By Hoole. 1672.

51. *The Gentlemen's Recreation.* By R. Blome. 1686.

52. *Pteryplegia, or The Art of Shooting Flying.* By G. Markland. 1727.

53. *The Chace.* By W. Somerville. 1735.

54. *British Zoology.* By Th. Pennant. 1770.

55. *A Sporting Tour.* By Col. Th. Thornton. 1804.

56. *The Sportsman's Dictionary.* By H. J. Pye (see under No. 20, above). 1807.

57. *The Sportsman's Directory.* By John Mayer. 1819.

58. *Bracebridge Hall.* By Washington Irving. 1822.

59. *Instructions to Young Sportsmen.* By Lt. Col. P. Hawker. 1830.

60. *The Art of Deer Stalking.* By William Scrope. 1838.

61. *Extracts from the Diary of a Huntsman.* By Th. Smith. 1838.

62. *An Encyclopaedia of Rural Sports.* By D. P. Blaine. 1840.

63. *Dictionary of Archaic and Provincial Words.* By J. O. Halliwell. 1847.

64. *A Tour in Sutherland* (etc.). By Charles St. John. 1851.

65. *Volume of Vocabularies.* By Th. Wright. 1857.

66. *Badminton Library.* 1886.
67. *Origin of the Thoroughbred Horse.* By Prof. W. Ridgeway. 1893.
68. *Fur and Feather Series.* 1896.
69. *Encyclopaedia of Sport.* 1897.
70. *English Sport.* By A. E. T. Watson. 1903.
71. *Bird Life and Bird Lore.* By R. Bosworth Smith. 1905.
72. *Shooter's Catechism.* By Col. Meysey Thompson. 1905.
73. *Old English Sports.* By F. W. Hackwood. 1907.
74. *Sport in Wildest Britain.* By Hesketh-Prichard. 1921.
75. *The Wild Red Deer of Scotland.* By A. G. Cameron. 1923.
76. *The Art of Shooting.* By Leslie Sprake (Middle Wallop). 1930.
77. *Lonsdale Library.* *c.* 1930.
78. *Falconry and Falcons.* By Arnold Fleming. 1934.
79. *Tunny Fishing for Beginners.* By F. Taylor. 1934.
80. *Deer-Stalking.* By Pat. R. Chalmers. 1935.
81. *History of Hunting.* 1936.
82. *The A.B.C. of Fox-Hunting.* By D. W. E. Brock. 1936.
83. *The Horseman's Week-end Book.* By Gordon Winter. 1937.
84. *The Shooting Week-end Book.* By Eric Parker. 1942.
85. *British Game.* By B. Vesey-Fitzgerald. 1946.

CHAPTER XXVII

THE BOOK OF ST. ALBANS

THIS INTERESTING book, printed at St. Albans by the 'school-master printer' (John Insomuch), in 1486, is commonly supposed to have been written by Dame Juliana Barnes, or Berners, sister of Lord Berners, and prioress of the nunnery of Sopewell. There was, however, according to Cox (1903), 'no such prioress . . . and the story of "Dame Julyano Barnes" being a sister of Lord Berners was an invention of Chauncy in his *History of Herts* (1700).' She was 'celebrated', says Daniel, 'by Leland, Holinshed, and other writers for her uncommon learning and accomplishments.' The book contains three treatises—on Hawking, Hunting and Cote Armour (Heraldry) respectively. It is probable that only the treatise on Hunting was written by Dame Juliana (Dame = Mistress or Mrs. in the fifteenth century), the remainder being compiled by the schoolmaster. The work is evidently not original; Sir H. Dryden suggests that it is a metrical version of Twici's *Le Art de Venerie* and of *The Master of Game*.

In 1881 William Blades brought out a Facsimile Edition, and in his Introduction refers to 'England's earliest poetess', to the 'mystery that has always enshrouded the nameless printer', and to the three alliterative subjects, Hawking, Hunting and Heraldry, 'just those with which, at that period, every man claiming to be "gentle" was expected to be familiar; while ignorance of their laws and language was to confess himself a "churl".' He sums up: 'She (the Dame) probably lived at the beginning of the 15th century, and she possibly compiled from existing MSS. some rhymes on Hunting.'

We are only concerned here with the portion called 'The Book of Hunting', which is all in metre and is addressed to 'My deare childe'. It deals with the varieties of beasts and their ages, the proper names by which to distinguish them, singly and together. There follows a portion dealing with hunting and dressing a Roe, Boar, etc.; cries and noises of animals; varieties of horns; the seasons of the year. Then comes an imaginary discourse between a Master of the Hunt and his man. A return is then made to the original style, with instructions on the dismemberment of various beasts, hunting the hare, and what to say to hounds.

The Prologue to 'The Book of Hunting' runs as follows:

'Likewise, as in the Book of Hawking aforesaid are written and noted the terms of pleasure belonging to Gentlemen having delight therein, in the same manner this book following showeth to such gentle persons the manner of Hunting for all manner of beasts, whether they be beasts of Venery, or of the Chace, or Rascal. And also it showeth all the terms convenient as well to the hounds as to the beasts aforesaid. And in certain there be many diverse of them as it is declared in the book following.'

At the end of the book on hunting comes a long list of terms, headed 'The Compaýnýs of beestýs and fowlýs'. This list contains a number of expressions which do not refer to animals or birds; it is given in full below.

The NED. explains them generally as 'fanciful', 'technical', or 'alleged' terms for a 'company', and as 'artificial terms invented in the fifteenth century as distinctive collectives'. Some of these terms can, however, by no means be called 'collective'. Blades, in his Introduction, gives the following explanation:

'The same idea controlled the arrangement of "The Book of Hunting", which, beginning on sig. ej, ends with Dame Juliana's "Explicit" on the recto of sig. tiiij. This left the last seven pages of the quaternion to be filled up. Now it was a common practice both with the scribes and with the early printers, when they got to the end of their text and found that a page or two of blank paper was left, to occupy the blank pages with such common household aphorisms or popular rhymes as came easily to the memory, or were at hand in some other book. So here the schoolmaster printer fills up his vacant pages with a number of odd sentences and rhymes, most of which occur over and over again in numerous manuscripts of early poetry.

'Among others we notice the well-known—

"Arise erly,
serue God deuouteli,
and the world besely," etc., etc.

'Also the folks proverb—

"Too wyues in oon hous,
Too cattys and oon mous,

Too dogges and oon boon,
Theis shall neũ accorde I oon."

'Then the list of proper terms to be used by gentlemen and those curious in their speech is of very common occurrence—

"An *herde* of Hertis
An *herde* of all man̄ dere
A *pride* of Lionẏs
A *sleuth* of Beeris," etc.

'This was evidently copied from some MS., and ends with "Explicit" and nothing more.'

Blades was clearly of the opinion that these terms were not exclusively company terms. The careless omission of the little word 'etc.' after 'fowlys' in the heading 'has probably been the cause', says Hodgkin, 'of the subsequent misinterpretation of the terms.'

In 1496, *The Book of St. Albans* was reprinted by Wynkyn de Worde, and in this there is a similar heading to the list. Altogether there were about fifteen editions in the sixteenth century.

The Book of St. Albans, 'the book of venery, of hawking, and hunting, is called the book of Sir Tristram' (Mallory) and is referred to as such by Turberville. (See No. 14.) Sir Tristram, the famous Knight of the Round Table, was 'a fictitious character held forth as the mirror of chivalry in the romance entitled *The Death of Arthur*, translated from the French by Sir Thomas Mallory (1481) . . . of all the terms of hunting and hawking he was, said King Arthur, the beginner'. (J. Strutt.)

The List of Terms from the 'Boke of St. Albans'. (1486)

The Compaẏnẏs of beestẏs and fowlẏs

128. An *Herde* of Hertis
118. an *herde* of all man*er* dere
52. an *Herde* of Swannys
9. an *Herde* of Cranys
11. an *Herde* of Corlewys
61. an *Herde* of Wrennys
2. a *Sege* of betouris
31. *a *Sorde* or a *sute* of malardis
36. a *Mustre* of Pecockys
48. a *Walke* of Snytis
*a *Congregacion* of peple
29. an *Exaltyng* of Larkis
*an *Herde* of harlottys
37. a *Nye* of ffesaunttys
a *Beuy* of Ladies
147. a *Beuy* of Roos
42. a *Beuy* of Quaylis
26. a *Sege* of heronnys
a *Superfluyte* of Nunnys
a *Scole* of clerkes
a *Doctryne* of doctoris
†a *Conuertyng* of prechouris
a *Sentence* of Juges
a *Dampnyng* of Jurrouris
†a *Diligens* of Messangeris

32. a *Wache* of Nyghtingalis
an *hoost* of men
a *ffelishippyng* of yomen
21. a *Cherme* of Goldefynches
a *Cast* of Brede
*a *Couple* or a *payer* of botillis
13. a *fflight* of Doues
43. an *vnkyndenes* of Rauenes
6. a *Clateryng* of choughes
1. a *Dissimulacion* of breddis
a *Route* of Knyghtis
134. a *Pride* of Lionys
105. a *Sleuth* of Beeris
104. a *Cete* of Graies
115. a *Bery* of Conyis
136. *a *Riches* of Martronys
122. a *Besynes* of ferettis
130.*a *Brace* of grehoundis of .ij
130. a *Lece* of Grehoundis of .iij
150. a *Coupull* of spaynellis
130.*a *Couple* of rennyng houndis
155. a *Litter* of Welpis
111.*a *Kyndyll* of yong Cattis
107. a *Synguler* of Boris
152. a *Dryft* of tame Swyne
129. an *Harrasse* of horse
114. a *Ragg* of coltis or a *Rake*
140. a *Baren* of Mulis
126. a *Trippe* of Gete
127. a *Trippe* of haaris
20. a *Gagle* of gees
25. a *Brode* of hennys
14. a *badelyng* of Dokis
*a *Noonpaciens* of Wyues
a *State* of Prynces
a *Thongh* of barons
†a *Prudens* of vikeris
24. a *cast* of haukis of ye tour .ij
24.*a *Lece* of thessame haukis .iij
24. a *Flight* of Goshaukes
51. a *Flight* of swalowes
45. a *beldyng* of Rookes
50. a *Murmuracion* of stares
156. a *Route* of Woluess
133. a *Lepe* of Lebardis
102. a *Shrewdenes* of Apis

†*an *Obeisians* of seruauntis
a *Sete* of vssheris
†a *Draught* of boteleris
*a *Proude shewyng* of taloris
†a *Temperans* of cokys
a *Stalke* of fosteris
a *Boost* of saudiouris
a *Laughtre* of Osteloris
a *Glosyng* of Tauerneris
a *Malepertnes* of pedleres
a *Thraue* of Throsheris
a *squatte* of Dawberis
a *Fightyng* of beggers
*an *vntrouth* of sompneris
†*a *Melody* of Harpers
a *Pauuerty* of pypers
*a *sotelty* of sergeauntis
*a *Tabernacle* of bakers
*a *Drifte* of fishers
*a *Disgysyng* of Taylours
a *Bleche* of sowteris
a *Smere* of Coryouris
a *Clustre* of Grapys
a *Clustre* of chorlis
†a *Example* of Maisteris
*a *Rage* of Maydenys
a *Rafull* of Knauys
*a *blush* of boyes
*an *vncredibilite* of Cocoldis
35. a *Couy* of partrichis
54. a *Sprynge* of Telis
28. a *Desserte* of Lapwynges
59. a *fall* of Woodecockis
39. a *Congregacion* of Pleuers
7. a *Couert* of cootis
13.*a *Duell* of Turtillis
30. a *Titengis* of Pies
49. an *Ost* of sparowis
300. a *Swarme* of bees
*an *Obseruans* of herimytis
an *Eloquens* of laweyeris
an *Execucion* of Officerys
†a *faith* of Marchandis
†a *preuision* of stewardes of hous
a *Kerff* of Panteris
*a *Credens* of Seweris
*an *vnbrewyng* of Kerueris
†a *Safegarde* of Porteris

a *Skulke* of Theuys
123. a *skulke* of ffoxis
144. a *Nest* of Rabettis
138. a *Labor* of Mollis
130.*a *Mute* of houndes
130. a *Kenell* of Rachis
130. a *Sute* of a lyam
117. a *Cowardnes* of curris
152. a *Soundre* of Wilde swyne
135. a *Stode* of Maris
103. a *Pase* of Assis
132. a *Droue* of Nete
148. a *fflocke* of Shepe
a *Gagle* of Women
5. a *Pepe* of chykennys
*a *Multiplieng* of husbondis
a *Pontificalite* of prelatis
a *Dignyte* of chanonys
a *Charge* of curatis
†a *Discrecion* of Prestis
a *Sculke* of freris
a *bhomynable sight* of mokis
201. a *Scoll* of ffysh

a *Blast* of hunteris
a *Thretenyng* of courteyeris
†a *Promyse* of Tapsteris
a *Lyeng* of pardeneris
*a *Misbeleue* of paynteris
a *Lash* of Carteris
a *Scoldyng* of Kemsteris
*a *Wonderyng* of Tynkeris
*a *Waywardness* of haywardis
*a *Worship* of Writeris
a *Neuerthriuyng* of Jogoleris
*a *ffraunch* of Mylneris
*a *Festre* of Brweris
*a *Goryng* of Bochouris
*a *Trynket* of Corueseris
*a *Plocke* of Shoturneris
*a *Dronkship* of Coblers
123. a *Sculke* of foxis
a *Clustre* of Nottis
*a *Rage* of the teethe
a *Rascall* of Boyes
a *Disworship* of Scottis

Explicit

[NOTE: The number before each term is the Index number, and is inserted to facilitate reference to the Notes in Part III.

* These terms are not contained in the Egerton MS. or in any previous list.

† A sarcastic term.]

APPENDIX I

A DIGRESSION

TOMMY, A pupil of Mr. Cathro, had competed for the Hugh Blackadder prize. The subject of that year's Essay was 'A Day in Church'. There were only two competitors; the other one was a boy called Lauchlan, trained by Mr. Ogilvie, who looked upon the Blackadder as his perquisite.

And 'Tommy was ignominiously beaten . . . for the gowk had stuck in the middle of his second page. . . . He had brought himself to public scorn for lack of a word. What word? they asked testily, but even now he could not tell. He had wanted a Scotch word that would signify how many people were in church, and it was on the tip of his tongue but would come no farther. Puckle was nearly the word, but it did not mean so many people as he meant. The hour had gone by just like winking; he had forgotten all about time while searching his mind for the word.

'When Mr. Ogilvie heard this he seemed to be much impressed. . . . "The right word—yes, that's everything." . . .

' "You little tattie doolie," Cathro roared, "were there not a dozen words to wile from if you had an ill-will to puckle? What ailed you at manzy, or—"

' "I thought of manzy," replied Tommy woefully, for he was ashamed of himself, "but—but a manzy's a swarm. It would mean that the folk in the kirk were buzzing thegither like bees, instead of sitting still." . . .

' "I thought of mask," whimpered Tommy, "but that would mean the kirk was crammed, and I just meant it to be middling full."

' "Flow would have done," suggested Mr. Lorrimer (one of the judges).

' "Flow's but a handful," said Tommy.

' "Curran, then, you jackanapes!"

' "Curran's no enough."

'Mr. Lorrimer flung up his hands in despair.

' "I wanted something between curran and mask," said Tommy, dogged, yet almost at the crying.

'Mr. Ogilvie, who had been hiding his admiration with difficulty, spread a net for him. "You said you wanted a word that meant middling full. Well, why did you not say middling full—or fell mask?"

' "Yes, why not?" demanded the ministers, unconsciously caught in the net.

' "I wanted one word," replied Tommy, unconsciously avoiding it.

' "You jewel!" muttered Mr. Ogilvie under his breath, but Mr. Cathro would have banged the boy's head had not the ministers interfered.

' "It is so easy, too, to find the right word," said Mr. Gloag (another judge).

' "It's no; it's as difficult as to hit a squirrel," cried Tommy, and again Mr. Ogilvie nodded approval....

' "And so, Cathro, you need not feel sore over your defeat," added Mr. Gloag; but nevertheless Cathro took Tommy by the neck and ran him out of the parish school of Thrums.

. . . .

'And then an odd thing happened. As they were preparing to leave the school, the door opened a little and there appeared in the aperture the face of Tommy, tear-stained but excited. "I ken the word now," he cried, "it came to me a' at once; it is hantle!"

'The door closed with a victorious bang, just in time to prevent Cathro——

' "Oh, the sumph!" exclaimed Mr. Lauchlan McLauchlan, "as if it mattered what the word is now!" ...

'But Mr. Ogilvie, giving his Lauchlan a push that nearly sent him sprawling, said in an ecstasy to himself, "He *had* to think of it till he got it—and he got it. The laddie is a genius!" '

(From *Sentimental Tommy*, by J. M. Barrie)

A. VARIOUS COMPANY TERMS

It will be noticed that the List of Terms from *The Book of St. Albans* (Chapter XXVII) contains a number of terms that do not refer to animals, birds, etc., or to 'sport' in any way. Examples of such are: an *Herde* of Harlottys, a *rage* of maidens, a *route*[1] of Knyghtis, a *cast* of brede. Most of them refer to Persons.

[1] Originally the word *route* was used generally for a multitude. '*Rout* (*routa*) is a French word signifying a company or flock.... It signifieth in our Common law, an Assembly of three persons or more, going on about forcibly to commit an un-

These terms were all probably in use at one time or another, though the majority of them are not true 'company terms'. A few, as 'a *host* of men', are common expressions at the present day. Some of them deserve to be perpetuated: e.g. a *charge* of curates, a *dignity* of canons, a *drift* of fishers,[1] a *blast* of hunters, a *rayful* of knaves, a *bevy* of ladies,[2] a *rascal* (or a *blush*) of boys,[3] a *boast* of soldiers, and a *skulk* of thieves. Surely 'a *worship* of writers' should be incorporated at once into our daily language? (The phrase refers to a common practice of poets in days gone by to seek the patronage of the great by dedicating to them empty panegyrics. Spenser may be cited as an example. Present-day 'readers' would not know of this, and might now give the expression its natural interpretation!)

From other ancient sources have come such expressions as:

A *route* of gentlemen (Eg.).
A *good advice* of burgesses (P.).
A *gaggle* of gossips[4] (Harl. 1.).
A *hastiness* of cooks, a *pity* of prisoners (S.).
A *knot* of astrologers, a *pack* of lazy, droaning devils, a *gang* of fiddlers (or of lovers), a *generation* of modest fools, a *regiment* of hypocrites (or of usurers), a *parcel* of mathematicians, a *gang* of poets, a *consort* of loud and tedious talkers, and a *troop* of women upon the high-way to hell.[5]

lawful act, but yet do it not.' (Cowell, *Interpreter*, 1658 ed.) Eventually the term seems to have been adopted as 'proper' for 'knytys' in company. The 'Nominale Sive Verbale' (about 1340), however, and the Femina MS. (1420) use *aray* for knights and *route* for squires. (See Chapter XXIV, No. 156, Notes.)

[1] A *drift* was the name for the recognized fishing-ground of a fisherman.

[2] *Bevy* was the proper term for a company of maidens or ladies, of roes, of quails, or of larks. (NED.)

[3] *Rascal* is one of the few genuine collective terms applied to persons. It originally meant 'rabble' or 'mob'. Sir Thomas Smith, in his *Commonwealth*, 1642, divides the English below the rank of Esquire into Gentlemen, yeomen, and *Rascals*. The word was also a hunting term, being applied to all beasts other than the four beasts of venery, and the four beasts of the chase (see Chapter I). 'As before I have shewed how the ill names of beasts in their most contemptible state, are in contempt applyed unto women, so is Rafcall, being the name of an ill-favoured, leane, and worthlesse Deere, commonly applied unto such men as are held of no credit or worth.' (Richard Verstegan's *Restitution of Decayed Intelligence*, 1634.) (See Chapter XXVI, No. 34.)

[4] *Gaggle* is the proper term for geese, but is also applied to women—'Ceux deus sunt associez' (Bibbesworth)—and to gossips.

[5] *The Visions of Dom Francisco de Quevedo Villegas, now made English by J. Dodington, Esq., The True Edition*, 1688.

Coming to more modern times, from *Word Lore* (vol. iii, 1928) come 'a *break* of hemp', 'a *plume* of trees', and 'a *laughter* of eggs', which seem worth preserving. *Gathered Together* (Chapter XXVI, No. 29) gives a large selection.

The derivation of all the group terms for persons (and objects) form as fascinating a study as those for animals and birds. The notes, however, would be too long for insertion in this work.

B. TERMS WITHOUT PRECEDENT

(Containing a collection of Improvised Terms, and an Extract from Rabelais' Works)

Much ingenuity has been expended in the invention of terms similar to the genuine ones quoted above. A selection of these follows.

(1) BIRDS, ANIMALS, FISHES AND INSECTS

400. Buffaloes	an *obstinacy* of	
401. Bullfinches	a *bellowing*	Letter in *Sunday Dispatch*
402. Crocodiles	*bask*	
403. Ducklings	*worseling*	P1.
404. Flies	*helluvalot*	RJN.
405. Flying-fish	*glitter*	B.
406. Greyhounds	*hazard*	P2.
407. Giraffes	*tower*	
408. Gulls	*screech*	B.
409. Hens	*holocaust*	P1.
410. Kittens	*concatenation*	P1.
411. Midges	*bite*	RJN.
412. Opossums	*malingering*	
413. Parrots	*pandemonium*	P1.
	psittacosis	P2.
414. Pekingese	*pomp*	P2.
415. Porpoise	*turmoil*	B.
416. Puppies	*huddle*	
417. Razorbills	*strop*	H.
418. Red Cardinals	*college*	B.
419. Rhinoceroses	*stubbornness*	
420. Sea-serpents	*slither*	B.
421. Swallows	*gulp*	RJN.
422. Turkey-buzzards	*stench*	B.
423. Turtles	*turn*	
424. Zebras	*zeal*	
425. Beasts	*caboodle*	H. Quinn
426. Canaries	*glitter*	
427. Earwigs	*perruque*	LDC.
428. Fleas	*irritation*	LDC.
429. Magpies	*scold*	CL.

430. Pythons	*posse*	FWL.
431. Robins	*sending*	LDC.

(2) PERSONS

500. Actors	a *condescension* of	RJN.
501. Aldermen	*guzzle*	P3.
502. Bachelors	*debauchery*	RJN.
503. Bandsmen	*furore*	*
504. Bishops	*psalter*	P1.
505. Bookmakers	*surge*	*
506. Bores	*geyser*	P1.
507. Boys	*riot*	*
508. Bridge fiends	*argument*	P2.
509. Children	*cluster*	*
510. Chorus Girls	*giggle*	RJN.
511. Clowns	*guffaw*	P2.
512. Conservatives	*stodge*	P3.
513. Company Promoters	*boodle*	P2.
514. Damsels	*spray* or *spring*	*
515. Fairies	*charm*	*
516. Flappers	*frolic*	P2.
517. Gate-crashers	*thrust*	P2.
518. Generals	*blather*	RJN.
519. Golfers	*gargle*	P2.
520. Gypsies	*pitch*	*
521. Highbrows	*altitude*	P2.
522. Husbands	*hubbub* or *futility*	RJN.
523. Laddies	*curn*	local expression in Angus
524. Liberals	*brace*	P3.
525. Loafers	*saunter*[1]	*
526. Mayors	*muddle*	RJN.
527. Mannequins	*slink*	P3.
528. Mermaids	*bevy*	B.
529. Miners	*muttering*	*
530. Peasants	*pool* or *sod*	*
531. Poets	*gush*	P2.
532. Prohibitionists	*gargle*	P3.
533. Punters	*fleece*	P2.
534. Socialists	*heckle*	P3.
535. Spinsters	*flutter*[2]	P3.
536. Virgins	*trace* or *trance*	*

From a Letter in *The Sunday Dispatch*

537. Councillors	*corpulence* of
538. Curates	*coyness*
539. Editors	*erudition*
540. Fathers	*fatuity*
541. Housewives	*haggie*
542. *Paupers*	pollution
543. *Scotches*	skinful
544. *Squaws*	squabble
545. *Vicars*	vicariousness

[1] And of chuprassis.

[2] Or a *singular*, JKA.

The following are from a list supplied by Lieut.-Col. C. Bartley-Denniss; those marked † appear rather better than slang.

546. Artists	†*school* of
547. Chorus Girls	*click*
548. Dacoits	†*gang*
549. Doctors	*emulsion*
550. Domestics	*dearth*
551. Gamblers	†*den*
552. Gods	*gatheration*
553. Graduates	*unemploy-ment*
554. Husbands	*unhappiness*
555. M.P.'s	*chatter*
556. Politicians	
(tame)	*plethora*[1]
(wild)	*gang*
557. Ragamuffins	*evil*
558. Rascals	*parcel*
559. Robbers	†*band*
560. Tourists	*drove*
561. Urchins	*mischief*
562. Vakils	*starvation*
563. Waiters	*dawdling*

SOME SERVICE TERMS

564. Generals	a *rage* of
565. Brigadiers	*blast*
566. Colonels	*cackle*
567. Majors	*morbidity*
568. Captains	*dash*
569. Subalterns	*simplicity*

A FEW MORE

570. Cooks	a *lack* of	ECH.
571. Film-stars	*galaxy*	JKA.
572. Fishermen	*exaggeration*	JHC.
573. Mowers	*mess*	
574. Physicians	*quack*	JHC.
575. Railway-shareholders	*fry*	
576. Rickshaw-coolies	*towing* or *tonk*	*

(3) VARIOUS

600. Aeroplanes	a *buzziness* of	
601. Casts	*tangle*	RJN.
602. Cocktails	*shake* or *scatter*	P2.
603. Lines	*rot*	RJN.
604. Motors	*stink*	P2.
	maze	
605. Sausages	a *sizzle* of	P2.
606. Waders	*leak*	RJN.
607. Whisky	*want*	RJN.
608. Bicycles	*wobble*	RJN.
609. Paratroops	*stick*	
610. Peace Treaties	*quiver*	
611. Road-hogs	*gadarene*	'Hickie'

[1] Or a *scandal*, JHC.

SOURCES OF ORIGIN

B.	= R. Beale	*	= The Author
H.	= A. Hopkins	ECH.	= E. C. Hare
P1.	= *Punch*, 6.3.29	FWL.	= Frank W. Lane
P2.	= *Punch*, 12.3.30	JHC.	= J. H. Caesar (*Field*, 10.9.38)
P3.	= *Punch*, 30.4.30	LDC.	= L. Dawson Campbell
RJN.	= R. J. Nicol	JKA.	= J. K. Adams (*Field*, 8.10.38)
CL.	= *Country Life*		

(4) EXTRACT FROM RABELAIS' WORKS

(Book III, Ch. 13—1546)

(Translated by Sir Thomas Urquhart, who expanded Rabelais' list of nine cries to no less than seventy-one. Rabelais' terms are printed in *italics*. It is curious that Urquhart omitted one, *braislent les asnes* (the braying of asses). The author is indebted for this correction to Mr. G. Legman (*American Notes & Queries*).

The translation was first published in 1693, but this extract is taken from a nineteenth century re-edition.)

How Pantagruel adviseth Panurge to try the future good or bad luck of his marriage by dreams, without, however, a previous long and pertinacious fasting. Pantagruel speaks:

'You may very well remember how my father Gargantua . . . gave us the example of the philosopher, who, when he thought most seriously to have withdrawn himself unto a solitary privacy, far from the rustling clutterments of the tumultuous and confused world, the better to improve his theory, to contrive, comment and ratiocinate, was, notwithstanding his uttermost endeavours to free himself from all untoward noises, surrounded and environed about so with the *barking of curs*, bawling of mastiffs, bleating of sheep, prating of parrots, tattling of jackdaws, grunting of swine, girning of boars, yelping of foxes, mewing of cats, cheeping of mice, squeaking of weasels, croaking of frogs, crowing of cocks, cackling of hens, calling of partridges, chanting of swans, chattering of jays, peeping of chickens, singing of larks, creaking of geese, chirping of swallows, clucking of moorfowls, cucking of cuckoos, bumbling of bees, rammage of hawks, chirming of linnets, croaking of ravens, screeching of owls, whicking of pigs, gushing of hogs, curring of pigeons, grumbling of cushet-doves, howling of panthers, curkling of quails, chirping of sparrows, crackling of crows, nuzzing of camels, whining of whelps, buzzing of dromedaries, mumbling of rabbits, cricking of ferrets, humming of wasps, mioling of tigers, bruzzing of bears, sussing of kitlings, clamoring of scarfes,[1] whimpering of fulmarts, booing of buffalos, warbling of nightingales, quavering of meavises, drintling of turkies, coniating of storks, frantling of peacocks, clattering of magpies, murmuring of stock-doves, crouting of cormorants, *cigling of locusts*, charming of beagles, guarring of puppies, snarling of messens,[2] rantling of rats, gueri-eting of apes, snuttering of monkies, pioling of pelicans, quack-ing of ducks, *yelling of wolves*, *roaring of lions*, *neighing of horses*, *barring*[3] *of elephants*, *hissing of serpents*, and *wailing of turtles*[4] that he was much more troubled, than if he had been in the middle of the crowd at the fair of Fontenay or Niort. Just so is it with those who are tormented with the grievous pangs of hunger.'

[1] Cormorants. [2] Lap dogs (Scottish). [3] (orig.) *crying*.
[4] i.e. Turtle-doves.

APPENDIX II

SOME DUTCH TERMS

EXTRACT FROM a letter from Mr. A. E. Th. de Bye Dolleman, of Holland: 'Perhaps these sayings in Dutch can give you any information on the subject. We say (translated from the Dutch):

A *herd* of cattle.
A *flock* of sheep.
A *yoke* of bullocks.
A *team* of oxen.
A *set* of horses.
A *swarm* of bees, grasshoppers, sparrows, starlings.
A *bevy* of larks.
A *covey* of partridges.
A *brace* of partridges (two).
A *pen* of hens.
A *shoal* of herrings, whales, etc.
A *roddel* of deer (comes from the German).
A *pack* of dogs, wolves, etc.
A *bouquet* of pheasants (when they come all together and more than twenty over the guns).

'Is it not funny that man always is compared with animals? We say:

He works like a horse.
He eats like a wolf.
He shoots out like a pike.
He is as slippery as an eel.
He is gluttonous as a shark.
He is proud as a lion, as a peacock.
He smells as a polecat.
He is stupid as an oyster, a duck, a donkey.
He is cunning as a fox.
He is afraid as a weasel.
He is red as a lobster (also in politics).
He is fat as a snail.
He is unwieldy as a boar.
He has the eye of a falcon.
He is blind as a mole.
He is lazy as a pig.
He is a real jelly-fish.
He is quick as a monkey, a hare.
He has got the little nose of a salmon (the best of the best).

He has haddock eyes.
He is faithful as a dog.
He is false as a cat.

And so hundreds more.

'I don't think you have all these sayings in English, perhaps it will interest you. . . .'

APPENDIX III

PET NAMES, PHRASES AND ORIGINS

'All local names were once words.' (Balch.)

THIS BRAN-TUB of terms has been purposely filled with gifts from a variety of sources, in the hope that all who dip may find something to their taste. Only those phrases and names that have *some* connection with sport or nature have been included. The list is by no means complete. More 'pet' names, and some provincial and nick-names, will be found in the Notes to Part III.

Alligator: The Spanish *el lagarto* means the lizard. Early English settlers to the Gulf Coast of North America corrupted the word to 'lagato', which finally became 'alligator'.

Anthony: There are well over 100 names for the smallest pig of a litter. *Anthony* (Thanet) is a common one. So also are *Nisgull* (Midlands) and *Dilling*.

Beanfeast: From the Bean-Goose (so called from the similarity of the *nail* (see p. 74) of its bill to a bean), which was formerly the invariable dinner dish.

Bruin: The bear in the old Flemish poem *Reynard the Fox* was called *Bruin*, which is a Dutch word meaning brown.

Camel-hair: Camel-hair brushes are made from squirrel hair. Camel was the surname of the first man to make them.

Cat call: A corruption of *Cat wail*, applied to the 'mewings' of the audience.

Catgut: A cord made, not from cats, but from the intestines of lambs. Fishing gut comes from Silkworms.

Chamois: The Alpine goat. Chamois or 'shammy' leather is from Sauland, a district on the Baltic.

Cock-a-hoop: Defiant; like a game cock with its crest erect.

Crocodile tears: Crocodiles were said to attract victims by moaning as if in profound woe; they would then shed tears over their prey while devouring it.

Dromedary: Does not refer to the two-humped camel, whic histhe Bactrian. It means 'a well-bred, finely-boned African camel', and is used for riding as distinct from one used for packs. Generally one-humped.

Essex Duck: A sheep's head.

Gibbon: From an ape called Gilbert.

Glow worm: Not a worm, but the female of the beetle; it glows in the dark.

Goatsucker: Only the harmless nightjar, which got its name from the belief in Aristotle's day that it sucked goat's milk. Also known as *fern owl*, because it lies in bracken during the day.

The Welsh call it the *Wheel Bird*, from the resemblance of its notes to a large spinning wheel. Other names: *Eve jar, dew-fall hawk, dor-hawk, moth owl, flying toad, lich fowl*, and *jerry-spinner* (from its *churring*).

The swift is its nearest relative in this country.

Gopher: The same name refers to different animals in four different American states. It means a turtle in Florida, a snake in Idaho, a rat-like animal in California, and a ground-squirrel in Montana. The inhabitants of Florida, by the way, call their real gopher a salamander and their true salamander a 'Congo eel'.

Halcyon: The kingfisher (*martin-pêcheur*); its breeding season was fabled to be always accompanied with calm weather, the 'halcyon days', i.e. the seven days before and after the shortest day.

Hell for leather: Originally used solely for riding 'all out' on horseback. It has been suggested that the phrase had a prior meaning—'all of a lather'.

Hobby-horse: A favourite recreation—from the smooth-going Irish *hobby*-horse of the Middle Ages.

Hobson's choice: The expression comes from an ostler of that name who hired out hacks as taxis are hired to-day—front one or none.

Hogshead: Corruption of Ox-head.

Humble-pie: See page 17.

Insect: From the root *seco* (cut) because insects are cut into three different parts: head, thorax, and abdomen.

'*In the soup*': 'In difficulties' or 'out of the running' (American). Originally referred to the hunting field when a rider got pitched into a ditch of dirty water.

Isle of Dogs: Corruption of Isle of Ducks, owing to the great number of wild fowl on the marshes.

Jackal: From the Turkish *chakal*, the gypsy *Jukel* (dog). It was fabled to forage for the lion, and so called 'the lion's provider'.

Jackanapes (Jack with an ape): A coxcomb, a 'mischief'. One who *apes* the manners of his superiors.

Jackass: The male of the ass (also, a blackhead; a brig). Arabic *Jackhsh* means 'one who extends his ears'. The Laughing Jackass is an Australian kingfisher.

Jenny Wren: A diminutive term of affection for the wren. (Jenny—a woman's name.) 'An excellent example of the people's poetry ("twopence coloured").' (E. Partridge, 1937.) Cf. Tom tit, etc.

Jocko: A familiar name for a monkey, from the native African *n'djecko*.

Joey: A young kangaroo; from the Australian word *Joé*.

John Dory: A fish; a corruption of the French *jaune-dorée*, golden.

Jumbo: Now a pet name for any elephant, it originally referred to a famous beast at the Zoo, about 1882.

Kangaroo: The word signifies 'What do you mean?' Readers could invent the reason for this name, and they would probably be right.

Katydid: N. American tree-grasshopper. The word does not derive from Katherine, but from the peculiar sound of the insect's wing-covers.

Kittiwake: A three-toed species of sea-gull. Not derived from Katherine either, but from the bird's cry.

Leopard: Supposed originally to be a cross between the *pard* (panther) and the lioness; hence its name. (The *jumar*, or *jumart*, supposed offspring of a bull and a mare, or a horse and a cow, is now known to be the mule.)

Lost shoes: A Leicestershire term meaning 'dead beat'.

'*Mad as a hatter*': Really means 'as venomous as a viper'; corrupted from 'mad as an atter', i.e. an adder.

Mare's nest: Something quite absurd; a hoax.

Martin: So termed from its migration at Martinmas (11th Nov.). Johnson suggests it is derived from the Latin *murten*, from *murus*, a wall.

Monkey: To put a monkey on is to bet £500.

Mother Carey's Chicken: The stormy petrel; protected by sailors from a superstition that they are the living forms of the souls of deceased sailors. Mother Carey = *mater cara*, and refers to the Virgin Mary, the patroness of sailors.

Neck and crop: Entirely; the crop is that of a bird. It has been suggested that the original phrase was Ncck and *croup*!

Osprey: Osprey feathers do not come from this bird, but from the Egret, a bird of the Heron family.

'*Pig in a Poke*': 'To buy a pig in a poke' is not to see what you are getting. It was the custom to take pigs to market in bags. *Poke* (now our diminutive 'pocket') was an old word for a sack. (Cf. poacher.)

Plover: Probably from the Latin *pluvia*, rain; the bird is mostly seen in the rain.

Poor man's goose: Sheep's head and liver, cooked to simulate goose.

Pop goes the weasel: This has nothing to do with our little Fairy-hound! The original phrase was 'Pop goes the whistle'. To *pop*=to pawn; and in rhyming slang 'whistle and flute' stands for 'suit'.

Popinjay: Parrot or *yaffle* (*q.v.*), from O.Fr. *papegau*, a parrot. (Also a shooting mark; a coxcomb.)

Puppy: Originally meant a puppet or doll; Fr. *poupée*=a doll.

Puss: Dim. pussy. A hare or cat. The word for cat is found in practically identical form in Gaelic, Irish, Swedish, Dutch, and German. Its origin is obscure, but is generally believed to be in imitation of its spitting. A correspondent writes that in Chitral (N.W. frontier of India) the word for cat is *Pushi*; and in Pushtu, the common language of Pathans, the word is *Pishu*. Perhaps they are all of a common onomatopoeic origin.

Balch (1889) says that it is the endearing corruption of *Pers*, the Persian cat.

The Latin name for hare is *lepus*; some took the word to be Norman and produced *le puss*!

Quail: Old Dutch *quackel*, a quacker. The bird was sometimes called *wet-my-lips*, or *wet-my-feet*, from the male bird's note.

Raven: From the A.S. *hrefn* (*h* silent), from the cry of the bird.

Redbreast: The European robin. Cf. *Red-eye*, the rudd; *Red-legs*, the purple sandpiper.

Red-herring: A point raised to divert attention from the subject at issue. Lit. a herring cured by smoking.

Renard (or Reynard): A colloquial name for a fox; derived from the German beast epic *Reinhard Fuchs*, a satire on the state of Germany in the Middle Ages.

Robin: Was the sheep's Christian name in old French. *Robinet* = Fr. for tap, and taps were first made in the shape of sheeps' heads.

Rout: From the Celtic *rhauter*, a crowd (Ger., *rotte*). (See Chapter XXIV, No. 156, and Appendix I.)

Scotch woodcock: A savoury egg dish.

Snack: A Lurcher; a poacher's dog.

Southern blunder: Holloaing a fresh fox.

Slow-worm: A legless lizard. A.S. *sla-wyrm*, the slay, or striking, worm, from confusion with the snake.

St. Peter's Bird: The Petrel, a sea-bird with the nostrils in a tube. The allusion is to St. Peter who walked on the sea, for this bird usually skims over the sea.

Tabby Cat: Not derived from *Tabitha*. The word is of Eastern origin. A kind of striped taffeta came from a certain part of Baghdad, whence the material took the name *Attabiya*, which in English soon became *Tabby*. The word was first used to refer to this striped or watered silk. Even in the eighteenth century 'tabbies' meant dresses, as often as cats. Towards the end of that century there came a new meaning: 'old maid'. Natives call Tigers *Tabby*.

Teddy Bear: A toy bear; named after Theodore Roosevelt in allusion to his fondness for big game hunting. The Australian 'teddy-bear' is the Koala.

Vixen: The only surviving example of the O.E. method of forming the feminine by adding *-en* to the masculine. *Vox* was the name for fox in S. England.

Whitechapel pheasant: A bloater.

Yaffle: The green woodpecker, so named from its 'laughter' in spring. Other pet names for this bird are: *rainbird*, *hewhole*, *wood-knocker*, *wood-spite*, *wood-pole*, *whet-isle*, *hufle*, *eccle*, *hecco*, *jar-peg*, and *popinjay*.

APPENDIX IV

TERMS WITH SEVERAL MEANINGS

Bag: (1) A *bag fox* is one turned out especially for hounds to hunt. (2) Total of game plus *various* shot in one day. (3) Old fishing term applied to line when one hair of it ran up more than the rest. (4) In badger-digging, the process of securing Brock in a bag.

Bar: (1) Of a horse's mouth, the bare portions of the gums on the lower jaw. (2) Of a horse's hoof, portions of the wall near the heels. (3) Crowbar for moving an otter from a strong holt.

Bay: (1) To chase a deer, etc., so as to make it stand *at* bay. (2) =Bez, part of the attire of a deer. (3) Colour of a horse. (4) The cry of a hound.

Beam: (1) Circumference of an antler. (2) Long feather of a hawk's wing.

Beating: (1) Of an otter; when he is driven to water he *beats* the stream. (2) A method of rousing game. (3) Of a hawk; fluttering the wings. (4) The cry of a hare at rutting time.

Bed: (1) Old term in fishing, e.g. of eels lying in the mud. (2) Proper term for a roe deer when it lodges. (3) Sometimes used of a cluster of young snakes.

Bend: (1) Fishing term, of a hook. (2) Otter's short cut between two reaches of a winding river.

Blind: (1) Of fences, or country, where ditches are overgrown and hidden. (2) American term for a hide. (3) 'To chuck and chance it' =to fish *blind*.

Bolt: (1) To force a fox, otter or rabbit into the open. (2) Of a hawk, to fly from the fist. (3) Of a horse, to gallop out of control.

Bore: (1) Calibre of a gun or rifle. (2) Of a horse, to lean heavily on the bit.

Bottom: (1) A big ditch with (usually) a fence on one side. (2) Hair (or gut) *cast* (old fishing term). (3) The bed of a river.

Break: (1) Of hunted game when they leave covert. (2) Old word for a knot in the joint of a fishing-rod.

Brown: (1) Colour of a horse. (2) To fire into the middle of a flock of birds.

Buck: (1) The male of the fallow deer, and of hare, rabbit. (2) A general term for goats and antelopes. (3) A hare or rabbit at mating *goes to buck.*

Butt: (1) A sort of *hide* for a 'gun'. (2) The thick end of a rod, gun.

Buttons: Of a deer's antlers, when they begin to grow. (2) The *crotiles* of a hare (old term). (3) Rubber protection on butt of fishing-rod.

Cap: (1) Black cap worn by M.F.H., etc. (2) Money collected at the Meet.

Carries: (1) Of ploughland, etc., when it is sticky; good scenting land *carries a scent.* (2) Of a hawk, when it flies off with the quarry. (3) A hound which works with its nose when the pack is running is said to *carry the scent.*

Cast: (1) When the hart became tired he *cast* his *chaule* (hung his head. (2) An effort to recover the scent at a check in fox-hunting. (3) '*Let slip* a greyhound; *cast off* a hound.' (4) Hawks were *cast*; goshawks *let fly.* (5) A pair of hawks. (6) Pellet of feathers given to a hawk to purge her gorge = *castings.* (7) The fisherman's familiar '*cast*'. (8) The *leader* at the end of the running line.

Catch hold: (1) of a huntsman, when he lifts the pack. (2) Of a horse that pulls.

Check: (1) When hounds throw up and temporarily lose the scent. (2) When a hawk changes bird in pursuit.

Chestnut: (1) Colour of a horse. (2) = Castor, horny growth on inside of horse's legs.

Cob: (1) A male swan. (2) A thick-set horse, not over 15 hands.

Cock: (1) The male of birds, or fish. (2) Colloquial name for Woodcock. (3) A float was said to *cock* when it was swimming perpendicularly in the water (old fishing term).

Cocking: (1) Making a fly sit up well on the water (dry fly fishing). (2) (or *Cocketting*) Noise made by pheasants when roosting.

Collar: (1) The greyhound has his *collar*—the hound his *couples.* (2) The twisted gut between running line and cast (in fishing).

Cope: (1) A hunting cheer. (2) To pare the claws or beak of a hawk. (3) To tie a string round a ferret's mouth.

Couple: (1) Two hounds. (2) Leather collar for coupling hounds together.

Cover: (1) An old term for a hart harbouring. (2) To get bait (or fly) over place where fish is lying. (3) General term fo copulation of animals.

Covert: (1) A wood that might hold a fox. (2) Company term for a flock of coots.

Crowned: (1) Old term for the first head of a deer (*crowned tops*). (2) Of a horse, with *broken* (hairless) knees—old term.

Curb: (1) Of a horse, an enlargement at back of hock. (2) Short for *curb-bit.*

Doe: (1) Female Fallow deer or Roe-buck. (2) Female hare.

Double: (1) Fence or bank with ditch on both sides. (2) Of an otter that has run out of the water and back again, leaving a loop of scent. (3) Of a hare that winds about to deceive hounds. (4) To blow a succession of quick notes on the horn. Also of a hound, to double the Tongue (old).

Drag: (1) *The* line of a fox leading to his kennel. (2) *An* artificial line laid over a country. (3) The trail of scent left by an otter. (4) The trail of a carcase that has been moved by big game. (5) Old term for the brush of a fox. (6) Fishing instrument for disentangling the line. (7) State when a fly is moving at a pace or in a direction different from that of the stream.

Draw: (1) Of the huntsman or hounds, when they seek for a fox in covert. (2) The area selected for a day's hunting. (3) Of a huntsman, when he separates a hound from the rest of the pack. (4) In Coursing, of the owner—to withdraw a dog. (5) The classifying of greyhounds prior to running.

Drift: (1) An old term for the ordure of 'stinking beasts'. (2) An old term for a herd of tame swine. (3) An old company term for four or more anglers together.

Dun: (1) Natural fly before its final change. (2) Colour of a horse.

Entry: (1) Old term (=*Rack*) for branches broken by deer's head. (2) Of a wet fly, into the water. (3) A batch of young unentered hounds.

Feathers: (1) Covering of birds. (2) Of a hound, when it drives uncertainly along the line, waving its stern.

Fetlock: (1) Of a horse, joint above pastern. (2) Tuft of hair behind this joint.

Field: (1) The mounted men and women hunting with a pack. (2) The horses in a race.

Flags: (1) The floor of the kennel courts. (2) Certain feathers of a hawk.

Flies: (1) Fences in Ireland which are not jumped 'on and off'. (2) A hawk *flies* at fur, plume or feather. (3) Artificial insects with hooks, dressed like flies, used by anglers.

Flight: (1) A number of birds together, e.g. of goshawks, pigeons. (2) Game birds produced in the same season. (3) Motion of birds through the air, e.g. ducks coming in to water. (4) In fishing, two or more triangles form a *flight* of hooks.

Foil: (1) A smell which obliterates the fox's scent. (2) A fox *runs his foil* when he doubles back on his track. (3) Otter hounds *swim the foil* when they follow the ream. (4) An old term for the trace of deer on hard grass.

Game: (1) Edible birds and animals that are objects of the chase. (2) An old term for a number of conies, and a *herd* of swans.

Gape: (1) Mouth of a pike. (2) Bend of a fishing hook. (3) A disease which occurs among pheasants, called *Gapes.*

Gaze: (1) Deer stand *at gaze,* when they stop to look. (2) To view the otter.

Gled: (1) Local name for a kite. (2) Another name for *baggot* (fishing term).

Gorge: (1) Of a fish, to swallow completely. (2) Crop of a hawk.

Grey: (1) (or *Gray*) The badger. (2) Colour of a horse.

Hack: (1) Early stage of training of young hawks. (2) A horse kept for hire, or one worn out.

Hackle: (1) Hair along hounds back—stands up, when angry. (2) Fly for angling. (3) Feathers at back of hawk's neck.

Hands: (1) The quality of a horseman's touch on the reins. (2) Measure of height for horses.

Hardel: (1) An old term meaning coupling hounds together. (2) An old term for the binding of a roe-buck's legs.

Harling: (1) Trolling with fly or bait (River Tay). (2) Preparing a rabbit's hind legs for slinging.

Hatch: (1) A grated weir. (2) Of flies.

Head: (1) In pigsticking, the steel point at the end of the spear. (2) Hounds carry a *good head* when they hunt fast on a broad front.

Hide: (1) The temporary retreat of a hunted otter. (2) A small structure, to conceal a watcher or a 'gun'. (3) The skin of a deer.

Hob: (1) A local name for a stoat. (2) The male of a polecat.

Hold: (1) A huntsman, in casting, may *hold* hounds *round, on,* etc. (2) Of a covert that contains a fox.

Hover: (1) Alternative name for the *hide* of an otter. (2) Of a 'shoal' of trout waiting for food near fast water.

Hurdle: (1) Of horses that take their cock fences too fast. (2) To bind up the legs of a roe-deer (cf. *Hardel*).

Jack: (1) One kind of snipe. (2) The male Hobby. (3) Alternative name for a male ferret. (4) A pike (fish). (5) Term for a male stonefly.

Jackass: (1) A male ass. (2) Local name for penguins.

Jerkin: (1) In coursing, an old term for a *trip*. (2) The male of the Gerfalcon.

Kennel: (1) A fox's bed above ground. (2) Alternative term for the *couch* or *holt* of an otter. (3) An old term for a pack of foxhounds.

Kid: (1) An old term for a roe-deer of the first year. (2) A young goat.

Leap: (1) Salmon falls. (2) Company term for leopards.

Leash: (1) Of hares, hawks, greyhounds, etc.—three. (2) In coursing, the line used to hold the dogs until slipped.

Line: (1) The trail of a fox. (2) Of a dog, to cover.

Mark: (1) Of hounds baying at the entrance to an earth or holt. (2) Sometimes used for the *seal* of an otter. (3) Of hawks, soaring above the quarry.

Mask: (1) The head of a fox. (2) The head of an otter.

Mew: (1) Of deer, to shed their antlers. (2) Of hawks, to moult. (3) The cry of a cat.

Mob: (1) To hunt a fox without giving it a fair chance. (2) In coursing, when the crowd presses a hare unfairly. (3) A *herd* of cattle.

Mort: (1) Old term for the call blown on the horn at the death of a deer. (2) Sea trout.

Mute: (1) The old term for a *pack* of hounds. (2) A term describing hounds that do not *throw their tongue* when on the line of a fox. (3) Another name for ordure, especially of birds, e.g. hawks.

Off: (1) (Opposite to *rising.*) Used in describing the age of horses, e.g. *three off*. (2) Old term applied to fish after spawning. (3) 'He's *off*' = Lost the fish!

Pad: (1) A fox's foot, or an otter's. (2) The cushion soles of hound's feet. (3) To track a fox.

Pass: (1) = *Ladder*, for assisting salmon over difficult falls. (2) Process of changing food over in the air by the male hawk to his mate. (3) *Passe* was the original term for a *pace* (herd) of asses.

Pate: (1) Another name for the mask of an otter. (2) An old name for *Brock* the badger.

Pelt: (1) The skin of an otter. (2) Prey hawk has killed.

Pipe: (1) A branch in a fox's *earth.* (2) Passage in the *sett* of an otter. (3) May describe the noise of song-birds, etc.

Point: (1) The tips of a deer's antler. (2) The distance, as the crow flies, of a hunting run. (3) When a gun dog checks and stiffens. (4) Top joint of a fishing rod. (5) A fine piece of gut tied to the end of the cast.

Pony: (1) The *shelt* used to carry the carcase in deer-stalking. (2) A small horse—up to about 14 hands.

Pricker: (1) The whipper-in (O.E.). (2) An old term for a hunter on horseback.

Pride: (1) Of a hawk, to be in good flesh and heart. (2) Company term for a number of lions.

Pudding: (1) Meal porridge fed to hounds. (2) Old coursing term for *Inchipin* or fat gut.

Pug: (1) Footmark; or to track a beast by its footprints. (2) Third year salmon.

Put down: (1) When a horse or hound has to be destroyed. (2) To drive an otter from its *holt* into the river. (3) Frightening a fish.

Put up: (1) Same as 'put on' a fly. (2) To cast off from the wrist (*put-over*) a hawk. (3) To disturb (*flush*) game.

Pye: (1) A descriptive colour. (2) A magpie.

Rattle: (1) Of a goat's cry at rutting time. (2) The sound of the horn at a kill (otter hunting). (3) Of hounds, when they hard press a fox.

Rights: (1) Perquisites at the *Curée*, where the rites were performed with great ceremony. (2) Term for the brow, bez and trez tines of a red deer.

Rouse: (1) An old term—of a hawk, to shake herself. (2) To dislodge the buck.

Rout: (1) Old term meaning to cheer or *rate.* (2) Old term for a flock of wildfowl. (3) Of boars = to *root* (old term). (4) *Route* is a company term for wolves.

Run: (1) Enclosed ground where poultry can peck. (2) A fox hunt. Hounds *run* when they are actually in pursuit of a fox. (3) A fast part of the river. (4) When a hooked fish takes out the line. (5) The flow of a lot of fishes.

Runt: (1) A form of plug bait in fishing. (2) A variety of pigeon.

Say: (1) To allow birds to feed undisturbed is to let them *get a say*. (2) An old term for cutting open the belly—to *take say*—at the *Curée*.

Seeling: (1) Closing the eyelids of a hawk with a thread. (2) Of a horse, when white hairs began to grow in his eye-brows (old term).

Sewin: (1) Alternative spelling for *Sewel*—a cord with rags tied on, to make pheasants fly. (2) Sea trout.

Shoal: (1) To drive an otter into shallow water. (2) A *school* of fishes.

Shoot: (1) Of a fish when it swam away in fright (old term). (2) To discharge, or hit with, a fire-arm. (3) Old term for a young boar.

Sore: (1) A male fallow deer in his fourth year. (2) Of a hare, when in the open field. (3) = *Sord* or *safe*; a *flush* (flock) of mallard.

Sound: (1) Of a fish, to swim to the sea-bed. (2) To sound the horn = to blow it.

Spayed: (1) Killing with a knife of a stag at bay. (2) Term describing bitch hounds that have had their ovaries removed.

Spear: (1) Weapon used in pig-sticking. (2) Spike affixed to end of fishing rod for inserting in ground.

Spinner: (1) Imago fly. (2) Spinning bait. (3) He who spins.

Spur: (1) An old term for the *seal* of an otter. (2) Claw of a cock pheasant. (3) To prick a horse with spurs.

Stare: (1) Of a horse'e coat, when it has a dull look. (2) Old name for a starling.

Stickle: (1) Formed by the Field standing across a shallow to prevent otter passing. (2) Small eddies in a river.

Stock: (1) Amount of game on an area of ground. (2) The wooden portion of a shot gun. (3) Wild pigeon (i.e. Stock-dove).

Stoop: (1) Of fox- or otter-hounds when they put their muzzles to the scent. (2) The sudden descent of a hawk on its quarry.

Stop: (1) To close foxes' earths when they are abroad at night. (2) A man posted on the flanks of a *beat*. (3) Name for a rabbit's nest burrow.

Strike: (1) Sharp jerk given to hook fish. (2) Of a pike when it seizes a bait. (3) Of a hawk when she breaks the neck of her quarry in the air and flies on (old term).

Strip: (1) To skin a hare. (2) To squeeze out ova or milt from a fish.

Stroke: (1) The feeling of the scent by hounds. (2) An old term for the blowing of the horn.

Summed: (1) Of a hart, when he has got his complete antler. (2) When a hawk has all its plumes. (*Full-summed* = completely 'moulted'.)

Sute: (1) Company term for a flock of mallard. (2) Old term used in connection with bloodhounds.

Tag: (1) Short tail of artificial fly. (2) The tip of a fox's brush.

Tail: (1) Of hounds which run behind the pack. (2) To catch an otter by his rudder, a badger by his tail, or a fish by the tail end. (3) Of fish, usually trout, grubbing on the bottom.

Teaser: (1) An old type of hound (small mongrel) to 'tease forth' game. (2) A wooden lure (for towing) used in Tunny fishing in America.

Trace: (1) Alternative to *slot*. (2) Footprint of the hare in snow. (3) Gut length between line and bait, used in spinning for fish.

Train: (1) Something tied to the lure to entice the hawk. (2) Correct term for the tail of a hawk is *trains*. (3) Dryden's term for a wolf retiring to rest. (4) Display of its upper tail coverts by a peacock.

Treading: (1) Old term for the dung of bears. (2) General description for the coupling of birds.

Tree: (1) Old term for a marten *lodging*. (2) To hunt an animal until it climbs a tree.

Trip: (1) Old term for a deer when he 'forceth by'. (2) In coursing, an unsuccessful effort to kill. (3) A small number of wildfowl. (4) Company term for a flock of goats, *down* of hares, or herd of tame swine.

Trumpeters: (1) A name for the largest Whooper swans. (2) A variety of pigeon.

Trussing: (1) Of a hawk, when she soars with a bird and at length descends to the ground. (2) Tying the wings of a hawk to the body. (3) A term for the dressing of a chicken.

Tushes: (1) The four projecting tusks of a boar. (2) The four permanent teeth which appear in a (male) horse at about five years.

Vent: (1) Of the otter, when it comes to the surface to breathe. (2) Old term for unkennelling the otter.

View: (1) The sight of, or to see, a fox. (2) Old term for the slot of a fallow deer.

Walk: (1) Of hound puppies, when they are cared for at farms, etc. (2) Or a *wisp*, of snipe.

Watch: (1) An old coursing term for *lurching*. (2) Old term for an otter retiring to rest. (3) Fancy term for a flock of nightingales.

Whelps: (1) Unweaned foxhound puppies. (2) Old term for otter or bear cubs.

Whistle: (1) Sound by which the falconer dispatched his hawk and lured her back again to the fist. (2) Cry of the chital and bachelor seal.

Wind: (1) Of hounds, when they smell a fox. (2) To blow the horn (O.E.). (3) The breathing of the horse.

Wisp: (1) Term for a flock (*walk*) of snipe. (2) Pad for massaging a horse's coat.

Wreath: (1) Fore part of a hawk's neck. (2) The tail of a boar.

INDEXES

NOTE :

(i) The Indexes do not cover Appendix II, and only include the sporting terms in Appendices I and III.

(ii) Where more than one page number occurs against a term, the definition of the term is indicated by **BOLD TYPE**.

INDEX TO SPORTING TERMS

INDEX TO ANIMALS, ETC.